STARTING AND RUNNING

A PROFITABLE

INVESTMENT CLUB

THE OFFICIAL GUIDE FROM

THE NATIONAL ASSOCIATION OF INVESTMENT CLUBS

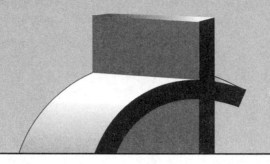

STARTING AND RUNNING A PROFITABLE INVESTMENT CLUB

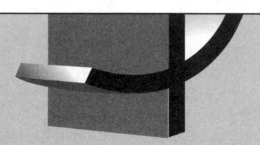

THOMAS E. O'HARA AND KENNETH S. JANKE, SR.

TIMES BUSINESS

T

RANDOM HOUSE

All rights reserved under International Pan-American Copyright Conventions. Published in the United States by Times Books, a division of Random House, Inc., New York, and simultaneously in Canada by Random House of Canada Limited, Toronto.

Library of Congress Cataloging-in-Publication data is available.

ISBN: 0-8129-2686-2

Printed in the United States of America on acid-free paper
98765432

A MESSAGE FROM THE CHAIRMAN OF NAIC'S BOARD OF ADVISORS

*I*nvestment clubs have existed in the United States for nearly a century. The oldest known club began operation in Texas in 1898.

Most of the early clubs were built around a combination of like social interests and a desire to try one's wings in the blue skies of investment and speculation. There was little, if any, attempt to establish uniform principles for guidance or education of members.

The modern investment club movement began in Detroit in 1940 because circumstances dictated a serious attitude toward investment results. Frederick C. Russell, unable to find a job and desiring to buy a small business, decided to form an investment club as the vehicle for accumulating capital. He became the inspiration for the investment club movement.

Being a serious undertaking, the Mutual Investment Club of Detroit, at my suggestion, determined to do three things: (1) invest every month, (2) reinvest all dividends, and (3) buy growth companies. Each principle in itself was adopted for the purpose of safety, but the three in combination produced aggressive results over the years.

Having observed the Mutual Investment Club of Detroit for over 50 years and the growth of the investment club movement, I believe it is possible for most people to achieve a goal of investing $20,000 in stock over 20 to 30 years by budgeting $20 to $25 a month for such a purpose. Russell's club members had realized a gain of more than $200,000 each by 1982 on $10 to $20 a month invested. This contributed to the education of their children, better housing, and supplements to retirement years.

The behavior of investment club members during the stock market declines has been essentially professional. Most uneducated investors panicked and suffered losses.

Seeing the progress of the Mutual Investment Club and noting the ways in which the club members advanced in their family finances and businesses, we first discussed the creation of a national association in 1949.

On October 20, 1951, the National Association of Investment Clubs (NAIC) was founded at the Rachham Building, Detroit, with the Mutual Investment Club of Detroit and three other Michigan clubs as charter members. One objective of the association was to transform investment clubs into a vast, nationwide educational project. This emphasis on education is one essential difference between the early days of the investment club movement and the modern-day clubs.

Having found a vigorous interest in investment club work abroad, NAIC took the lead in establishing the World Federation of Investment Clubs on July 8, 1960, in London. The founding associations were: NAIC, United States; NAIC, Great Britain; the National Bureau voor Beleggings Studieclubs, the Netherlands; and the Federation of New Zealand Investment Clubs.

Realizing the vital significance of the widespread ownership of industry and its dependence on effective investment education, NAIC launched the Investment Education Institute in February 1961. The International Investment Education Institute was established in London in August 1966. Investment education worldwide has been gradually broadening from its investment club base to include growing numbers of individual investors.

With billions of dollars going into pension funds for retirement years, with world industrialization requiring increasing supplies of capital, with inflation making us all conscious of the need to maintain purchasing power, and with Japanese competition and their concept of government, business, and labor cooperation creating trade tension, the question of "who owns industry" is of deep significance. Capitalism can exist only to the extent that equity money is made available to business—small, medium, and large—in all areas, here and abroad. Capitalism will work better if people (1) understand investing, (2) are educated to invest successfully, and (3) intelligently provide capital to expanding industries. Investment education is essential to good citizenship in the modern world.

George A. Nicholson, Jr.
Chairman of the Advisory Board
National Association of Investors Corporation

ACKNOWLEDGMENTS

NATIONAL ASSOCIATION OF INVESTORS CORPORATION

INVESTMENT EDUCATION FOR INDIVIDUALS AND CLUBS SINCE 1951

711 W. Thirteen Mile Road • Madison Heights, Mich. 48071
810-583-NAIC

NAIC is a Michigan Not-for-Profit Corporation founded by and served by a group of volunteer officers whose sincerity, diligent service, and devotion to sound investment principles have produced the tremendous growth and success of the Investment Club movement and made it an outstanding force for investment education.

vii

Robert V. Blailock
Emma Dimpfel
Gordon L. Hakes
Evonne A. Hurst
Lennart H. Width
Billy M. Williams

Past Chairmen
Lewis A. Rockwell
Helen Stege
Leland Finkbeiner
William T. Mabee
Ralph L. Seger, Jr.
Warren B. Alexander
Leroy F. Mumford
James L. Agee
William R. Sandvig
Cynthia P. Charles
Wagar A. Glass
Richard G. Horak
Robert L. Tice

Securities Review Editorial and Advisory Committees
James L. Agee
Robert M. Bilkie, Jr., CFA
Donald E. Danko, CFA
Maury Elvekrog, CFA
Kenneth S. Janke, Sr.
Walter J. Kirchberger, CFA

George A. Nicholson, Jr., CFA
Thomas E. O'Hara
Ralph L. Seger, Jr., CFA

NAIC Computer Group
Philip Keating, CFA, Chairman
Herbert K. Barnett, President
Hans D. Steinke, Vice President
Werner H. Wahl, Ph. D., Treasurer
William C. Thomas, Secretary
Richard D. Becker
Christopher T. Collins
Jerome C. Cooper
Joseph N. Craig, Ph. D.
Kenneth J. Morris
G. Kenneth Wood

NAIC Corporate Advisory Committee
John D. Tyson, Chairman
Lisa Sikora, Vice-Chairman
Sandy Upperman, Secretary
Jonathan W. Booraem, Treasurer
John Baker
Gutte Carr
Marsha Gordon
J. Kevin Helmintoller
Mike Klodnicki
Mark Rozelle
Barbara VenHorst

CONTENTS

STARTING AND RUNNING
A PROFITABLE
INVESTMENT CLUB

LEARNING AND EARNING WITH AN INVESTMENT CLUB

*E*veryone interested in the stock market wants to find the key to consistently profitable investment. There *is* a way. In forming an investment club, you are joining hundreds of thousands of other men and women who are following the profitable path of learn-by-doing investing in common stocks. You share with them the opportunity to enhance your knowledge of business and investing, accumulate a significant amount of capital over time, and have fun, too.

What is an investment club? It's a group of like-minded people, interested in investing in the stock market. They agree to a few basic investing goals and principles, and they each take on part of the job of research. The modest investment of each individual, the limited time each puts into research, and the devotion to three basic principles collectively add up to a formidable investing force.

But why the stock market? The chart from the Ibbotson Study (Figure I-1) demonstrates quite clearly that few investments compare with stocks in rate of return. What's more, stocks are easily bought and sold and have a universally recognized value.

WHAT MEMBERSHIP CAN MEAN

You can make more money through your investment club than you might have thought possible. Of course, in the first year or two, many clubs show losses or only small gains. However, as members become more knowledgeable

Figure I-1
**Comparison of Total Returns on Different Kinds
of Investments**

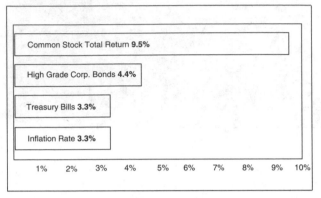

*This sixty-year study (1936–1996) from Ibbotson Associates
clearly shows that common stocks have been twice as profitable as corporate bonds. What is more, common stocks have earned enough to
outpace inflation by almost three times.*

and the amount of money under management grows, gains often begin to
increase exponentially.

Consider someone who joined the Mutual Investment Club of Detroit,
the "granddaddy" of the investment club movement, shortly after its formation in February 1940 (Figure I-2). After paying in $20 monthly for five
years, he interrupted that schedule for two years. He then resumed his contributions, making up some back payments.

Almost forty-one years later, at normal retirement age, he had paid in
$8,120. His share of club assets amounted to $158,962. This savings program enabled him to spend most of his income throughout his working years
while accumulating, by means of small but regular investments, a substantial
supplement to his pension and Social Security income.

The knowledge of investing he had gained through his club enabled
him also to invest wisely for his own personal account, adding to his modest
fortune. (Typically, when a club forms, only two members own personal portfolios. After five years, almost all do. Currently, nine out of ten NAIC club
members buy securities for their own accounts in addition to making club
investments.)

Figure I-2
A History of the Mutual Investment Club of Detroit

Year Ended Dec. 31	Total Deposit by Members	Earnings from Both Dividends & Sales of Securities — Dividends	Sales	Accumulated Total Deposits & Reinvested Earnings	Withdrawals	Liquidating Value Feb. 28 of Following Year
1941	$ 800			$ 800		$ 812
1942	1,920			1,920		1,915
1943	3,220			3,220		3,405
1944	4,860			4,860		8,847
1945	5,080			5,080		9,844
1946	5,080	$ 1,489*		6,569	$ 2,519	15,347
1947	5,620	978		8,087		11,854
1948	7,310	1,004	$ 693	11,474	825	12,401
1949	9,761	1,196	(525)	14,794	200	13,439
1950	8,741	1,100	167	15,041	3,000	20,690
1951	10,190	1,670	2,513	20,673	800	27,471
1952	11,460	1,433	1,937	25,313		33,222
1953	15,025	1,690	806	31,374	1,606	43,233
1954	18,430	2,073	(459)	36,393	7,631	50,125
1955	21,770	2,200	3,618	45,551		75,975
1956	26,642	2,991	7,707	61,123	5,689	85,001
1957	30,542	3,355	2,600	70,978		94,121
1958	35,282	3,074	3,737	82,529		91,323
1959	35,935	3,367	3,114	89,663	6,695	132,690
1960	40,885	3,701	11,012	109,326		151,515
1961	45,470	4,369	174	118,454	1,026	171,655
1962	49,870	3,731	2,867	129,452	5,000	188,738
1963	53,960	4,568	2,311	140,421	1,000	172,577
1964	57,085	4,258	3,621	151,425	800	211,801
1965	61,685	6,069	6,102	168,196		246,738
1966	59,040	5,599	5,146	176,296	21,302	268,829
1967	62,308	6,411	1,500	187,196	8,142	270,994
1968	67,056	10,139	21,968	224,330	17,340	386,558
1969	75,327	11,815	2,967	247,383	5,175	535,604
1970	84,083	11,696	3,498	271,333	2,955	394,434
1971	93,493	11,541	2,599	294,883		439,849
1972	90,819	11,524	(2,092)	301,641	43,658	436,413
1973	97,219	9,560	13,493	331,094		430,081
1974	103,584	12,241	3,026	351,726	3,925	382,959
1975	108,983	15,621	429	374,175	14,300	470,675
1976	115,076	13,840	2,739	396,847	13,000	503,916
1977	112,250	18,443	6,779	419,243	29,000	478,418

Figure I-2 (Continued)
A History of the Mutual Investment Club of Detroit

Year Ended Dec. 31	Total Deposit by Members	*Earnings from Both Dividends & Sales of Securities* Dividends	Sales	Accumulated Total Deposits & Reinvested Earnings	Withdrawals	Liquidating Value Feb. 28 of Following Year
1978	118,589	22,073	5,378	453,033	12,000	559,419
1979	126,860	24,630	70,183	556,117	15,000	759,038
1980	133,640	19,003	67,171	649,035	25,750	915,726
1981	142,136	24,122	80,542	762,231	38,086	891,196
1982	145,716	25,988	1,653	783,452	25,750	1,124,038
1983	167,952	26,767	33,127	875,582	7,210	1,235,893
1984	195,954	29,328	10,937	943,846	78,280	1,474,266
1985	211,659	31,094	55,283	966,018	10,300	1,600,543
1986	211,489	25,761	62,904	1,064,513	386,094	1,754,924
1987	233,159	22,390	48,356	1,266,832	90,640	1,602,599
1988	248,524	41,562	102,943	1,386,702	105,957	1,729,620
1989	262,530	47,838	29,916	1,478,462	109,150	1,682,569
1990	275,130	59,865	55,951	1,606,878	105,321	1,833,368
1991	291,045	58,594	47,842	1,729,229	106,295	2,109,917
1992	310,797	56,987	30,002	1,835,980	41,928	2,377,930
1993	331,777	51,541	65,089	1,973,580	59,988	2,413,378
1994	371,802	55,065	113,798	2,182,468	23,800	2,701,399
1995	425,960	59,581	100,593	2,396,800	445,285	3,002,181
TOTALS	$425,960	$874,925	$1,095,915	$2,396,800	$1,881,412	$3,002,181

* The amount of dividends shown here is the accumulation from the beginning of this club through 1946. Note that the club members invested $425,960 in 56 years, withdrew $1,881,412, and had a liquidating value of $3,002,181 as of February 29, 1996, the 56th anniversary of the club's founding.

SET YOUR OBJECTIVE

The National Association of Investment Clubs (NAIC) recommends that your investment objective should be to double your money every five years. To do so, you must achieve an average 14.9 percent compounded annual growth rate. This same growth will not come every year, but you should expect to achieve that average from one stock market peak to the next. In the past ten years, NAIC's surveys have seen the average club exceed that figure three times. In the 1995 sampling of 629 clubs, the average club (which was nearly nine years old) had earned 12.3 percent over its lifetime.

Of course, you need not meet the typical return of NAIC members to prosper. Figure I-3 shows what you can accumulate over various spans of time

Figure I-3
Building Your Next Egg

Rate of Return	5	10	Years 20	30	40
3%	$19,442.50	$42,027.23	$ 98,736.83	$175,258.12	$ 278,512.39
5	20,486.83	46,778.79	123,823.89	250,717.91	459,713.57
8	22,190.01	55,249.70	177,884.17	450,088.55	1,054,284.37
10	23,424.71	61,965.61	229,709.07	683,797.60	1,913,034.07

Use this table to see how much you would save over a period of years at various rates of return if you invested $300 a month.

at different rates of return by investing $300 monthly. An 8 percent return is a conservative objective, since the stock market overall has attained a long-term annual growth of roughly 10 percent. Were you to invest $300 monthly for 20 years at 8 percent, you would amass total capital of $177,884. In 30 years, you would wind up with $450,088.

To make consistent overall returns, you will need to invest in down markets, when virtually all stocks are underpriced, as well as in up markets, when most stocks are fully valued. And at all times, good stock selection is vital.

YOUR CLUB ACCOUNT HELPS BUILD YOUR PERSONAL ACCOUNT

For many people, the investment club is their introduction to the stock market. If you're one of these people, your club experience will lead you to open a personal investment account in addition to your club shares, and here you will build your individual portfolio.

Having a personal account doesn't mean you should abandon membership in an investment club. Continuing club membership can be very valuable. Members look at stocks at least once a month, which serves as a reminder to pay attention to their own personal portfolios as well. Many investment ideas come from club meetings, even for the most experienced investor.

The Mutual Investment Club of Detroit celebrated its fifty-fifth anniversary in 1995. Some of the original members still participate actively, despite the fact that their personal portfolios have grown to substantial sums.

Figure I-4 Taking the Long-Term View: The Ibbotson Associates Study

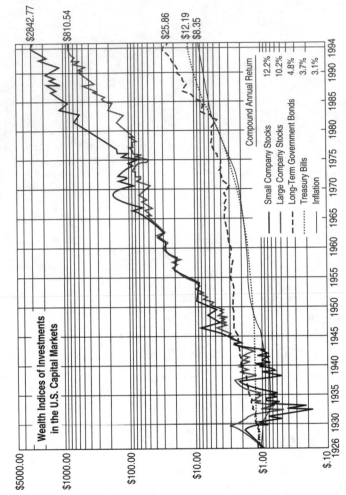

This Ibbotson Associates study covers 1925–1994. Over time, certain trends appear, mainly that stocks have the highest annual return (12.2% for small-company stocks and 10.2% for large-company stocks) compared with long-term government bonds (4.8%), Treasury bills (3.7%), and inflation (3.1%). Source: © Stocks, Bonds, Bills, and Inflation 1996 Yearbook™, Ibbotson Associates, Chicago (annually updates work by Roger G. Ibbotson and Rex A. Sinquefield). Used with permission. All rights reserved.

8

Investment club membership can be a lifelong experience. Through the club, experienced help is at hand.

It only works, though, if you can stick with it. Fully 40 percent of new investment clubs are out of business within two years, victims of a poor selection of members and a "get rich quick" mentality. Everyone needs to agree at the outset to common goals, meaning entering into a long-term program with a long-term investment philosophy. Short-term trading simply doesn't work in an investment club.

LOOK FOR INVESTMENT IDEAS

With this book, you and your fellow club members will gain ideas on selecting investments. If you also become a member of NAIC, you can receive additional useful information, including NAIC's monthly publication, *Better Investing.* Over the years, securities featured in the magazine's "Stock to Study" feature have on average met NAIC's goal of doubling their value within five years. Your broker may have suggestions for you as well. But don't accept anyone else's word as final. Using NAIC's tools, after learning how from this manual, you and your fellow members should make your own informed judgments about what and when to buy and sell. Tips are great, but put every stock to the test of the NAIC Stock Selection Guide and Report before making a purchase.

This book will show you how to organize your club properly and guide its operation though the years to come. Left to its own devices, your club might falter and fall back on highly speculative concepts. In adhering to the principles we present, you will follow the same time-tested techniques used by many others to finance their children's educations, travel the world, and avoid money worries in retirement.

Figure I-5
**Taking the Long-Term View: The Dow Jones Industrial Average
(1920–1994)**

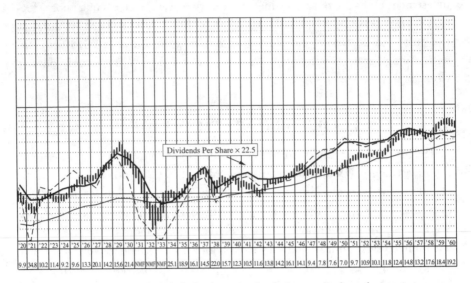

'20	'21	'22	'23	'24	'25	'26	'27	'28	'29	'30	'31	'32	'33	'34	'35	'36	'37	'38	'39	'40	'41	'42	'43	'44	'45	'46	'47	'48	'49	'50	'51	'52	'53	'54	'55	'56	'57	'58	'59	'60
9.9	34.8	10.2	11.4	9.2	9.6	13.3	20.1	14.2	15.6	21.4	NMF	NMF	NMF	25.1	18.9	16.1	14.5	22.0	15.7	12.3	10.5	11.6	13.8	14.2	16.1	14.1	9.4	7.8	7.6	7.0	9.7	10.9	10.1	11.8	12.4	14.8	13.2	17.6	18.4	19.2

Long-term trends provide a great deal of information for the investor. Perhaps the most important observation for the investor to make is that stock prices have followed an upward trend for approximately 200 years. Second, prices do fluctuate. Downward trends can continue for a while, but the overall movement has been upward. Of course, you want your investments to keep pace with or,

Figure I-5 (Continued)
Taking the Long-Term View: The Dow Jones Industrial Average
(1920–1994)

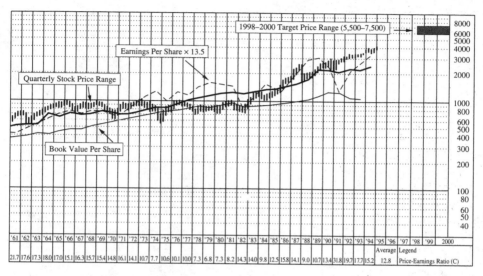

better yet, *outperform inflation. The records suggest that stock prices do indeed exceed the rate of inflation over time. As a club member, you will purchase stocks when they are high and low. But the general upward trend will most likely continue, and investors will benefit from that trend. The important thing is not to concentrate on the short term, but to keep the total picture in mind.*

INVESTING THE NAIC WAY

CHAPTER 1

A PROVEN INVESTMENT PHILOSOPHY

There is no rapid route to riches. Today's most successful investment clubs—with assets of hundreds of thousands of dollars, a million dollars, or more—started out, years ago, with only a few dollars. Most of the members in those clubs had no previous stock market experience, and their investment funds were limited, as was the time available to devote to club activities. Yet they've achieved results that would make many professional investors envious.

You can apply the same philosophy that has made them prosperous. All you need is the patience to follow a few tested and proven standards, while avoiding the traps so many investors fall into. David Babson, the noted investment counselor, has written:

> It is surprising how few investment portfolios are based on a consistent philosophy aimed at meeting long-term objectives. Most are merely collections of securities assembled over time for a variety of reasons which seemed compelling at the moment of purchase, but are no longer clearly remembered.
>
> Even among those investors who develop a basic plan, far too many do not stick with it through thick and thin. In periods of pessimism, they end up selling stocks when they should be buying. And when optimism prevails, they become lured by rumors, greed or bad advice into speculating when they should be investing.

With the basic principles recommended by NAIC and practiced by successful clubs in the past, you can apply a consistent philosophy aimed at long-term, proven investment objectives. Since 1951, these simple rules have led investors to consistently superior results. Here they are.

Principle 1: Invest Regularly, Regardless of the Market Outlook.   When you start investing, you may be nervous about timing. What if you commit your capital and the market immediately heads south? Could there be another Black Monday, or worse, after your money is invested?

Time and experience will help allay these fears. The market's overall trend for decades has been upward, at an average annual compound rate of about 10 percent—despite intermittent cycles of boom, recession, depression, and recovery. Once you recognize the rhythm of market cycles, fluctuations will no longer distract you; instead, you'll welcome market dips as buying opportunities.

Investors minimize risk when they purchase shares they intend to hold as long as the business operates successfully. In contrast, *speculators* who try to forecast near-term market fluctuations magnify their risk tremendously. We've found that half of all investment clubs go out of business within the first eighteen months because of conflict between those who believe in long-term investing and those advocating speculative trading. Be sure your members agree on a long-term philosophy before you get started.

Principle 2: Reinvest All Earnings.   Put your investment earnings back into the market. This will let you maximize your profits through compounding, so you'll earn more than you would have just by keeping your original capital at work. In the examples presented in coming chapters, you will see the amazing effect of compounding made possible by reinvestment.

Principle 3: Invest in Growth Companies.   Buy shares in businesses whose sales and earnings are moving ahead faster than the gross domestic product, and whose records suggest they will be far more valuable five years in the future. We'll show you later how to identify growth companies with the best potential.

Principle 4: Diversify to Reduce Risk.   Some of your selections will be great successes, while others will post disappointing results. Since it is impossible to predict the future with certainty, you cannot expect every outcome to reach your forecast. With diversification, you need only realize an *average* advance that meets your goal; an occasional mistake will not prove disastrous.

Diversification is a basic principle in investing. The idea is that, because you cannot possibly know which stocks will perform better or worse than average, you cannot afford to put all of your money into one company, or even in companies within a single industry. You have to spread the risk—and the opportunity. Only by diversifying will you be able to realize your average return objective. It's true that diversification also limits the upside potential, but that's important in order to balance risk and opportunity.

By applying these four principles, you will be in an especially good position to succeed as an investor. You should also seek out an experienced investor who subscribes to this philosophy and is equipped to serve as your club's coach. The individual might be an experienced investment club member, an individual investor, or your broker.

THE FOUR PRINCIPLES IN ACTION

Here's an example of how the principles work in a real situation. Everyone who approaches the stock market begins with the question: Is the market today high or low? This question is more complex than it seems at first glance. Perhaps the market is high compared with last week or last month, but lower than a year ago. Maybe it will prove to be low now compared with its level a year hence. But who knows? It is virtually impossible to find someone who has built a fortune over a lifetime by forecasting short-term movements in the market. In contrast, millions have found purchasing sound stocks regularly to be a profitable pursuit, as the market has advanced over the long term. That's where our investing principles come in.

When you make regular purchases with a set sum, regardless of the market's level, you are utilizing an idea called *dollar cost averaging.* You'll buy more shares when prices are depressed, and fewer when they are high. That's because, when prices are lower, your investment dollars get more shares for the same amount; and when those same shares are more expensive, the set amount buys fewer shares (Figure 1-1).

When is it time to sell? When you buy carefully, you should sell very seldom. When you own quality companies with continuing high growth potential, you should continue to hold. When a company becomes grossly overpriced, you should take one quarter to one third of your profits. We'll talk about how to recognize overvalued stocks in more detail later. However, when you purchase a company whose growth is driven by management, you may hold it for as long as that management remains in control. One company

Figure 1-1

Regular Investing Can Lower Your Average Cost per Share

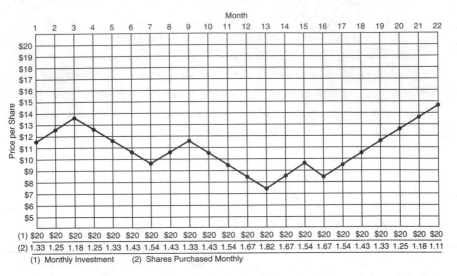

(1) Monthly Investment   (2) Shares Purchased Monthly

If you invested $20 each month in a particular stock, the fluctuating nature of the stock market would allow your $20 investment to buy more of the stock at some times and less of the stock at others. However, because of the nature of dollar cost averaging, you are at an advantage. Your average cost per share is actually lower over time. The figures on the bottom line show the number of shares purchased each month with the $20 fixed amount of investment. The $440 invested over a twenty-two-month period bought 31.228 shares. At the latest price of $18, the 31.228 shares are worth $562.10. As you continue to invest, your advantage will increase.

widely held by NAIC members has just completed forty-nine successive years of increasing sales and earnings per share.

But why dollar-cost-average in the first place? Why not just "buy low and sell high"? The answer is that you don't know with foresight when those situations really exist. Hindsight tells all, but as investors, you don't have that luxury. Combining dollar cost averaging with the policy of reinvesting all of your dividends will let you, over time, buy more shares "low" and fewer shares "high," without the benefit of hindsight.

SETTING INVESTMENT GOALS

Your club's goal should be to attain average growth in prices and dividend income of 14.9 percent, compounded annually. At this rate, you will double the value of your holdings every five years. Still, an 8 percent per year increase over an extended period of time would be an excellent result.

An important component of your increase in value is dividends. Your aim should be to realize a 4 to 6 percent yield over time on your investment from dividend income, particularly in the early part of the business cycle, when stock prices tend to be lower and yields consequently higher. Often this will prove difficult, perhaps even impossible, but keep that standard in mind. Remember: It's a standard, not a hard and fast rule.

When you join or start an investment club, plan to stay a member until your retirement years. A fifteen-member club in which each member pays in $20 per month should reach a worth of $22,190 in five years. The longer you invest, and the wiser your choices, the better your results will be. The compound interest table (see Figure I-3) shows how the value of $300 invested monthly at varying rates of return for different periods of time can grow.

Club members who begin their program in their twenties and maintain it until their departure from the labor force forty years later could amass $1,913,034 at a rate of return of 10 percent, barring withdrawals over the four decades, especially if those clubs follow our advice to invest in growth companies. It is thrilling to invest in companies and see them subsequently grow in size, stature, and, of course, value. Buying shares in such concerns, whose sales and earnings outperform those of business as a whole, typically means you will reap a higher price for your shares.

This increased price stems not only from growing earnings, but also from the propensity of investors to pay a premium for growth. Growth company shares typically sell at higher price/earnings multiples than do other issues. Be aware that a company must attain growth over a period of years to warrant the growth designation. Growth comes in a number of ways. It comes when an industry is new and has a new market to satisfy. It may come from a new product. Growth may also be produced by vigorous, talented, driven management. It is the last type of growth that is the most dependable and long lasting. A five-year history should be minimum, to ensure that the company is established and that management has encountered varying conditions in which to prove its mettle. A short period of growth may be a lucky accident, not the indication of management drive that we are looking for.

The charts in Figure 1-2 show how the consistent growth records of American Home Products and Sigma Aldrich have been accompanied over the years by higher prices.

Figure 1-2
Two Companies Showing the Potential for Continued Growth

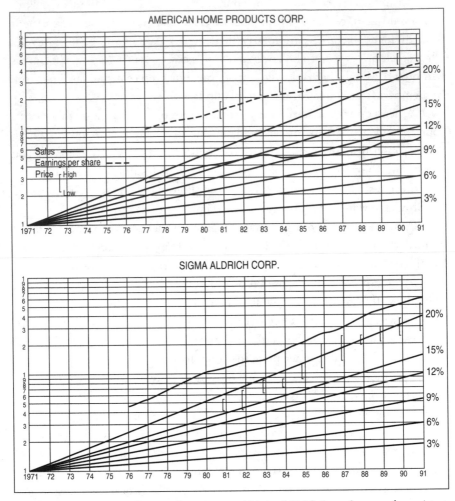

The charts for American Home Products Corp. and Sigma Aldrich Corp. document the consistent growth in sales and earnings per share that identify a company as a good prospective investment.

CHOOSING GROWTH STOCKS

From the charts in Figure 1-2 the investor can readily see that when sales increase nearly every year and earnings per share follow roughly the same pattern, the price of the stock usually continues to advance. That is what all of us are seeking.

NAIC believes that the investor profits most dependably by placing money in a company whose history suggests that it will be worth substantially more five years in the future.

Growth in a business comes in many ways. For example, there are growth industries. These occur where a new product, material, or service is offered and the companies satisfying this need grow as they fill the new market. In some cases, such as electronics, the growth seems likely to continue indefinitely, spurred by the steady development of new products. Some new products offer growth for just a few years. Sometimes the growth comes from a new use for an old product. The investor who understands where the growth is coming from is in a good position to understand how long it may continue and the potential in the investment.

NAIC members have found that the most reliable growth is a result not so much of the industry as of a management that is driven to produce growth. Such growth will last the lifetime of the management. And some such managements are able to instill a growth culture in their corporations that will be carried on for years after the originating management is gone. A well-known example is Minnesota Mining and Manufacturing. The idea of replacing the product line with new items within a short time span has carried forward from one management to the next and has given the company an outstanding record of growth. The two companies in Figure 1-2 are other examples of this sustained growth.

NAIC's Stock Selection Guide is designed to help you recognize this kind of management. Such a management produces a fairly consistent increase in sales and earnings per share, superior pre-tax margins, and high earnings on invested capital. These features are clearly shown on the Guide. When the investor identifies these features, the remaining job is to figure out a reasonable price. That's the purpose of the third section of the Guide.

Diversify to reduce risk. Most investment clubs purchase eight to twelve stocks in the first year. Later, they concentrate on increasing their ownership of the best performers and substituting better stocks for the laggards. How many stocks should your club own? No more than you can remain informed about. Clubs under ten years of age are likely to own no more than twenty to twenty-five stocks; twelve issues should be sufficient diversification for a relatively new club. Your main concern is not how many or how few stocks you own, but that each has the qualifications enabling it to be worth substantially more at the next market peak.

These totals presuppose an active membership. One active member can probably keep current on four stocks. If only two or three members are thus involved, the club's portfolio will clearly be restricted in size.

As part of the diversification process, we recommend including big, small, and medium-sized companies in your portfolio. Large companies (generally those with annual sales of $4 billion or more) tend to have a more predictable rate of growth and offer more resistance to price decline during down markets. On the other hand, small companies (those with sales of $400 million or less) are able to achieve more rapid rates of growth. Their shares may advance sharply in buoyant markets. When the market goes down, their prices tend to fall more than the average amount. The in-between companies provide further balance and range of market interest.

Historically, there have been extended periods when, in spite of increasing sales and earnings, stock prices remained virtually unchanged. In such periods, while the market overall may stand still, groups of stocks will attract attention. A range of large, medium, and small companies offers your club sufficient variety in securities so that something in your portfolio will get market attention and thus help keep interest in your club alive during a dull period.

In selecting stocks for your club's portfolio, try to put one third of your holdings in major companies in major industries and another third in small companies. The latter companies can be selected from corporations headquartered in your area, making it easier for you to obtain information concerning them.

The remaining third of the portfolio should be mid-sized companies. Aim for growth potential of 5 to 7 percent a year among the major companies, and at least 12 percent among the small concerns. The mid-range organizations should offer a 7 to 12 percent rate. If these guidelines are followed, your overall portfolio should yield 10 to 12 percent in price appreciation. This, coupled with dividends, will enable you to attain the 14.9 percent overall gain we suggest you seek.

KEY FACTORS IN INVESTMENT ANALYSIS

Club members should agree that no stock will be purchased without advance analysis. Members are not expected to become professional stock analysts— although many investment club members have done so. However, you should become proficient in applying a few essential tests to enhance your prospects for success and reduce your risk in buying and selling stocks.

As you pursue your goal of achieving 100 percent appreciation within five years, your members should analyze every prospective purchase for (1) the company's management capability, as evidenced by growing sales and earnings, pre-tax profit margin, and superior return on stockholders' equity; and (2) a reasonable current share price that can be expected to rise as financial results improve in the future.

Management Capability.   The drive of a corporation's management is the single most influential element of growth. When investment clubs give undue attention to industry outlook ("Health care is bound to grow") or the product of a company ("Fat-free food ingredients are certain winners"), they ignore, to their later regret, that only the best-led companies succeed over the long run. Growth is most reliable when it is produced by good management.

Apply these three tests of management:

1. *Rate of growth:* Other factors being equal, over the long term an investment is likely to increase in value at about the same rate that sales grow. The companies you select as possible investments for your club should be those whose sales have increased at least at the expected rate for their size as described above. Further, each company should offer the promise of continuing advances.

2. *Pre-tax profit margin:* This margin is calculated by deducting costs from sales and then dividing the result, profit before taxes, by sales:

$$\frac{\overset{\text{Pre-tax profit}}{\text{(Sales} - \text{Costs)}}}{\text{Sales}} \;=\; \% \text{ Pre-tax profit}$$

Comparison with other companies in the same industry will show whether the margin is average, better than typical, or under par. Obviously, a higher margin is preferable. Warning bells should ring if the margin is far above the averages of other companies. That could mean there's a distortion in the way profits are being reported, and chances are the high rate won't be repeated. If the high margin is for real, competition will be quickly attracted.

3. *Earnings on stockholders' equity:* Another mark of good management is a high percentage of earnings on stockholders' equity (which is net earnings divided by the sum of the value of preferred stock, common stock,

and retained earnings). Compare the company being considered with others in the same industry. The same caveat applies as before: An unusually high rate of return may indicate distortion in the numbers or a temporary advantage.

You will learn to apply other means of appraising management as your investment experience grows. The three basic tests above should be employed from the outset on every stock you study.

Another important basic to keep in mind in your review is share price. Quality and growth potential mean nothing in a security if you pay an exorbitant price. Use the Stock Selection Guide in assessing the high and low limits of the stock's price over the next five years (see Chapter 7). Then relate current price to this range and to your objective of doubling your money.

There are three ways to test for reasonableness of price.

1. *Earnings per share.* Earnings should be growing on a per-share basis at approximately the same rate as sales. Under occasional market conditions, you will find growing companies—particularly smaller ones— that can be bought for no more than the sum of the estimated earnings per share for the next five years. This situation is rarely found, but when it is, you have an exceptional buying opportunity.

2. *Dividends.* Generally speaking, a quality growth company pays out no more than half of its earnings; the remainder is retained to build the business. If you as an investor can expect over the years a dividend yield of 4 to 6 percent on the price paid for the stock, with retained earnings devoted to fueling growth, you can also anticipate stock price appreciation. When the stock you're considering has a track record of rapid growth in sales and earnings per share, be content with a relatively modest payout. The company can probably achieve greater value for you in building the business than you can attain elsewhere with your dividends.

3. *Price range.* Study the price range of the stock over the past five years. If you review the lows, you'll get a sense of where the stock might be bought at some point during the year to come. Looking at the highs, you'll see where the stock might be sold, should the club wish to sell. Although this is admittedly a rough test, it gives you a good general guideline for recognizing an excessively high current price.

In the world of investments, as elsewhere, rewards reflect the quality and quantity of the effort you and your fellow investors expend. You get out of investment club study just what you put into it—no more and no less.

As you continue to develop your investment background, you should know that there are two broad procedures used by investors to select stocks and decide when to invest and when not to. One is called the *fundamental procedure*, and the other is called the *technical procedure*. Investors usually choose one or the other procedure for their method of operation, but some combine parts of the two procedures. In the fundamental approach, the investor studies the company, its industry, and its market and tries to understand what makes the company run and what its future will be. The technician pays more attention to the stock market than to the individual company, expecting to make more money from the price movement caused by different stock market forces than by the progress achieved by a particular company through business processes. Both of these procedures enable investors to make money, but there are great differences.

In the fundamental approach, the investor is looking for companies to grow and increase in value over a long time period. The pie gets bigger and everyone benefits—customers, employees, and shareowners. Three companies widely held by NAIC members are good examples of fundamental growth. NAIC members started buying these companies fifteen to twenty years ago with the expectation that they would continue to grow, and the companies are now many times the size they were when the clubs made their first purchases. The companies are AFLAC, McDonald's, and RPM. Clubs started to buy McDonald's when it had a couple hundred stores; now it has thousands. Its stock price has multiplied many times. We have seen clubs' portfolios showing the cost per share of AFLAC at 75 cents. Recently it has sold as high as $45. Members have thousands of shares of RPM that they bought for 20 cents and that are now selling for $17. Members, of course, hold many other companies as well. The company whose growth is driven by management can produce tremendous results for the investor. NAIC's stock study procedures are designed to help you identify such companies.

In the technical approach, the goal is usually to catch fairly quick price moves. These moves are caused more often by conditions in the stock market itself than by the nature of the individual security, although there are technical procedures involving market factors concerning only one particular company. Usually profits of 20 to 50 percent are taken when they become

Figure 1-3
Reinvesting Dividends

Month	Amount Paid-in	Dividend Added	Total Invested	Shares Purchased	Total Shares Owned
1	$ 20	—	$ 20.00	1.333	1.333
2	20	$ 0.27	20.27	1.267	2.600
3	20	—	20.00	1.176	3.776
4	20	—	20.00	1.250	5.026
5	20	1.00	21.00	1.400	6.426
6	20	—	20.00	1.428	7.854
7	20	—	20.00	1.538	9.392
8	20	1.88	21.88	1.563	10.955
9	20	—	20.00	1.333	12.288
10	20	—	20.00	1.428	13.716
11	20	2.74	22.74	1.749	15.465
12	20	—	20.00	1.667	17.132
13	20	—	20.00	1.818	18.950
14	20	3.79	23.79	1.983	20.933
15	20	—	20.00	1.538	22.471
16	20	—	20.00	1.667	24.138
17	20	4.83	24.83	1.910	26.048
18	20	—	20.00	1.428	27.476
19	20	—	20.00	1.333	28.809
20	20	5.76	25.76	1.610	30.419
21	20	—	20.00	1.176	31.595
22	20	—	20.00	1.111	32.706
	$440	$20.27	$460.27	32.706	@$18= $588.71

Dividend is $0.80 per share per year, $0.20 per quarter. Stock is bought at prices shown on preceding chart.

You can compound your earnings even more quickly by reinvesting dividends. The additional amount earned is small at first but grows to sizable sums as you continue to invest. Plus, when you take into consideration that many companies increase their dividends regularly, you begin to see the power of dividend reinvestment. If you look at column 3 of the chart, you can see how the amount earned increases at each dividend payment. In this case, the investor ended up with 32.706 shares in twenty-two months—about 1½ shares more than in the preceding example (Figure 1-1).

available, and holding the stock for long-term growth is not contemplated. The result is that the first investors to start following a trend and the first to bail out reap the largest profits. The latest in and slowest out make less or lose.

A study made by Dr. Jess H. Chua and Richard S. Woodward at the University of Calgary under the auspices of the Saloman Brothers Center for the Study of Financial Institutions found that individuals who followed short-term, technical techniques over a sixty-year test period had to be right 80 percent of the time to achieve the same results as the investor who bought good-quality growing companies, held them for long periods of time, and made few changes. Based on the experience of NAIC, this is the type of procedure that the great mass of individuals can learn and follow and benefit from greatly.

The stock study program detailed in this book has proven beneficial to investors for half a century. If you resolve now to utilize the program consistently, your club will reap rewards as well.

CHAPTER 2

FINDING COMPANIES TO STUDY

*I*n launching your investment program, your club's first challenge is identifying suitable stock candidates for purchase. Your plan is to invest in growth stocks. Remember the definition of a growth company: one whose earnings per share and sales are growing at a rate higher than that of the economy as a whole. With thousands of public companies available, where should you start?

FINDING GROWTH COMPANIES

Growth stems from management. While growth companies are normally found in growing industries, they are also located in stagnant and declining industry groups. Growth of sales and earnings happens to almost everyone in a growth industry and is not as reliable a factor in identifying a growth management as in other situations. When growth stops, there is a shake-out, and poorly managed companies go bankrupt.

When buying into companies in rapidly growing industries, try to select the best-managed companies within those industries; usually those are the ones with the highest pre-tax profit margins and earnings on invested capital. While this is a logical method, it can be dangerous. Growth industries frequently attract many marginal performers that start strong but are destined to decline during periods of severe competition. Ordinarily, a shake-out period follows, where a third of the industry is lost or absorbed by the stronger units. Only after such a shake-out period does the ultimate leader emerge. All companies tend to have good figures in the first stage of a new industry.

29

A more practical approach is to look for companies, regardless of industry, where management has achieved a growth of 10 percent or more compounded annually. This method entails less risk, since your attention is focused on able management within one company rather than on a strong industry with ever-changing companies, the real leader of which might not yet be firmly established.

Each month, *Better Investing,* NAIC's own magazine, features a "Stock to Study," which has been selected because it appears to possess the potential to double in price within five years. Companies mentioned by columnists in the magazine may also prove worthy of investigation.

USING BUSINESS PUBLICATIONS

Your reading of business and financial publications will bring to your attention companies that merit exploration. *The Wall Street Journal, Barron's, Business Week, Fortune,* and *Forbes* are among the helpful sources.

Many advisory services are dedicated to the monitoring of stocks with prospects of growing value. NAIC's own Investors Advisory Service has an outstanding record. It presents stock selection guides and comments on three growth stocks each month. Two other services are *Growth Stock Outlook,* published by Charles Allmon, and Standard & Poor's *The Outlook,* which monthly highlights 200 fast-growing companies. Both may be available at your local library.

Don't overlook the importance of "backyard" investment opportunities. Local companies featured in your own community's paper, where some of your neighbors may work, could offer outstanding potential not yet recognized by the world at large.

Your broker or other business acquaintances, including suppliers and customers, and your friends who work in different industries from your own and in other areas can offer suggestions worth pursuing.

PUT IDEAS TO THE NAIC TEST

The source of an idea is not important; how you react to it is crucial. No purchase should be made at any time without formal analysis. Logical thought, not raw emotion, leads to success in the market. A great story does not produce a profitable investment. There has to be a management capable of producing growing earnings per share.

A mistake frequently made by new and inexperienced clubs is concentrating on so-called cheap stocks—those selling at a low price per share. Members deem it advantageous to own more shares for their monthly contributions. Of course, stocks may or may not be "cheap" at any price; it depends on what you're getting for your money. From the very beginning of your investment activity, emphasize the purchase of quality stocks at a reasonable price.

In performing your analysis of stocks, you'll be using the NAIC tools described later in this manual. It's also important to obtain a copy of each company's annual report to review as a prospective stockholder. The next chapter tells you how.

THE NAIC LOW-COST INVESTMENT PLAN

NAIC offers a valuable service to its members, enabling them to reinvest earnings and additional funds in additional partial shares of stock with little or no expense—a feature critical to success if your club intends to follow the reinvestment recommendation. To learn the details of this program, contact NAIC and ask for the Low-Cost Investment Plan folder, which will be accompanied by a complete list of companies in the program.

Under the program, you pay NAIC a one-time $7 charge for each stock purchased, to meet setup and handling expenses. Some companies make a small charge for each purchase you make, but most do not—every dollar you forward goes to the purchase of shares. Certain companies even sell you stock at a discount from market or reinvest your dividends at a discount. When you let NAIC know which companies are of interest, you will receive the Plan prospectus with full details of the cost associated with each company. You can make changes or terminate the program at any time.

There are three advantages to investing in one or more of the dozens of companies comprising NAIC's Low-Cost Investment Plan:

1. Information on all Plan companies is readily available for your investment analysis.
2. As a Plan participant, you will be following NAIC's proven philosophy by investing a set amount regularly, reinvesting your dividends, and buying into companies with characteristics suggesting that they can be worth substantially more five years in the future.

3. The low costs associated with the Plan will permit your club to show a profit more quickly than if you, rather than the company, were paying the commissions. NAIC has joined the dividend reinvestment programs of a number of corporations. You pick the company in which you wish to invest. Send your money to NAIC. Once your initial purchase is registered, you'll send future payments directly to the corporation's agent.

You will be surprised at how quickly your monthly payments and reinvested dividends grow into sizable holdings of the stocks you have selected. Figure 2-1 shows what would have happened had you elected to invest $100 per quarter for the last ten years in one Plan company. The initial dividend was 27 cents quarterly, and it increased five times, to 43 cents quarterly by the end of the decade of investing.

Figure 2-1
Results from NAIC's Low-Cost Investment Plan

Time Period	Amount Invested at $100/Quarter	Dividends Received	Total of Shares Bought	Total of Shares Now Owned
1st Q	$ 122.07	$ 0.27	6.2470	6.2470
2d Q	100.00	1.69	5.7582	11.9852
3d Q	100.00	3.24	6.5177	18.5029
4th Q	100.00	5.00	6.9399	25.4428
2d year	400.00	41.02	22.1677	47.6105
3d–5th years	1,200.00	307.16	58.4990	106.1095
6th–10th years	2,000.00	1,176.97	81.9142	188.0237
Totals	$4,022.07	$1,535.35	188.0237	188.0237

NAIC's unique low-cost investment plan is perfect for a new club that doesn't want to spend lots of money in transaction fees. With only a $7 setup fee, your club will show a profit more quickly. The initial purchase of one share was $22.07. At the end of five years, the stock was selling at $32 and the portfolio value amounted to $3,395.50 on an investment of $2,022.07. After ten years, the stock price was $52.50, for a value of $9,871.24 on an investment of $4,022.07.

CHAPTER 3

ANNUAL REPORTS: THE BALANCE SHEET

The annual report constitutes an essential piece of information concerning any company. Typically, the report includes financial highlights for two years, although tables of financial statistics may cover ten or more years of performance. The more years presented, the more easily you can spot and follow financial trends.

The annual report inevitably includes the President's "Message to Stockholders," reviewing the past year and looking ahead to the next. Financial statements are always included, along with an independent auditing firm's certification. Financial statements include a balance sheet and income statement, and a statement of cash flows. Reports usually also include narrative sections focusing on different product lines, research activities, foreign operations, and other subjects of interest to would-be and current owners of the business, often accompanied by photographs.

You may not derive much meaning from the financial statements when you begin analyzing them because of the terminology barrier. What is a "current ratio"? What does "shareholders' equity" mean? We'll help you clear this hurdle in the next few chapters, as we explain basic financial terms every investor should know. You'll discover that all you need to put these ratios and terms to good use is simple arithmetic. You'll even discover that many companies have done at least some of the calculations for you, offering key ratios for your immediate interpretation.

BALANCE SHEET TERMINOLOGY

The *balance sheet* reports the financial condition of a company at a specific point in time. You can evaluate the company's solvency, or ability to meet its debts, by studying the balance sheet.

Assets are properties and accounts owned by the company, while *liabilities* are the debts and claims against the company. The difference between assets and liabilities is called *shareholders' equity.* The *balance sheet* is so named because it shows the two sides of the company's condition. On one side are the assets; on the other are liabilities and shareholders' equity. The two sides are always equal in total value:

Assets = Liabilities + Shareholders' equity

Shown in Figure 3-1 is the balance sheet for a (fictitious) firm, Manic Manufacturing Company, as of December 31, 199X. Let's look more closely at the meaning of the key terms found on this balance sheet and the relationship of various entries.

Current assets constitute assets owned by the company that can be converted into cash within a year. They will not necessarily be converted; the word "current" defines these assets as "liquid," or readily available. Current assets are listed in the order of their "closeness to cash," meaning ease of convertibility. Since "cash" is immediately available for use, it ranks first. In this example, cash on hand and in the banks equals $4,500,000.

Accounts receivable is the sum of accounts due from customers for goods already sold. Practically all business transactions are conducted on a credit basis, with payment due at the end of thirty or sixty days. On occasion, the company encounters slow payers; in some instances, accounts prove to be uncollectible. For this reason, companies establish a reserve for bad debts. The amount of accounts receivable shown on the statement represents the amount due from customers, minus the reserve for bad debts. Manic's accounts receivable balance is $6,750,000.

Inventories are the balances of materials at various stages of manufacture: raw materials, work in process, and finished goods. Inventory balances are considered current assets on the theory that, on average, they will be sold, or "turned over," within one year or less. Inventory balances will not be converted into cash until the goods are sold and the resulting receivables collected. Being furthest from cash, inventories rank last in the list of current assets.

Figure 3-1

Manic Manufacturing Company Balance Sheet, December 31, 199X

CURRENT ASSETS

Cash	$ 4,500,000
Accounts receivable—less	
allowance for doubtful assets	6,750,000
Inventories	22,500,000
Total current assets	$33,750,000

PROPERTY, PLANT, AND EQUIPMENT

Cost	$40,000,000	
Accumulated depreciation	7,300,000	
Net property		32,700,000
Total assets		$66,450,000

CURRENT LIABILITIES

Accounts payable	$ 3,000,000
Accrued taxes	2,000,000
Accrued wages, interest, and other expense	1,225,000
Total current liabilities	$ 6,225,000

LONG-TERM DEBT

Mortgage bonds	$12,000,000	
Debentures	6,000,000	
Total long-term debt		$18,000,000

SHAREHOLDERS' EQUITY

Preferred stock, 100,000 shares,	
$100 par value	$10,000,000
Common stock, 6,750,000 shares,	
no par value	20,000,000
Amounts contributed above stated value	
(arising from sale of stock)	7,000,000
Retained earnings	5,225,000
Total shareholders' equity	$42,225,000
Total liabilities and shareholders' equity	$66,450,000

Companies usually value their inventories at cost or market value, usually using the lower of the two figures or values suggested by their auditors with the intent of presenting an inventory value that is consistent, conservative, and in line with economic facts, as well as with tax law. Manic values its inventories at $22,500,000.

In some cases (although not in this example), companies list *securities* among their current assets. Some companies invest surplus cash in short-term government bonds and other investments. Since these holdings are closer to cash than either accounts receivable or inventories, securities follow cash in the ranking of current assets and are normally reported at their cost value. An accountant's note will show the other value if any adjustments are made to the cost of securities.

The terms *fixed assets, long-term assets,* and *property, plant, and equipment* are used interchangeably. These are capital assets owned by the company that are expected to be employed on a continuing basis and not converted into cash within a year. Included are land, buildings, office equipment, production machinery, delivery trucks, and other long-term assets.

Except for land, all fixed assets are depreciated over a prescribed *recovery period,* set by tax law. Depreciation is a means of writing off expensive capital assets over a period of years. It is reported by way of a reserve for depreciation. This appears as a reduction to capital asset values on the balance sheet, so that the final amount shown is the net value of assets, minus accumulated depreciation. For example, if a machine is purchased for $1,000,000 and is subject to depreciation over a period of seven years, a portion is deducted from the value each year for depreciation, until the full purchase price is deducted.

For some types of assets, companies are allowed to deduct a higher amount in the first few years and less later on. Companies also have the option to claim the same amount of depreciation each year—*straight-line depreciation.* For example, suppose that some machinery a company bought cost $140,000 and has a recovery period of seven years. Applying the straight-line method, the company would be allowed to deduct one seventh of the cost, or $20,000, each year. At the end of the seven years, the asset will be fully depreciated and its book value will be zero.

If and when the company sells that equipment, it has to "recapture" the depreciation it paid. That means it will have to pay tax on its profits. Since the book value is zero after the equipment is fully depreciated, the sales price of the fully depreciated machinery in the example above would be fully taxable—at capital gains rates. For example, let's say the company sells the machinery after it's fully depreciated for $90,000:

Cost	$140,000
Less: depreciation	−140,000
Book value	$ 0
Sales price	90,000
Taxable profit	$ 90,000

Manic values its property, plant, and equipment at cost ($40,000,000) minus accumulated depreciation ($7,300,000), resulting in a net property value of $32,700,000.

Depletion is a term you'll encounter on some balance sheets. It is similar to depreciation, but recognizes the exhaustion of a natural resource. Lumber companies set up depletion accounts for their timberlands, and oil companies claim accumulated depletion on their oil reserves.

Combining the total current assets and net property of Manic, we find the company's total assets to be $66,450,000.

LOOKING AT LIABILITIES

Let's look now at the other side of the balance sheet: liabilities and stock-holders' equity.

Current liabilities include debts that come due within one year. That includes the next twelve payments on any long-term loan. Mortgages or debentures are usually payable periodically over a number of years. Payments due in the coming year are considered current.

Accounts payable are those accounts owed by the company to its creditors. Manic states its indebtedness as $3,000,000 for materials, supplies, and services. If the firm owed money to a bank or other lender that would fall due within a year, this sum would be shown under the heading "current portion of long-term debt."

Accrued taxes, which in Manic's case come to $2,000,000, represent the sum the company estimates it owes for taxes for the past year, including federal, state, and local income taxes; personal property taxes; real estate taxes; and all others.

Accrued wages, interest, and other expense is the account showing the current balance of money owed by the company to its employees, interest on money borrowed from bondholders and banks, contributions due to the company's pension plan, and other debts that must be paid within a year. For Manic, the total in this category is $1,225,000.

Taken together, all of the debts Manic must pay within the next twelve months—the current liabilities—come to $6,225,000.

Manic has two types of bonds outstanding. First, there are *mortgage bonds,* which represent debt secured by company property. These amount to $12,000,000. The second are *debentures.* Investors buy these unsecured bonds based on the company's general credit and reputation. The company has issued debentures totaling $6,000,000. Total long-term debt, the amount due beyond the coming year, amounts to $18,000,000.

EQUITY: THE OWNERSHIP OF THE COMPANY

Next we review the shareholders' equity section of the balance sheet, which represents the ownership of the company.

Manic has issued two types of stock: *preferred stock* and *common stock*. Manic has 100,000 shares of preferred stock outstanding. Holders of these shares, which have a par value (the price at which they were sold) of $10,000,000, have prior claim over common shareholders to both dividends and assets. This means that, if the earnings of Manic are insufficient to pay anticipated dividends to both preferred and common holders, the preferred stockholders will get their due and the common holders will receive less than expected, or nothing. In the event that the company files bankruptcy, preferred stockholders get paid first and common stockholders come last—if there's enough left over for them.

Both classes—preferred and common shareholders—are owners of the company. By contrast, holders of bonds are creditors. Interest payments to the bondholders must be met before even preferred holders receive dividends; and if Manic should go out of business, all claims of the bondholders would have to be met before the shareholders would be entitled to any payment.

You can see the difference between bondholders and stockholders: When investors buy bonds in a company such as Manic, they are lending money to the company. The are paid interest and, when the bond becomes due, they will get their principal back as well. When a bond is secured by mortgages on property or by other collateral, the bond investor is reasonably sure of getting his or her money back. Debentures pay higher interest because they are unsecured—so the investor's risks are greater.

Stockholders are not lenders; they are owners of the corporation. Capital stock, whether common or preferred, represents the sum total of assets, less liabilities. Preferred stockholders have priority for dividends and claims on assets, but common stock share prices are where the real action is, especially for growth companies. Together, the debt investors in the company (lenders) and the stock investors (shareholders) hold the company's total *capitalization*. Most companies are capitalized, or funded, by a combination of debt and equity.

In Manic's case, the outstanding 6,750,000 shares of common stock are valued on the company books at $20,000,000. This sum may have little or no relationship to the market value of the stock, or even to the amount of money the holders of the shares would receive if the company is dissolved. It's just the value that was originally assigned to the capital stock of common shares when the company was first organized.

Two types of surplus are listed by Manic. The first is *capital surplus,* which might also be called paid-in surplus, listed at $7,000,000. This means that the first stock was sold for $7,000,000 more than had been assigned to it in the incorporation process. In this case, the stock brought in $27,000,000 when it was sold. It had been assigned a value of $20,000,000, so the extra $7,000,000 becomes capital surplus. Adding together the stated value of the common stock and the capital surplus, we obtain $27,000,000. Dividing the number of common shares—6,750,000—into this amount, we find that the company received an average of $4.00 net per share for the common stock when it was sold.

The other type of surplus is *retained earnings,* which may also be called *earned surplus.* This is the sum total of each year's net income from operations that the company has retained for the growth of the business, rather than paying it out to shareholders as dividends. Of course, these retained earnings belong to the shareholders whether or not they are paid out. Some corporations try to keep some (or most) of their retained earnings as working capital to fund expansion.

There are other balance sheet items you may encounter.

Prepaid expenses or *deferred charges* refer to bills the company has paid in advance. What that means is that some expenses were paid before they were incurred, so they cannot properly be put into the books. For example, just before the end of the year, a corporation pays $27,000 representing facilities rent for the first month of the following year. That payment should be included in next year's expenses, so it will be set up as a prepaid expense or deferred charge. These accounts are also used to *amortize* expenses paid in one month but applicable over a longer period. For example, a corporation pays for thirty-six months of insurance in a single payment. It sets up the payment as a prepaid expense, and amortizes (or writes down to general expenses) one thirty-sixth of the payment each month.

Some companies list intangible assets, such as *goodwill.* While such assets have value, it's clearly difficult to quantify. For example, suppose a corporation purchases a competitor and, as part of the negotiation, agrees to pay $50,000 for goodwill—an admittedly arbitrary value assigned to the company's reputation and the value of name recognition. Because this is clearly an asset, it is entered as such. However, it has no physical value, so it is classified as an *intangible asset*.

On the liabilities side, take a good look at *reserves for contingencies*. It could be important to understand more about goodwill and contingencies if these are significant amounts. A contingent liability is a debt or claim that might or might not materialize. Depending on the industry, companies may set up reserves for such contingencies. For example, a company might know that a lawsuit is pending against it. In the event of a loss, or to set aside some funds for legal defense, a contingency reserve is set up and shown as a liability.

CHAPTER 4

ANALYZING THE BALANCE SHEET

*T*he balance sheet supplies you with a wealth of information about the company whose stock you're thinking of buying. But, as with anything else, you need to know what to look for.

First, let's check the *working capital* of the company, the amount of money available for use in its current operations. Working capital is derived by subtracting current liabilities from current assets; Manic has working capital of $27,525,000. This seems to be an amount sufficient to permit the company to stay out of financial difficulty if business falls off for a period, and enough to take advantage of any opportunities that require ready cash. Working capital is the lifeblood of the company. It's needed to make payroll; to pay and remain current on taxes, rents, note and interest payments, and mortgages; and for the purchase of raw materials. With working capital problems, a company will not be able to sustain itself—and that means it won't make money, either.

Now we'll turn to the *current ratio*, or the current assets divided by the current liabilities. Manic's ratio is better than 5.4 to 1. About 2 to 1 is typical of manufacturing companies; among those whose inventories are subject to wide price fluctuations, a higher current ratio is desirable. A ratio of less than 2 to 1 is a danger sign. Such a company could run short of working capital in meeting its near-term cash requirements. However, a ratio far in excess of 2 to 1, as is true with Manic, is not necessarily a plus. This may indicate that the company is not employing its cash to full advantage in income-producing assets.

While a ratio of 2 to 1 is normal for manufacturing, utilities often oper-ate successfully with current ratios of 1 to 1 or even less. If the company car-ries no inventories—for example, a non-manufacturing concern—a current ratio of 1 to 1 is normally considered an acceptable standard.

You should track the current ratio of the company you're examining back a few years. Also plan to keep an eye on this in the future. Look for changes in the current ratio trend, to ensure that management is remaining fiscally responsible in controlling cash flow. Also see how your candidate com-pares with its competitors, especially other companies in the same industry. If the current ratio for your candidate seems out of line with those of its com-petitors, you might question it.

Another ratio is the *acid test*, also called the *quick assets ratio*. This is found by dividing current assets (excluding inventories) by current liabilities. For some companies, the acid test more realistically evaluates the company's ability to meet its current debts. This might be especially important for cor-porations that keep an inventory of high-priced items, where conversion to cash might not be readily possible, or when a company's inventory seems exceptionally high. Manic's acid test ratio stands at 1.8 to 1. Thus we can see that about two thirds of the firm's current assets are tied up in inventories, and its ability to meet current cash needs seems reasonable.

Track the acid test ratio over a period of years, and compare it with those of competitive firms. A large inventory position may cause losses if materials prices drop. That would mean the company purchased its materials at a higher rate than current market value, which certainly affects its profit mar-gin. An overly large inventory may show that the company has a considerable amount of unsalable merchandise or that it has overinvested working capital in materials.

TURNOVER

One important test of inventory position is *inventory turnover*, which is deter-mined by dividing cost of goods sold (from the income statement, discussed in Chapter 5) by average inventory at cost. If the average inventory figure is unavailable, you can use the ending inventory figure shown on the balance sheet. You may compute an average by adding together the company's begin-ning and ending inventory, and dividing by 2. If inventory levels are fairly consistent, this is dependable. However, if seasonal fluctuations are wide, this method could distort the true picture.

Manic has an inventory of $22,500,000; its cost of goods sold is $45,000,000 (see Chapter 5 for Manic's income statement). Thus, the inventory turnover is precisely two times. This ratio shows, on average, how many times during the period the inventory is entirely sold and replaced. In reality, of course, the warehouse isn't emptied out and restocked. Like all aspects of financial analysis, the turnover ratio is an estimate. The higher the turnover, the better, as an indication of both quality merchandise and proper pricing. You might want to check if the company you are analyzing is improving its inventory turnover, and how it stacks up with its competitors in this respect. Some industries, such as foods, are characterized by high turnover levels; others, such as tobacco, characteristically have low inventory turnover.

Another figure worth computing is *plant turnover*, or sales (from the income statement) divided by property. plant, and equipment. In the case of Manic, this is $67,500,000 divided by $40,000,000, so plant turnover amounts to about 1.7 times.

The higher this ratio, the better, and we would like to see it increasing over time. If the company expands its plant without a corresponding growth in sales, there is clearly a problem with asset utilization.

BOOK VALUE

Another useful figure is the *book value* of the common stock. To find it, add the par or stated value of common stock to retained earnings and any surplus reserves. (As noted earlier, companies occasionally earmark part of their retained earnings for contingencies or other purposes.) For Manic, we add the $20,000,000 stated value of common stock, $7,000,000 capital surplus, and $5,225,00 in retained earnings to derive a book value for the common stock of $32,225,000. We'll use this figure in a computation in the next chapter. Keep in mind that book value has no direct relationship to market value; the shares of well-regarded companies with rising sales and earnings may sell at many times their book value, while other firms with lackluster results may actually sell at a discount to book.

One other item to review is the *capital structure* of the company, or what proportion is represented by each component of capitalization—bonds, preferred stock, and common stock. A high proportion of bonds may make both forms of stock less attractive, while a sizable amount of preferred stock could make the common stock less appealing.

The *bond ratio* is found by dividing the face value of bonds by the total value of bonds, preferred stock, common stock, capital surplus, and retained earnings. In Manic's case, $18,000,000 divided by $60,225,000 shows that bonds constitute about 30 percent of total capitalization.

The *preferred stock ratio* results from dividing the stated value of the preferred stock by the total value of bonds, preferred and common stock, capital surplus, and retained earnings. For Manic, we divide $10,000,000 by $60,225,000 and determine that the preferred stock ratio is about 16.5 percent.

To calculate the *common stock ratio*, divide the stated value of common stock plus capital surplus and retained earnings by total capitalization, or $32,225,000 divided by $60,225,000. Common stock represents about 53.5 percent of total capitalization.

In general, an industrial company should have no more than half of its capitalization represented by *senior securities*—bonds and preferred stock. They are so called because in the event of bankruptcy, bonds and preferred stocks are senior; holders of these investments will be paid before investors in common stocks.

It is also considered desirable for no more than one quarter of total capitalization to be represented by bonds. Manic meets the senior securities test, but its bond ratio of 30 percent is a bit higher than the standard.

Utilities typically carry a much higher load of debt and preferred to total capital ratio—up to 70 or 75 percent—and can do so successfully because of their relative stability of earnings. For this reason, though, such industries are said to be interest-sensitive. Because they are so heavily capitalized by debt, their earnings are adversely affected when interest rates rise.

LEVERAGE

A company with a high ratio of bonds and preferred stock is said to be highly *leveraged*. Leverage may or may not be an advantage to common stockholders, depending on the success of the company in utilizing the other forms of securities to enhance earnings.

As an example, consider ABC Company, which has long-term debt or bonds outstanding in the amount of $50,000. The company pays interest of 5 percent, or $2,500 per year. Shareholders' equity in the company totals $100,000. The total capital structure amounts to $150,000. The interest charge on the bonds does not vary; as income increases, more money will go to the value of common stock. However, when income falls, the portion available to stockholders will drop. Here's how leverage can impact stockholders in a good year and in a bad year (Figure 4-1).

Figure 4-1
Impact of a Good versus a Bad Year on ABC's Leverage

Capitalization	*Rate of Return*	
	Good Year	Bad Year
Long-term debt $50,000 at 5% interest	$2,500 or 5%	$2,500 or 5%
Shareholders' equity $100,000	$12,500 or 12.5%	$4,000 or 4%
Capital structure $150,000	$15,000 or 10%	$6,500 or 4.3%

Debt has the effect of magnifying a company's performance and shareholder profit. In a good year, debt actually benefits the shareholder. Once the long-term debt at a rate of 5 percent is paid off, the shareholder receives a very good 12.5 percent return. However, in a bad year, the long-term debt must be paid off at the same rate of 5 percent, and the shareholder receives only a 4.3 percent return.

The company earned $15,000 in the good year, but just $6,500 in the bad year. In the good year, after paying bond interest of $2,500, ABC has a net profit after taxes of $12,500. The rate on long-term debt is 5 percent. The rate of return on the total capital structure is 10 percent, and the rate of return on shareholders' equity is 12.5 percent. The additional return to the stockholders through use by the company of money borrowed is 2.5 percent, or the difference between earnings on stockholder money and earnings on total capital structure.

But what about a bad year? What if net after interest payment had amounted to just $4,000? In this scenario, the rate on long-term debt remains at 5 percent. The rate of return on the total capital structure stands at 4.3 percent, but the rate of return on shareholders' equity is only 4 percent. Thus, the owners of the company would have fared better had no bonds been outstanding.

If the company you are analyzing is leveraged, check to see if the return on equity is higher than the return on total capital structure. Look for a trend rather than analyzing one year in isolation. If equity tends to be higher, then shareholders are benefiting. If it is not, the shareholders would be better off if the company had no debt.

Now that you are familiar with the essentials of the balance sheet, we will turn our attention to another key financial report: the income statement.

CHAPTER 5

ANNUAL REPORTS: THE INCOME STATEMENT

While the balance sheet depicts a company's solvency or financial position at a specific date, its *income statement,* also called *profit and loss statement,* reports income, costs, expenses, and profits (or losses) over a period of time, usually one full year. The income statement, considered along with the balance sheet, is of crucial importance to stockholders—and to you and your club, if you're considering becoming stockholders.

INCOME STATEMENT TERMINOLOGY

The first item on Manic's income statement (Figure 5-1) is *net sales* of $67,500,000; this is money collected for all goods sold by the company (gross sales) minus returns and allowances. If you're studying such non-manufacturing companies as utilities or transportation concerns, the term "revenues" corresponds to sales.

The first deduction from sales is *cost of goods sold,* also termed *cost of sales.* (A utility or insurance company might refer to this as "operating expenses.") Subtracted here are all $45,000,000 in costs attributable to units produced by the company during the period being reported. It includes wages of production workers, costs of raw materials used in production, and expenditures for electricity required to keep production lines moving. Another item in this cost is the change in inventory levels.

Subtracting cost of sales from sales, we arrive at Manic's gross profit of $22,500,000. Next *selling, general, and administrative expenses,* or *non-manufacturing*

47

Figure 5-1

Manic Manufacturing Company Income Statement for the Year Ending December 31, 199X

Net sales	$67,500,000
Cost of sales	45,000,000
Gross profit	$22,500,000
Selling, general, and administrative expenses	15,000,000
Operating profit	$ 7,500,000
Other income	900,000
	$ 8,400,000
Other expenses	945,000
Net income before taxes	$ 7,455,000
Provisions for federal income taxes	3,877,500
Net income after taxes	$ 3,577,500

costs, of $15,000,000 are subtracted. These include executive compensation, sales commissions, and staff department outlays—including legal, rent, office supplies, advertising, and public relations expenses.

Deducting these items from gross profit results in an operating profit of $7,500,000. This is the amount Manic made from the manufacture and sale of its products.

The next line (not shown in Manic's statement) is *non-operating income.*

OTHER INCOME

Manic's *other income* of $900,000 includes sources of income beyond the primary business. For example, here the company reports interest and dividends on securities owned, royalties on patents, profits on foreign exchange, and other such items.

The total of operating profit plus other income for Manic is $8,400,000. Next, *other expenses* are deducted. This amount is $945,000 and could include expenses such as interest paid on the company's mortgage and debenture bonds, settlements of lawsuits, and losses on foreign exchange.

Manic's *net income before taxes* figure is $7,455,000. After the deduction of $3,877,500 in federal taxes, net income amounts to $3,577,500. The company may declare and pay out dividends to preferred and common shareholders, and add the remainder to retained earnings.

ANALYZING THE INCOME STATEMENT

One of the most important relationships that can be determined from the income statement is *pre-tax profit margin,* arrived at by dividing profit before taxes by net sales. Manic's profit margin is 11 percent.

What does this mean? If you examine the operating profit margin of a company over a period of years, you can learn if it is rising or falling. It does not have to rise consistently, but the company should be able to achieve the maximum practical net operating margin for the industry, year after year. Each industry has natural limitations on the percentage it can achieve, so it is always worthwhile to compare your target company's statements with those of its competitors. Look for a trend over many years. If the company has been able to produce consistent profits at the peak levels for the industry, that's a sign the corporation is well managed.

Do not use net (after taxes) profit margin as your basis of comparison. Taxes fluctuate for different companies from year to year, and this variation makes such a comparison less meaningful. In addition, state income taxes distort any such comparison. A company with its major operations in a state with a relatively high income tax should not be compared on an after-tax basis with a company operating in a state assessing a lower income tax.

The other important computation to be made from the income statement is *return on book value,* or *return on equity.* As you learned in examining the balance sheet, the book value of Manic common stock is $32,225,000. Dividing the company's net income of $3,577,500 by this figure, we obtain 11 percent. That means that, collectively, the stockholders earned 11 percent on their money.

Whether this result is favorable depends on Manic's trend over time; as with the operating margin, look for consistency rather than ever-growing returns. Don't expect unrealistically that a company is a worthwhile investment only if such results improve every year.

Also review how return on equity compares with that of other companies in the same industry. Any company you're considering should be at least average or above in this regard with respect to similar companies in the same industry, as an indication of average or superior management.

Another figure of interest is *sales per employee;* typically, the annual report lists the number of employees. If it doesn't, call the investor relations department and ask. Then compare the productivity of the company over time with the results of other companies in the same industry. The higher the ratio between sales and employees, the more efficiently the company is operating. Be aware, however, that these ratios will vary considerably by industry. An industry that is more labor-intensive, such as a manufacturing concern, will not be comparable to one that is less dependent on labor for its product or service.

EVALUATING MANAGEMENT

From examining the balance sheet and income statement, you already know something about the firm's management. Pre-tax profit margin and return on equity are two of the best statistical measures of managerial efficiency. What else can the annual report and other corporate publications reveal concerning management? Don't follow the example of the club member who wanted to buy a company's shares because the chief executive officer looked good! Far too many folks are overly impressed by expensively produced reports with good design and lots of color, not to mention Robert Redford look-alikes smiling at the reader. Remember, companies spend a lot of money producing annual reports. They're not going to report gloomy news or use poor-quality photographs, and they're not going to show you a picture of a depressed, unhappy president. The annual report is very much a public relations document. But it also includes full financial disclosures, and that's why it's valuable to you.

Take a logical approach in studying the information available to you. If you were a professional analyst, you could get answers to specific questions and gain definite impressions about company leadership from face-to-face meetings. Although such an opportunity is likely to be closed to you, there are still conclusions to be drawn. (Incidentally, the brokerage firm your club uses probably publishes reports prepared by their own professional analyst or analytical department on companies you are interested in. Be sure to ask if they have a report on the company you're reviewing.)

What can you ask on your own? First of all, what is the age composition of the top officer cadre? If ages aren't furnished, you can find them in *Standard & Poor's Register of Directors and Executives.* There should be a mix of ages, representing a combination of experience and new thinking. Too many senior citizens may mean less drive, just as an abundance of young men and women may signal insufficient seasoning in the crucible of depressed economic conditions.

Check the names of leaders, and be wary if several appear to be members of the same family. When nepotism is being practiced, make sure the management figures meet our previously mentioned tests.

What is the size of executive compensation? The corporate proxy statement should provide this information, but often it's difficult to identify with precision. The increasing complexity of executive pay options—different types, paid out at varying times—adds to the confusion. Fortunately, you can access other sources to find reasonable approximations, if not exactly accurate data. *The Wall Street Journal, Business Week,* and *Fortune* conduct surveys. A chief executive's remuneration should be in line with the size of the company and the profits attained. Check the degree of correlation between pay and performance.

What is the stock ownership of the top executive group? Here again, the proxy statement is the source of this information. A substantial number of shares in management's hands generally provides evidence of their confidence in the company's future. What about the board of directors? The board should have a majority of outsiders whose principal occupations and reputations indicate that they can make a real contribution to the company's results.

For further information on management, consult those who know the company best: its employees, suppliers, customers, stockholders, and direct competitors. Their attitudes should be factored into your decision making.

Don't overlook the notes in any annual report you review. Although customarily set in small type, these dull-appearing sentences contain important information about litigation, unusual liabilities, new pension or stock option plans, and other news you won't find elsewhere. Check the auditor's opinion to determine if there is routine approval or only a qualified endorsement. If the latter, the reason for any reservations is important, and you need to inquire further.

To summarize, always review income statement information in comparative form. How does this year look compared with last year? With five years ago? Dynamic information is always more revealing than the static profit and loss report, which is revealing only to the extent that it shows the latest entry in a trend.

You now know the essentials of annual report study. You may obtain an annual report on any publicly held company free of charge by calling the company's shareowner relations executive, listed in the Standard & Poor's or Value Line Survey corporate reports.

CHAPTER 6

THE NAIC TOOLS FOR SMART INVESTING

The stock study program of the National Association of Investment Clubs embraces five essential tools that will help you to make informed decisions about your portfolio. These tools will be explained in detail in the following seven chapters.

You'll get an overview of the program in this brief introduction. You'll learn what each tool looks like, the reason for its use, what it includes, when it should be used, and when it should be updated.

In investing, you have three basic tasks:

1. To judge a company's potential value by studying its record.
2. To compare several companies and select for investment the one that most nearly meets your objective.
3. To stay current on stocks you own so that you can make good decisions concerning whether to purchase additional shares, hold, or sell.

STOCK CHECK LIST

The simplest of NAIC's forms is the *Stock Check List*. Even the inexperienced club member can put it to good use immediately. The Stock Check List allows you to pursue the first of the three basic tasks of investing—recording and reviewing a company's sales and earnings record as well as its price history. From these data you can decide if the stock is a suitable candidate for purchase now or whether it might be a good choice in the future.

STOCK SELECTION GUIDE

The Stock Check List does not provide a thorough analysis. It is designed for use only until you have learned how to use the more sophisticated *Stock Selection Guide and Report*. Typically, you should be using this within six months of starting your investment club.

Like the Check List, the Stock Selection Guide and Report (SSG) addresses the first basic task of investing. The SSG helps you to learn facts about a company's past, take a look at how it's doing in the present, and form a judgment about its likely value in the future. The SSG ranks as the single most important weapon in the investment club member's arsenal. It should be completed before you purchase any security, and it should be updated annually as long as the stock is held.

The Stock Selection Guide comprises four different sections. In the *Visual Analysis of Sales, Earnings, and Price* you record sales, earnings, and price figures for the past ten years. This produces trend lines that show you quickly if you have a stock worth further study. Looking at the trend lines also helps you project future earnings.

The second section concerns management. Management is evaluated on the basis of two factors: (1) the sales and earnings-per-share trend lines and (2) the pre-tax profit margin and return on shareholders' equity. You will remember these concepts from Chapter 5.

In Section 3 you record the last five years' high and low prices, earnings per share, high and low price/earnings ratios, dividend payout, and yield figures to enable you to make estimates of the future.

In Section 4 you make adjustments to these figures based on the knowledge you have developed and estimate future price action.

In Section 5 you check whether the results you have estimated enable you to reach your goal.

STOCK COMPARISON GUIDE

The *Stock Comparison Guide* (SCG) addresses the second basic task of investing. When your club reviews several different investment opportunities, this tool helps you make an informed decision on which stock, if any, should be purchased.

The SCG lets you review quickly and easily the important differences in the same data on several companies. All of the figures needed are already available to you from the Stock Selection Guide.

There are four sections to the SCG: *Growth Comparisons, Management Comparisons, Price Comparisons,* and *Other Comparisons.* The more similar the businesses of the companies being studied, the more meaningful the SCG becomes.

PORTFOLIO MANAGEMENT GUIDE

The Portfolio Management Guide and the *Portfolio Evaluation Review Technique* are the two NAIC forms devoted to the third basic task of investing—staying current on stocks you already own. As your club grows older and the size of your portfolio expands, portfolio management becomes increasingly significant.

The Portfolio Management Guide is a memory jogger that requires you to record the stock's price every month. NAIC recommends that you also compare the current price with previously established price zones on a monthly basis.

Section 1 records price/earnings zones, Section 2 is devoted to price zones, and Section 3 permits you to record current price and price/earnings ratios. Section 4 lets you place the same information in a chart for easier review.

If you review each of your stocks in this guide at each meeting, you are unlikely to miss opportunities to add to your holdings at favorable prices.

PORTFOLIO EVALUATION REVIEW TECHNIQUE

The Portfolio Evaluation Review Technique (PERT) consists of a form and two worksheets. The form allows you to record quarterly and annual change rates in earnings per share and to calculate the current P/E ratio and compare it with historical P/Es. Worksheet A lets you register the percent change in earnings per share, pre-tax profit, and sales on an annual and a quarterly basis. Worksheet B is concerned with price, price/earnings ratios, and dividend and yield information on a monthly basis.

There is a PERT report to be updated and reviewed at each monthly meeting.

Is all of this overwhelming? It may look formidable to the beginner, but after a few times you and your fellow club members will be surprised at how easily and quickly the forms can be completed. Your skills at interpretation will improve rapidly.

In NAIC's 1991 survey of member clubs, 61.9 percent of them were found to have equaled or bettered the S&P 500 over their lifetimes (averaging nearly 10 years). In contrast, only 19 percent of the professional managers at equity mutual funds outperformed the S&P over the same time period.

Regular use of NAIC tools will permit you and other members of your club to make the best possible investment decisions and significantly enhance your prospects for profitability.

The next seven chapters will discuss how to go about putting the tools to use in your club.

CHAPTER 7

THE STOCK
CHECK LIST

*T*he NAIC *Stock Check List* is designed to help you complete a basic stock analysis. After completing the form, you will know the recent history of sales and earnings per share, and whether the stock's current price makes it a good buy.

The Check List is not meant to provide a thorough, detailed analysis. Rather, the form serves as "training wheels" for using the more detailed NAIC Stock Selection Guide and Report. Use the two tools together and, after no more than six months, you will have the experience to move beyond the Check List. After that, the NAIC Stock Selection Guide and Report can serve as your basic analytical tool.

PREPARATION
Section 1
Past Sales Record

First let us see how to fill the form out. Information on a specific company is available at your broker's office, at your public library, or from the company itself. A call to a company's shareholder relations department can usually get you a copy of the company's annual report and a number of broker reports about the company. The major services that provide information about corporations are Standard & Poor's (S&P) and Value Line. Standard & Poor's reports prior to January 1, 1996, do not provide information for the time period needed; reports issued since that date are satisfactory. The reports of Value Line meet the NAIC investor's needs, and are widely used.

A copy of the Value Line Survey form for Motorola appears in Figure 7-1. As of this writing, fairly reliable estimates are available for 1995, so we will use 1995 as our beginning year and work backward. Motorola's source of income is referred to as "sales." Some businesses use the word "revenues," and other businesses—utilities, banks, and insurance companies, for example—have other terms for their sources of income. Some have more than one source of income. The main item is usually shown on line 11 of the Value Line report. On this sheet we see that sales for 1995 are expected to be $28.250 billion, and we record that figure on our Stock Check List at Section 1, line 1. The next year back is 1994, for which we see $22.245 billion in sales on the Value Line report. This amount goes in Section 1, line 2 on the form. (See Figure 7-2.)

In Section 1, line 3 we have added these two figures to get $50,495. The amount on line 4 is the result of dividing line 3 by 2.

To get the figure for line 5 we return to line 11 of the Value Line report and count back five years from 1995. (We count 1994 as the first year because we want to include five full years of operations.) That takes us to 1990 and the figure $10,885 for line 5. The next year back is 1989, and $9,620 goes in line 6.

Completing the calculations called for in items 7, 8, 9, and 10, we see that sales have increased 146 percent over the last five years. The figure we want is the compound annual rate of growth over this five-year period. The conversion table at the end of Section 1 helps us estimate that. The table shows the percent increase on the first line and the corresponding one-year compound growth rate on the second line. We do not need an exact figure; a "ballpark" figure meets our need. We see that 146 falls between 129 and 148 on the upper line of the table and it is very close to 148. The figures corresponding to 129 and 148 are 18 and 20. Since 146 is very close to 148, we will choose 20 percent as our compound rate of growth. It would probably calculate out to 19.7 or 19.8 percent, but whole figures are good enough for these estimates.

Section 2
Earnings-per-Share Record

Section 2 is filled in using the same procedure as for Section 1. Use the earnings-per-share figures from line 3 of the Value Line report.

Figure 7-1
Value Line Report for Motorola

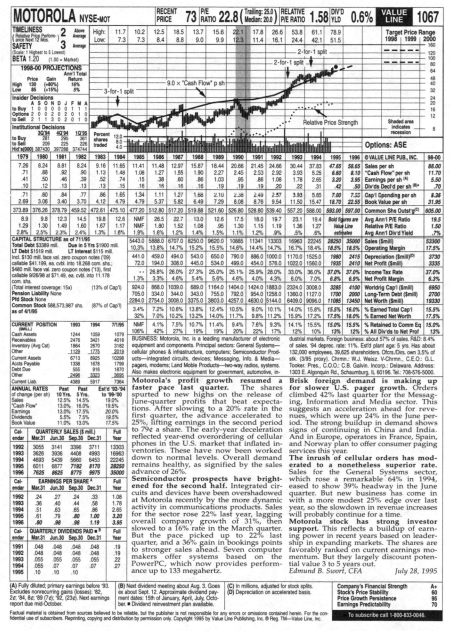

Figure 7-2
Stock Check List for Motorola, Page 1

NATIONAL ASSOCIATION OF INVESTORS CORPORATION **NAIC**® INVESTMENT EDUCATION FOR INDIVIDUALS AND CLUBS SINCE 1951	*Stock Check List* **for Beginning Investors**	Company __MOTOROLA, INC.__ Prepared by __G.O.M.__ Date __12-11-95__ *See Chapter 7 of Investors Manual.* *While Investors are learning to use NAIC's Stock Selection Guide, it is suggested the following Check List be used for each stock considered for investment.*

1 PAST SALES RECORD

Sales for most recent year were .... (1) $ __28,250__

Sales for next most recent year were .... (2) $ __22,245__

Total of above (1 + 2) .... (3) $ __50,495__

Figure above divided by 2 .... (4) $ __25,248__

Sales 5 years ago were .... (5) $ __10,885__

Sales 6 years ago were .... (6) $ __9,620__

Total of above (5 + 6) .... (7) $ __20,505__

Figure above divided by 2 .... (8) $ __10,253__

Increase in sales in above period (8 from 4) .... (9) $ __14,995__

Percentage increase in sales (9 divided by 8) .... (10) __146__ %

CONVERSION TABLE

This % Increase in Sales Gives ➜	27	33	46	61	76	93	112	129	148	205	271
This % Compounded ➜ Annual Growth Rate	5	6	8	10	12	14	16	18	20	25	30

Look for the percent increase that meets the objective you have set.

COMPOUND ANNUAL RATE OF SALES GROWTH WAS __20__ %

2 PAST EARNINGS PER SHARE RECORD

Earnings Per Share for most recent year were .... (1) $ __3.20__

Earnings Per Share for next most recent year were .... (2) $ __2.65__

Total of above (1 + 2) .... (3) $ __5.85__

Figure above divided by 2 .... (4) $ __2.93__

Earnings Per Share 5 years ago were .... (5) $ __.95__

Earnings Per Share 6 years ago were .... (6) $ __1.03__

Total of above (5 + 6) .... (7) $ __1.98__

Figure above divided by 2 .... (8) $ __.99__

Increase in Earnings Per Share in above period (8 from 4) .... (9) $ __1.94__

Percentage increase in earnings (9 divided by 8) .... (10) __196__ %

See **Conversion Table** above to determine ⟶

Earnings Per Share have increased _____ **more** _____ than sales in this period.
(more)   (less)

COMPOUND ANNUAL RATE OF EARNINGS PER SHARE GROWTH WAS __24__ %

Explain Apparent Reason for Difference in Sales and Earnings Per Share Growth: __A look at the Net Profit Margin line and Percent Earned on Total Capital on the Value Line report shows that margins increased and consequently produced more earnings per dollar of sales.__

Section 3
Price Record of the Stock

The price figures needed to fill out the price table in Section 3 come from the top of the Value Line report following the words "High" and "Low." (Data for 1995 in this section is based on updated figures from newspaper reports.) The earnings per share are found on line 3 of the report. The price/earnings ratios are calculated as indicated in the column headings in Section 3 (Figure 7-3).

INTERPRETING THE FIGURES

Now that we have recorded all the figures the form calls for, the question is what they tell us about Motorola. Section 1 tells us that Motorola has increased its sales by 146 percent in five years, which is 20 percent compounded annually. Our goal is 100 percent appreciation in five years, which is 14.9 percent compounded annually. Thus, Motorola more than meets our goal. The company's figures show that if it continues to grow the way it has in the past five years, it will double its sales in less than four years. Thus, Motorola has been an outstanding company in growing its sales. We probably should not expect such a high rate of growth to continue indefinitely.

Looking at Section 2, we see that earnings per share grew 196 percent in five years. That is almost twice our goal of 100 percent. The compound annual growth rate of earnings per share is 24 percent. That rate will double our money in just over three years. Clearly, we have a company with an outstanding rate of growth. This is doubly impressive when you realize that Motorola's sales are at $30 billion per year.

We note that Motorola's earnings per share are growing faster than its sales. We also know that earnings come from sales and therefore over an extended period cannot grow faster than sales. This suggests that we should not estimate future growth in earnings per share at a higher rate than we project sales growth. When we graduate to NAIC's Stock Selection Guide and Report, we will review the history of Motorola's pre-tax profit margins and earnings on invested capital. These figures will help us judge when we can expect further earnings growth to be limited to the sales growth rate.

Answering the questions between Sections 2 and 3 requires that we learn a little about the company. Your public library may have a folder of articles written about the company. You will want to read what Value Line, Standard & Poor's, and the company annual report have to say. The company's

Figure 7-3
Stock Check List for Motorola, Page 2

Discuss Possible Reasons for Past Growth:
A new product was very successful___✓_____.
A cyclical business that experienced recovery_____.
A research program has produced several new products or uses for older products___✓_____.
Purchase another company_____.
Has taken larger share of business in its field__✓_____.
Skill of management __✓_____.

Will Factors Which Produced Past Growth Continue Effective
for the next five years __✓____ yes, _____ yes, but less effective, _____ no.

3 PRICE RECORD OF THE STOCK

Present Price $ ___76 ⅛___ . Present Earnings Per Share _3.20_____ .

List Last 5 Years	High Price Each Year (A)	Low Price Each Year (B)	Earnings Per Share (C)	Price Earnings Ratio at High (A ÷ C)	at Low (B ÷ C)
1991	17.8	11.4	0.86	20.7	13.3
1992	26.6	16.1	1.08	24.6	14.9
1993	53.8	24.4	1.78	30.2	13.7
1994	61.1	42.1	2.65	23.1	15.9
1995	82.1	51.5	3.20	25.7	16.1
Totals	241.4	145.5		124.3	73.9
Averages	48.28	29.1		24.9	14.8

Average of High and Low Price Earnings Averages for the past five years.	19.9

Present Price is ___higher_____ than high price five years ago.
(higher)   (lower)

Present Price is _328___% higher than the high price 5 years ago. Compare this figure with the percent sales increase in 1 (10) and percent earnings per share increase in 2 (10).
The price change compares with sales growth and earnings per share growth ___favorably_____.
(favorably or unfavorably)

This stock has sold as high as the current price in ___1___ of the last 5 years.
In the past five years the stock ___has_____ sold at unusually __high___ price earnings ratios.
(has)   (has not)   (high)   (low)

The Present price earnings ratio is ____23.8_____ .
In relation to past price earnings ratios the stock is currently
_____ selling at a higher ratio
___✓___ selling about the same
_____ selling lower
The average price earnings ratios of the past might be expected to continue _____,
or should be adjusted to _22____ high, _13____ low.

4 CONCLUSION

1. The past sales growth rate ____does_____ meet our objective.
(does)   (does not)

2. The past earnings per share growth rate ____does_____ meet our objective.
(does)   (does not)

3. Our conclusion has been that possible earnings per share growth rate___will_____ meet our objective in the coming five years.
(will)   (will not)

4. The price of the stock is currently ___too high_____ .
(acceptable)   (too high)

This form is not meant to give you an adequate analysis of the stock, but is meant to help the beginner ask questions to indicate whether the company is likely to become more valuable and if it can be purchased reasonably. As Investors gain practice, a more thorough study of the stock is suggested using NAIC's Stock Selection Guide and Report as a guide.

shareholder relations department may send you copies of articles published about the company.

From this reading we learn that Motorola is a leader in producing chips for computers and in wireless communications research. It is also a leader in the production of various wireless communications instruments and systems. We would ascribe these superior positions to skill of management. This knowledge enables us to answer the questions concerning the reasons for Motorola's growth record.

The table in Section 3 shows us a great deal about Motorola's price. Our belief is that if a company grows in sales and earnings, the price of the stock will rise to reflect that increase in value. In 1991 Motorola earned 86 cents per share. In 1995 it earned $3.20. That is a 272 percent increase. The high price of the stock in 1991 was $17.8. In 1995 it was $82.1. That is a 361 percent increase. In 1991 Motorola sold at 20.7 times earnings at its high. In 1995 it sold at 25.7 times earnings. The stocks in the Dow Jones Industrials are selling at 15.8 times earnings. This indicates that we should be cautious about buying Motorola. It is selling at 10 P/E points above the average, which is high but not unusual for a stock with such a high growth rate.

Now let us answer the questions in Section 3. Motorola's price is $76^1/8$, and five years ago it was 17.8. That's an increase of 328 percent. From the front page of the Check List we see that sales are up 146 percent and earnings per share are up 196 percent. The price increase substantially exceeds our two basic growth indicators. This suggests that a great many investors have been impressed with Motorola's growth and have been paying very good prices for it. As we look at the record, we see that just this year it has sold for as high as 82.1 and as low as 51.5. We should be cautious in making a purchase.

The stock's price has been as high as it is only in the current year. In the past five years it has sold for more than 20 times earnings in each year, and in one year its P/E was over 30. Currently the stock is selling at 23.8 times 1995 earnings. Value Line estimates that 1996 earnings will be $3.95 per share. That makes the P/E 19.3 at $76^1/8$ on next year's earnings.

The figures show that Motorola is selling at about the same P/E for the average high as it has sold at for the past five years. The company more than meets our requirements for growth in sales and earnings, but the risk at $76^1/8$ is high. We should watch the stock. Its price is very volatile. We would recommend not buying it until the P/E on 1995 earnings of $3.20 is below 19.9 or until it is 14.8 or lower on estimated 1996 earnings of $3.95.

CHAPTER 8

THE NAIC STOCK SELECTION GUIDE AND REPORT: PAGE 1

The most important act that any investor takes is the selection of the individual stock to put his or her money in. You as an investor never buy the stock market, no matter how much you talk about it. We repeat: You never buy the stock market. What the stock market does is always interesting, but as an investor you buy a particular company, and the success of that company determines whether or not you make money.

The NAIC *Stock Selection Guide and Report* (*Stock Selection Guide* for short) is a tool to help you make that selection. We use the Stock Selection Guide with a definite objective in mind. We are looking for a company with a record of growth. We know that a record of growth does not guarantee future growth, but we believe a company is more likely to grow in the future if it has a record of growth in the past. It is growing sales and earnings per share that make a company increase in value and make its stock price go up.

If the company meets our growth objective, we next look at its pre-tax profit margin and earnings on invested capital. We compare these figures with those of its competitors and the standards of the industry. We want a company for which these figures are in the top half of its industry.

If a company meets these tests, we check to see if we can buy it at a favorable price. If it is too high-priced, we postpone action until the price is right.

Recording the information needed to make these tests on the NAIC Stock Selection Guide is the subject of this chapter. It cannot be overemphasized that completion of a Stock Selection Guide in one form or another, permitting review of operating data and computation of financial ratios, should be performed for every prospective purchase.

The NAIC Stock Selection Guide and Report has been in use for five decades and has gained wide acceptance among both professional and amateur security analysts as an aid to making informed and profitable investment decisions.

Completing your first Guide may require several hours' time. After some experience, you'll find that you need to devote no more than half an hour to the task for each company. Remember, the Stock Selection Guide contains no "magic formula" to ensure investment success. The form is only a guide to judgment, and is no more useful than the interpretation you make.

WHAT DOES "DATA" MEAN?

Many clubs are not sure how to interpret all the information captured by the Stock Selection Guide. For example, you and other members may energetically complete Guides for any number of companies, attend meetings, and make presentations summarizing each Guide. Then, however, you and your fellow members discover that nobody knows what to make of the findings.

Where does a high growth rate come from? Is it a short-term accident? Does it come from a temporary or long-term advantage of product or procedure? Is it the product of management skill and drive? If so, the growth can probably continue as long as present management is in charge. How high is a high profit margin? When is a P/E ratio high? What is the significance of book value? Is corporate debt a bad sign? Your ability to interpret the data will improve as you gain knowledge. Of course, you can always refer to this book to find the answers you are looking for.

The Guide allows you to use the past as a basis for estimating the progress of a company and the price of its stock. You have space to record ten years of history. Every decade the economy typically undergoes both up and down cycles. Using the Guide, you can review how effectively management has functioned under varying economic conditions. The Guide is really a judge of management.

It is always a good idea to look at a company's past performance and then make your prediction of where the company is moving. Of course, there is no guarantee your forecasting will prove accurate. If investing could be reduced to a formula, everyone would be a millionaire. However, in making predictions, as in interpreting the Guide, you will definitely improve.

IS THE GUIDE VALUABLE?

Is the Stock Selection Guide worthy of your time and attention? Just one example (Figure 8-1) should suffice.

A new member joined the Midwest-based First Ladies Investment Club in its eleventh year of operation. Over the initial decade, club members had paid in $19,000. Their investment was worth just $20,585. That's a return of less than 1 percent annually. The club members could have made several times that much simply by putting their deposits into a guaranteed bank savings

Figure 8-1
First Ladies Investment Club

Year	Cumulative Deposits	Cumulative Withdrawals by Members	Club Value, Year-end
10	$ 19,000	—	$ 20,585
11	20,920	—	29,229
12	22,960	—	42,381
13	25,480	—	44,672
14	28,540	—	40,615
15	31,600	—	45,658
16	34,840	$ 10,830	63,750
17	37,960	—	70,298
18	40,800	39,330	88,859
19	44,160	56,430	83,560
20	48,000	72,878	NA
21	51,440	86,478	84,581
22	55,320	—	88,890
23	59,880	—	108,223
24	63,860	—	113,451
25	68,420	95,478	154,769
26	74,650	105,478	159,900
27	79,450	125,478	180,569

At the end of year 27, the club had cumulative deposits of $79,450; club value was $180,569. Members had also withdrawn $125,478, a sum substantially greater than the deposits.

account. Members were less than enthusiastic about their club's performance and were persuaded by the newcomer to join NAIC, follow NAIC principles, and use NAIC tools. Figure 8-1 shows what's happened since.

Remember, in the first decade, the First Ladies had achieved a razor-thin profit. After the introduction of NAIC principles and tools, the women earned an average return of 17.7 percent compounded annually. How many professionals could rival that result over a similar period of time? Using the NAIC Stock Selection Guide doesn't guarantee such success, but it definitely improves your odds.

Note that the NAIC Stock Selection Guide does not make reference to any balance sheet items, which are used to determine the financial strength of a corporation. We are assuming that in using the Guide, you have first determined from your own analysis that the corporation is financially sound. One important factor you shouldn't overlook is company debt. If you consider financial condition and debt structure together, you may discover threats to the company's long-term progress. If debt is sizable, you might calculate a few of the key ratios from the balance sheet, which you learned about in Chapter 4. These include working capital, current ratio, acid test, and bond ratio. And remember, as with all forms of financial analysis, be on the look-out for trends.

RECORDING INFORMATION
ON THE GUIDE

Let us first discuss how to enter information on the NAIC Stock Selection Guide and Report. Then we will discuss what this information means and how it helps us judge the investment potential of a stock.

We will use Motorola to illustrate the use of the Guide, as we did for the NAIC Stock Check List. A copy of the Value Line report was included as Figure 7-1 on page 59. We will refer to that illustration as we discuss how to record information on the Guide. (*Note:* After the Value Line report was printed, Motorola released its actual sales for 1995 as $27,050 million and earnings per share as $2.93. We have used these actual figures in our illustrations.)

The graph in Section 1 of the Stock Selection Guide is a ratio chart or a semi-logarithmic graph. The horizontal scale is in familiar arithmetic proportion. It is used to show time. The vertical scale is based on logarithms.

Equal vertical distances represent equal percentage changes, regardless of absolute values. It is designed to show compound growth rates.

There is no zero point. That's because the chart is designed to show comparisons in terms of percentage of change, and positive numbers are required for this operation. (If the semi-log chart is new to you, refer to Appendix B, "How to Use the Ratio Chart and Calculator.")

With the semi-log chart, a consistent rate of growth is represented by a straight line. The slanted guide lines on the graph beginning in the lower left-hand corner represent compound growth rates ranging from 5 percent to 30 percent.

In analyzing companies of varying size, it makes far better sense to compare rates of growth than absolute increases in dollars. A large company might have year-to-year gains far greater, dollar-wise, than a small company; yet on a percentage increase basis, the smaller company might have a superior record of growth.

The five vertical time lines on the right-hand side of the heavier line of the graph are reserved for projecting results five years into the future.

The Guide was designed to analyze the figures of manufacturing, sales, and similar businesses. Banks, insurance firms, and utility companies have different names for their key operating figures. The Guide can be used for these companies also as long as you use the figures that are pertinent for those types of companies.

For instance, four classes of revenues are shown in the Value Line report for CNA Financial (Figure 8-2), an insurance company. These are life premiums, property/casualty premiums, total investment income, and other revenues. It is always helpful to note the trend of each revenue class to see what areas are growing and which ones are receding. One segment may be dominant and determine the course of the business. In CNA's case, we would use the total of all four items to draw our trend line and judge the growth of the company.

The loss/expense ratio of an insurance company indicates the company's profit margin. The farther the ratio is below 100, the better.

In studying the record of a bank, we look at different figures. Banks vary greatly in the way they earn their income. Traditional banks loan money and earn interest income. Some earn a great deal from trading financial instruments. Some are like computer services and collect fees for servicing mutual funds and credit cards. You first must determine the nature of the bank's

Figure 8-2
Example of a Value Line Report for an Insurance Company

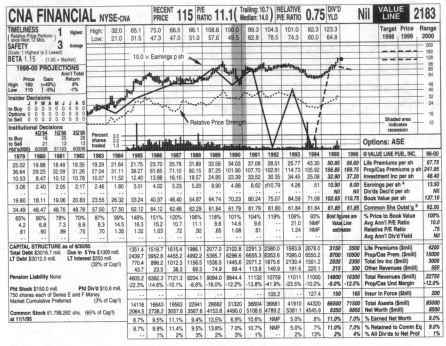

For this insurance company, revenues are categorized as life premiums, property/casualty premiums, total investment income, and "other revenues." Source: © 1996 by Value Line Publishing, Inc. Reprinted by Permission; All Rights Reserved.

business and then note which items are the important elements in its income. First Chicago Bank in our illustration (Figure 8-3) shows two sources of revenues: net interest income and non-interest income. You should add the two together and use the sum to plot annual revenues. Return on total assets for banks is typically below 1 percent; 1 percent or more is considered good.

Our second bank illustration is State Street Boston Corp (Figure 8-4). This bank's loan business is small but has grown by processing shareowner accounts for mutual funds. Its non-interest income is the figure to plot.

In the case of a real estate investment trust (Figure 8-5), rental income or total income is the figure to use for revenues. With an electric utility (Figure 8-6), the correct figure to use is listed as revenues in Value Line and often as operating revenues in other sources. The operating margin represents

Figure 8-3
Example of a Value Line Report for a Bank

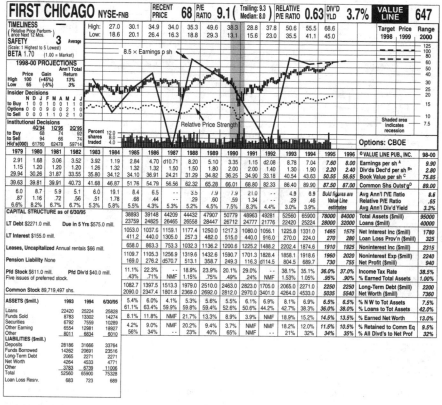

First Chicago Bank revenues are designated net interest income and non-interest income.
Source: © 1996 by Value Line Publishing, Inc. Reprinted by Permission; All Rights Reserved.

the percent of operating costs to revenues; the lower the figure, the more favorable the company's situation.

These examples should help you decide which data to use regardless of the type of business you are examining.

PLOTTING THE FIGURES

Now let's return to our analysis of Motorola. The first four items in the heading are self-explanatory. The place where the stock is traded is shown after the

Figure 8-4
Example of a Value Line Report for a Bank

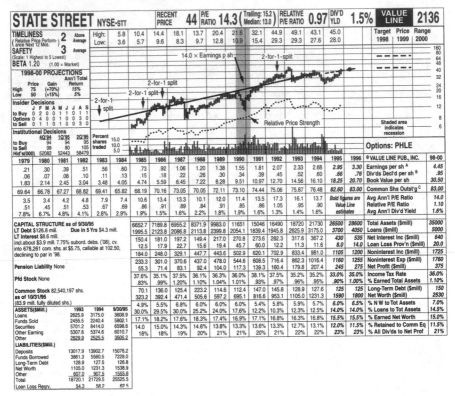

For this bank, specializing in mutual fund accounts, revenues are classified as non-interest income.
Source: © 1996 by Value Line Publishing, Inc. Reprinted by Permission; All Rights Reserved.

company's name at the top left part of the Value Line report. This is followed by the trading symbol. The nature of the business is described in the middle of the page following the heading "Business."

The box labeled "Capital Structure" provides a lot of information. Common stock is 87 percent of capital. The total debt is stated, and the dilution that would result from the conversion of notes does not seem to be significant. The number of common shares is recorded at the bottom of the box.

The quarterly figures called for in the space at the upper left of the graph in the Stock Selection Guide are found at the lower left of the Value Line report. We use the latest actual figures available except when we are making

Figure 8-5
Example of a Value Line Report for a Real Estate Firm

NEW PLAN REALTY NYSE-NPR | RECENT PRICE **22** | P/E RATIO **17.6** (Trailing: 18.8 / Median: NMF) | RELATIVE P/E RATIO **1.21** | DIV'D YLD **6.2%** | VALUE LINE **1180**

TIMELINESS **3** Average (Relative Price Performance Next 12 Mos.)
SAFETY **1** Highest (Scale: 1 Highest to 5 Lowest)
BETA .75 (1.00 = Market)

	1998	1999	2000
High:	9.2 11.9 15.3 18.4 16.8 18.8 18.6 24.5 26.1 26.4 24.4 22.6		Target Price Range
Low:	7.3 9.2 11.0 10.8 13.3 15.3 13.8 16.1 19.6 21.5 18.8 19.6		

1.50 × Dividends p sh divided by Interest Rate

2-for-1 split / 3-for-2 split

Relative Price Strength

Shaded area indicates recession

1998-00 PROJECTIONS

	Price	Gain	Ann'l Total Return
High	35	(+60%)	17%
Low	25	(+15%)	9%

Insider Decisions

	A S O N D J F M A
to Buy	2 0 0 0 0 0 1 0
Options	0 0 0 0 0 0 0 0
to Sell	0 0 0 0 1 0 0 0

Institutional Decisions

	3Q'94	4Q'94	1Q'95
to Buy	21	30	20
to Sell	28	32	38
Hld's(000)	6903	6607	6386

Percent shares traded 3.0 / 2.0 / 1.0

Options: ASE

1979	1980	1981	1982	1983	1984	1985	1986	1987	1988	1989	1990	1991	1992	1993	1994	1995	1996	©VALUE LINE PUB., INC.	98-00
1.28	1.40	1.45	2.37	2.49	3.44	3.66	4.40	5.98	6.03	7.90	7.95	9.83	10.46	10.22	10.74	10.85	10.70	Book Value per sh A	12.50
.30	.39	.40	.54	.59	.71	.80	.85	.84	.89	.98	1.01	1.03	.97	1.02	1.27	1.48	1.62	Funds from Ops per sh B C	2.20
.21	.31	.31	.46	.50	.60	.70	.74	.73	.70	.87	.91	.92	.86	.87	1.04	1.20	1.30	Earnings per sh A B	1.75
.25	.30	.34	.39	.51	.57	.65	.73	.81	.89	.97	1.05	1.13	1.21	1.28	1.32	1.37	1.41	Div'ds Decl'd per sh D ■	1.60
2.10	1.94	2.05	1.73	2.40	2.53	2.68	3.47	2.93	3.46	3.61	4.56	3.90	6.28	7.64	11.32	14.10	16.05	Loans & Real Est per sh	21.65
9.20	9.91	9.96	12.83	13.25	16.62	17.26	20.67	26.64	26.85	34.71	35.15	44.49	48.38	48.96	52.59	53.10	56.00	Common Shs Outst'g E	60.00
136%	121%	166%	85%	194%	123%	163%	170%	157%	135%	104%	114%	81%	105%	131%	115%			Premium over Book	125%
14.1	9.9	12.5	9.5	14.5	12.8	13.8	30.9	21.0	20.4	18.4	18.7	19.3	25.0	27.2	22.3	Bold figures are Value Line estimates		Avg Ann'l P/E Ratio	17.0
10.0	7.9	9.7	8.1	12.3	10.9	12.0	14.0	18.4	16.0	15.9	16.8	17.3	22.2	23.1	18.2			Avg Ann'l P/FFO Ratio	13.0
8.3%	9.7%	8.8%	8.9%	7.0%	7.4%	6.8%	6.2%	5.3%	6.2%	6.2%	6.1%	6.4%	5.6%	5.4%	5.7%			Avg Ann'l Div'd Yield	5.3%

CAPITAL STRUCTURE as of 4/30/95
ST Debt Nil   Due in 5 Yrs $20.0 mill.
LT Debt $129.1 mill.   Total Interest $15.0 mill.
(18% of Cap'l)
(Total interest coverage: 13.5x)
Pension Liability None
Pfd Stock None
Common Stock 53,105,634 shs.   (82% of Cap'l)
as of June 2, 95

				1985	1986	1987	1988	1989	1990	1991	1992	1993	1994	1995	1996		98-00
				19.7	21.9	26.2	28.5	33.8	38.0	41.4	47.6	65.3	96.4	127	160	Rental Income ($mill)	225
				6.6	9.5	9.2	8.9	9.8	16.1	16.0	17.1	11.0	4.6	3.5	5.0	Other Income ($mill)	5.0
				67.0%	70.2%	68.7%	62.4%	69.0%	68.4%	71.4%	71.0%	67.2%	64.3%	64.5%	65.5%	Operating Margin	64.5%
				11.8	14.9	16.5	18.7	25.0	31.8	35.1	39.4	42.3	51.3	63.5	73.0	Net Profit ($mill)	105
				44.8%	46.2%	46.0%	50.1%	57.4%	58.3%	60.7%	60.9%	55.4%	50.8%	50.0%	45.5%	Net Profit Margin	47.0%
				..	.7	1.5	2.2	2.2	3.3	4.8	10.1	.9	1.0	Nil	Nil	Capital Gains	Nil
				46.3	71.7	78.2	92.6	125.5	160.3	173.5	304.1	374.2	595.1	750	900	Loans & Real Est ($mill)	1300
				44.3	96.3	26.7	22.5	22.7	22.7	18.6	17.5	23.3	28.1	210	200	Long-Term Debt ($mill)	200
				63.1	90.9	159.4	161.9	274.2	279.5	437.2	506.3	500.6	565.5	575	650	Net Worth ($mill)	750
				81.3%	86.1%	96.7%	100.0%	98.7%	103.5%	109.7%	125.2%	125.4%	103.9%	93.5%	86.0%	% Div'ds Decl'd to FFO	73.5%
				8.0%	6.2%	5.9%	7.5%	6.6%	5.7%	4.6%	3.9%	4.7%	6.3%	6.5%	6.5%	% Expenses to Assets	6.5%
				15.1%	14.1%	11.6%	13.8%	14.5%	12.4%	11.8%	10.7%	8.6%	9.7%	9.0%	10.5%	% Earned Total Cap'l	12.5%
				19.7%	18.4%	15.2%	14.6%	15.3%	12.7%	12.0%	10.7%	8.6%	9.8%	11.0%	11.0%	% Earned Net Worth	14.0%

FUNDS FLOW ($mill.)	1992	1993	1994
Net Profit Plus			
Noncash charges	54.5	50.8	63.7
Investments Repaid	2.5	..	2.0
Net New Debt	-5.9	-6.2	.5
New Equity	74.8	11.7	77.0
Investments Funded	123.8	63.2	218.3
Dividends Declared	55.2	62.0	64.7

New Plan Realty Trust classifies revenues as rental income and "other income."
Source: © 1996 by Value Line Publishing, Inc. Reprinted by Permission; All Rights Reserved.

a study near the end of the year. Then we are inclined to use estimated full-year figures. The percentage change is calculated by subtracting the quarterly figure from the previous year by the amount for the current quarter and dividing the year-ago figure by the result.

The first figures we record on the semi-log graph are the sales for the past five years. We note from the sales line on the Value Line report that Motorola's sales figure grew by one digit in the past ten years. That means we will need to use two cycles of the graph. We number the lines in the bottom cycle from 1 to 10 billion and the lines in the second cycle from 10 to 100 billion. Figure 8-7 illustrates how to plot the sales of Motorola on the graph from the Value Line sheet. Once we have plotted a mark for each year's sales

Figure 8-6
Example of a Value Line Report for a Utility

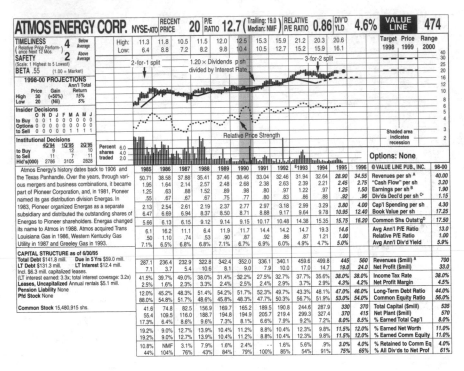

Atmos Energy Corp. revenues are listed simply as "revenues," although other services use the term "operating revenues." Source: © 1996 by Value Line Publishing, Inc. Reprinted by Permission; All Rights Reserved.

on the graph, we connect the marks with a line to get a picture of how sales have grown. A quick look suggests that our plotted data are roughly parallel to the 20 percent line on the graph. (See Figure 8-8.)

To get a better picture of the historical growth rate, we draw a trend line over our plotted data.

Statisticians draw lines in several different ways. The most frequently used are the inspection or best judgment method, the mid-point method, the peak method, and the area method. In the inspection or best judgment method, you look at the plotted data and just let your eye direct you in drawing a line that seems to best represent the trend of the plotted data. This is

Figure 8-7
Plotting Revenues

MOTOROLA NYSE-MOT			RECENT PRICE	**73**	P/E RATIO	**22.8**	(Trailing: 25.0 Median: 20.0)	RELATIVE P/E RATIO	**1.58**	DIV'D YLD	**0.6%**	VALUE LINE	**1067**

| TIMELINESS 2 Above Average | High: | 11.7 | 10.2 | 12.5 | 18.5 | 13.7 | 15.6 | 22.1 | 17.8 | 26.6 | 53.8 | 61.1 | 78.9 | |
| Relative Price Perform-ance Next 12 Mos. | Low: | 7.3 | 7.3 | 8.4 | 8.8 | 9.0 | 9.9 | 12.3 | 11.4 | 16.1 | 24.4 | 42.1 | 51.5 | |

1979	1980	1981	1982	1983	1984	1985	1986	1987	1988	1989	1990	1991	1992	1993	1994	1995	1996	© VALUE LINE PUB., INC.	98-00
7.26	8.24	8.81	8.24	9.16	11.65	11.41	11.48	12.97	15.87	18.44	20.66	21.45	24.66	30.44	37.83	47.65	58.65	Sales per sh	88.00
.71	.88	.92	.90	1.13	1.48	1.08	1.27	1.55	1.90	2.27	2.45	2.53	2.92	3.93	5.25	6.60	8.10	"Cash Flow" per sh	11.70
.41	.50	.46	.39	.52	.74	.15	.38	.60	.86	1.03	.95	.86	1.08	1.78	2.65	3.20	3.95	Earnings per sh (A)	5.50
.10	.12	.13	.13	.13	.15	.16	.16	.16	.16	.19	.19	.19	.20	.22	.31	.42	.50	Div'ds Decl'd per sh (B)	.70
.71	.80	.84	.77	.86	1.65	1.34	1.11	1.27	1.68	2.10	2.38	2.49	2.57	3.93	5.65	7.60	7.55	Cap'l Spending per sh	8.25
2.69	3.06	3.40	3.70	4.12	4.79	4.79	5.37	5.82	6.49	7.29	8.08	8.76	9.54	11.50	15.47	18.70	22.55	Book Value per sh	31.95
373.89	376.26	378.79	459.52	472.61	475.10	477.20	512.80	517.20	519.88	521.60	526.80	528.80	539.40	557.20	588.00	593.00	597.00	Common Shs Outst'g (C)	605.00
8.9	9.8	12.3	14.5	19.8	12.6	NMF	26.5	22.7	13.0	12.6	17.5	18.0	19.7	23.1	19.4	Bold figures are		Avg Ann'l P/E Ratio	19.5
1.29	1.30	1.49	1.60	1.67	1.17	NMF	1.80	1.52	1.08	.95	1.30	1.15	1.19	1.36	1.27	Value Line		Relative P/E Ratio	1.50
2.8%	2.5%	2.3%	2.4%	1.3%	1.6%	1.9%	1.6%	1.2%	1.4%	1.5%	1.1%	1.2%	.9%	.5%	.6%	estimates		Avg Ann'l Div'd Yield	.7%

CAPITAL STRUCTURE as of 7/1/95		5443.0	5888.0	6707.0	8250.0	9620.0	10885	11341	13303	16963	22245	28250	35000	Sales ($mill)	53300
Total Debt $3389 mill. Due in 5 Yrs $1900 mill.		10.3%	13.8%	14.7%	15.2%	15.5%	14.6%	14.4%	14.7%	16.7%	18.4%	18.5%	18.5%	Operating Margin	17.5%
LT Debt $1519 mill. LT Interest $115 mill. Incl. $130 mill. face val. zero coupon notes ('09) callable $41.199, ea. cvbl. into 18.268 com. shs.; $480 mill. face val. zero coupon notes ('13), first callable 9/26/98 at $71.49, ea. cvbl. into 11.178 com. shs.		441.0	459.0	494.0	543.0	650.0	790.0	886.0	1000.0	1170.0	1525.0	1980	2415	Depreciation ($mill) (D)	3730
		72.0	194.0	308.0	445.0	534.0	499.0	454.0	576.0	1022.0	1560.0	1935	2410	Net Profit ($mill)	3335
		1.3%	3.3%	4.6%	5.4%	5.6%	4.6%	4.0%	4.3%	6.0%	7.0%	6.8%	6.9%	Net Profit Margin	6.3%
(Total interest coverage: 15x) (13% of Cap'l)		924.0	868.0	1039.0	689.0	1164.0	1404.0	1424.0	1883.0	2324.0	3008.0	3285	4100	Working Cap'l ($mill)	6950
Pension Liability None		705.0	334.0	344.0	343.0	755.0	792.0	954.0	1258.0	1360.0	1127.0	1700	2000	Long-Term Debt ($mill)	2700
Pfd Stock None		2284.0	2754.0	3008.0	3375.0	3803.0	4257.0	4630.0	5144.0	6409.0	9096.0	11085	13450	Net Worth ($mill)	19330
Common Stock 588,573,987 shs. (87% of Cap'l) as of 4/1/95		3.4%	7.2%	10.6%	13.8%	12.4%	10.5%	9.0%	10.1%	14.0%	15.8%	15.5%	16.0%	% Earned Total Cap'l	15.0%
		3.2%	7.0%	10.2%	13.2%	14.0%	11.7%	9.8%	11.2%	15.9%	17.2%	17.5%	18.0%	% Earned Net Worth	17.5%

CURRENT POSITION	1993	1994	7/1/95	NMF	4.1%	7.5%	10.7%	11.4%	9.4%	7.6%	9.3%	14.1%	15.5%	15.5%	15.0%	% Retained to Comm Eq	15.0%
(SMILL.)				106%	42%	27%	19%	19%	20%	22%	17%	12%	10%	13%	12%	% All Div'ds to Net Prof	13%
Assets	1244		1079														
40				BUSINESS: Motorola, Inc. is a leading manufacturer of electronic equipment and ...												

Sales figures for Motorola are transferred from the Value Line sheet to the Visual Analysis graph.

Figure 8-8
Estimating Sales Growth

NATIONAL ASSOCIATION OF INVESTORS CORPORATION

NAIC ®

INVESTMENT EDUCATION FOR INDIVIDUALS AND CLUBS SINCE 1951

Stock Selection Guide

The most widely used aid to good investment judgment

Company			Date
Prepared by			Data taken from
Where traded		Major product/service	

CAPITALIZATION	Authorized	Outstanding
Preferred		
Common		
Debt	Potential Dilution	

1 VISUAL ANALYSIS of Sales, Earnings and Price

RECENT QUARTERLY FIGURES

	SALES	EARNINGS PER SHARE
Latest Quarter		
Year Ago Quarter		
Percentage Change		

See Chapters 8, 9 and 10 of Investors Manual for complete instructions. Use this Guide as working section of NAIC Stock Selection Guide & Report.

(1) Historical Sales Growth _____ %
(2) Estimated Future Sales Growth _____ %
(3) Historical Earnings Per Share Growth _____ %
(4) Estimated Future Earnings Per Share Growth _____ %

Marks representing yearly sales are connected to show the pattern of sales growth.

also referred to as "eyeballing." After some experience, this is the method most of us settle on. (See Figure 8-9.)

The peak method calls for using the most recent peak as a fulcrum and pivoting a straight-edge down to the next peak. In Motorola's case, that takes us all the way back to our first year and does not look very representative. (See Figure 8-10.) Experience has shown that the peak method works well for a cyclical growth company. The theory is that the company's next peak year will fall somewhere along the line projected from the last two peaks.

New analysts like the mid-point method because it gives precise results with a minimum of figuring. In this method, you divide the ten-year history of sales into two five-year periods. Average the five sales figures for the first period and place the result on the line for the third year, or the mid-point, of that period. Repeat the procedure for the second five-year period and then draw the trend line through the two points. When the figures show a fairly regular rate of increase, as Motorola's do, the result tends to look much like a precisely calculated line would. But if the figures are irregular, the results can be wild. (See Figure 8-11.)

In the area method, you inspect your plotted data and attempt to draw the trend line so that the plotted data enclose equal areas of space above and below the drawn line. This will produce a line close to the one drawn in Figure 8-12.

Of course, you can calculate each year's growth and average the figures to get the exact rate of growth. This is done by the computer programs available for the Guide, but such precision is not necessary. We are just looking for ballpark figures.

If we decide that the inspection method gives an adequate picture of the past rate of growth, how do we determine what rate of growth it represents? We compare it with the trend lines drawn on the graph. First we go to the left side of the graph and measure the distance from where our trend line intersects the line for 1986 down to the corner where the guidelines start. Then we take a ruler and measure down that same distance from the trend line at the right side of the graph. This point falls about midway between the 15 percent and the 20 percent growth guidelines, or about 17.5 percent. See Figure 8-13. Using NAIC's Tool-Kit, the computer-calculated rate is 17.9 percent. As we said earlier, exact rates are not important. Approximate figures are an adequate guide.

Our next step is to record earnings per share on the graph. We find these figures on line 3 of the Value Line report. Again we see that earnings start at

Figure 8-9
Best Judgment Method

			Company_____ Date_____
NATIONAL ASSOCIATION OF INVESTORS CORPORATION **NAIC** ® INVESTMENT EDUCATION FOR INDIVIDUALS AND CLUBS SINCE 1951	*Stock Selection Guide* The most widely used aid to good investment judgment		Prepared by_____ Data taken from_____

Company		Date
Prepared by	Data taken from	
Where traded	Major product/service	
CAPITALIZATION	Authorized	Outstanding
Preferred		
Common		
Debt	Potential Dilution	

1 VISUAL ANALYSIS of Sales, Earnings and Price

RECENT QUARTERLY FIGURES

	SALES	EARNINGS PER SHARE
Latest Quarter		
Year Ago Quarter		
Percentage Change		

See Chapters 8, 9 and 10 of Investors Manual for complete instructions. Use this Guide as working section of NAIC Stock Selection Guide & Report.

(1) Historical Sales Growth _____ %
(2) Estimated Future Sales Growth _____ %
(3) Historical Earnings Per Share Growth _____ %
(4) Estimated Future Earnings Per Share Growth _____ %

The trend line for recording and projecting the rate of growth is fitted to the plotted data using the estimator's judgment.

Figure 8-10
Peak Method

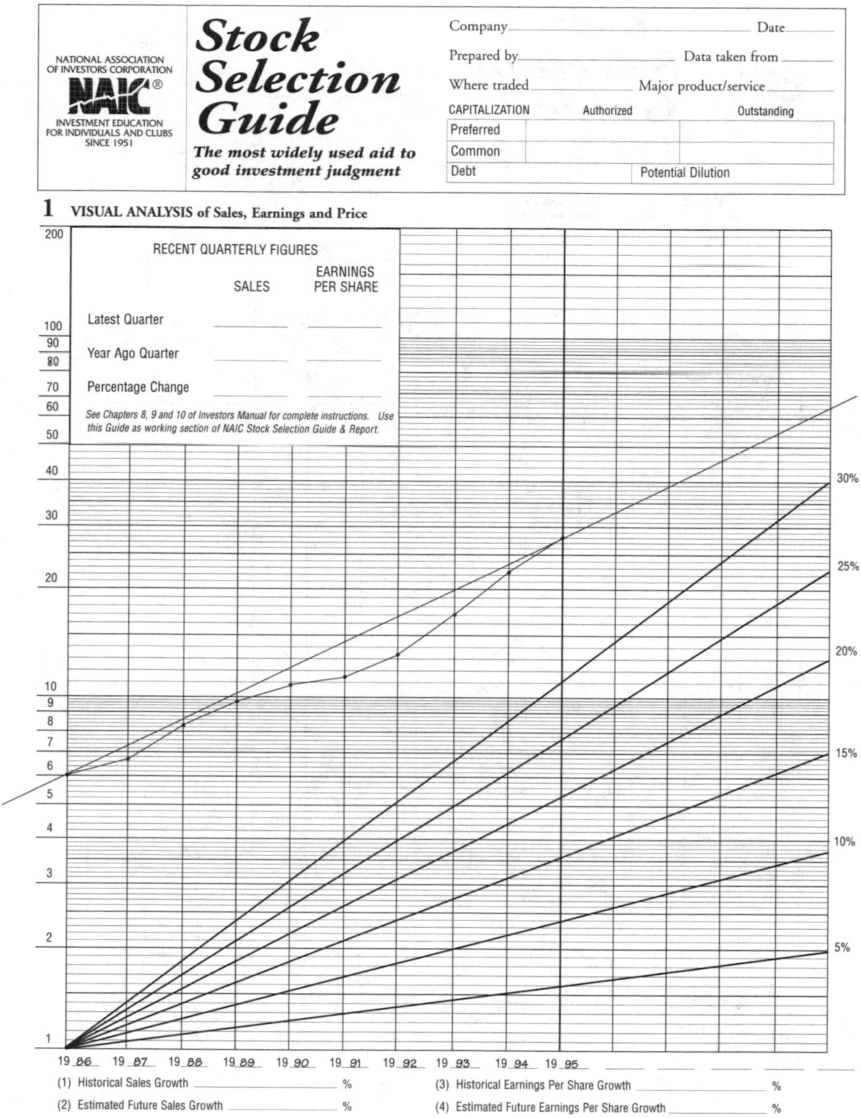

The trend line is drawn using the two most recent market peaks.

Figure 8-11
Mid-Point Method

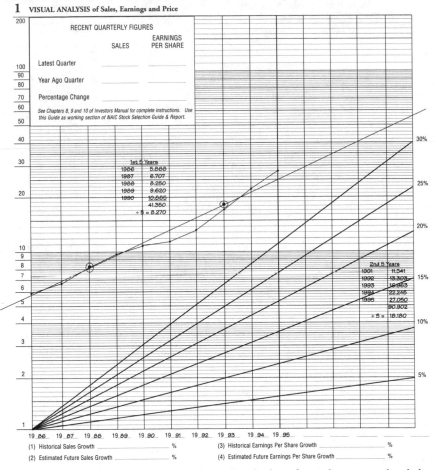

	Company		Date
NATIONAL ASSOCIATION OF INVESTORS CORPORATION	Prepared by		Data taken from
NAIC®	Where traded		Major product/service
INVESTMENT EDUCATION FOR INDIVIDUALS AND CLUBS SINCE 1951	CAPITALIZATION	Authorized	Outstanding

Stock Selection Guide

The most widely used aid to good investment judgment

Preferred		
Common		
Debt	Potential Dilution	

1 VISUAL ANALYSIS of Sales, Earnings and Price

RECENT QUARTERLY FIGURES

	SALES	EARNINGS PER SHARE
Latest Quarter		
Year Ago Quarter		
Percentage Change		

See Chapters 8, 9 and 10 of Investors Manual for complete instructions. Use this Guide as working section of NAIC Stock Selection Guide & Report.

1st 5 Years	
1986	5.888
1987	6.707
1988	8.250
1989	9.620
1990	10.885
	41.350
÷ 5 =	8.270

2nd 5 Years	
1991	11.541
1992	13.303
1993	16.963
1994	22.245
1995	27.050
	90.902
÷ 5 =	18.180

19 86 19 87 19 88 19 89 19 90 19 91 19 92 19 93 19 94 19 95

(1) Historical Sales Growth _____ %

(2) Estimated Future Sales Growth _____ %

(3) Historical Earnings Per Share Growth _____ %

(4) Estimated Future Earnings Per Share Growth _____ %

The sales history is divided into two five-year periods, sales for each period are averaged and plotted on each period's mid-point, and the trend line is drawn between the two mid-points.

Figure 8-12
Area Method

	Stock Selection Guide	Company_____ Date_____
NATIONAL ASSOCIATION OF INVESTORS CORPORATION **NAIC**® INVESTMENT EDUCATION FOR INDIVIDUALS AND CLUBS SINCE 1951	*Stock* *Selection* *Guide* **The most widely used aid to good investment judgment**	Prepared by_____ Data taken from_____

Stock Selection Guide form with plotted trend-line chart:

Company_____ Date_____
Prepared by_____ Data taken from_____
Where traded_____ Major product/service_____

CAPITALIZATION   Authorized   Outstanding
Preferred
Common
Debt   Potential Dilution

1   VISUAL ANALYSIS of Sales, Earnings and Price

RECENT QUARTERLY FIGURES

	SALES	EARNINGS PER SHARE
Latest Quarter		
Year Ago Quarter		
Percentage Change		

See Chapters 8, 9 and 10 of Investors Manual for complete instructions.   Use this Guide as working section of NAIC Stock Selection Guide & Report.

19 86   19 87   19 88   19 89   19 90   19 91   19 92   19 93   19 94   19 95

(1) Historical Sales Growth _____ %
(2) Estimated Future Sales Growth _____ %
(3) Historical Earnings Per Share Growth _____ %
(4) Estimated Future Earnings Per Share Growth _____ %

The trend line is drawn so that equal areas are encompassed by the plot above and below the trend line.

Figure 8-13
Determining Sales Growth Rate

		Company		Date
NATIONAL ASSOCIATION OF INVESTORS CORPORATION **NAIC**® INVESTMENT EDUCATION FOR INDIVIDUALS AND CLUBS SINCE 1951	*Stock Selection Guide* *The most widely used aid to good investment judgment*	Prepared by		Data taken from
		Where traded		Major product/service

CAPITALIZATION	Authorized		Outstanding
Preferred			
Common			
Debt		Potential Dilution	

1 VISUAL ANALYSIS of Sales, Earnings and Price

RECENT QUARTERLY FIGURES

	SALES	EARNINGS PER SHARE
Latest Quarter		
Year Ago Quarter		
Percentage Change		

See Chapters 8, 9 and 10 of Investors Manual for complete instructions. Use this Guide as working section of NAIC Stock Selection Guide & Report.

19 86   19 87   19 88   19 89   19 90   19 91   19 92   19 93   19 94   19 95

(1) Historical Sales Growth _____ %
(2) Estimated Future Sales Growth _____ %
(3) Historical Earnings Per Share Growth _____ %
(4) Estimated Future Earnings Per Share Growth _____ %

The distance below the beginning of the trend line is used on the other end of the graph to estimate the percentage of sales growth.

two digits in 1986 and increase to three digits in 1995. We will therefore need two cycles of the graph to record them. The lines in the bottom cycle will stand for cents and those in the second cycle from the bottom for dollars. Once we have recorded the earnings-per-share figures on the year lines, we connect them with a dotted line to distinguish them from the sales line. See Figure 8-14.

The final step in completing the graph is to record the high and low prices for each year on the vertical year lines. We find these prices at the top of the Value Line report across from the words "High" and "Low." We connect the high and low marks with a straight line so that the high and low prices look like bars on the graph. See Figure 8-15.

Figure 8-14
Plotting Earnings per Share

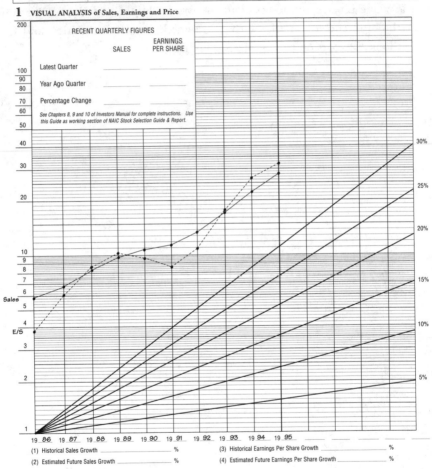

Stock Selection Guide	Company _____ Date_____
	Prepared by _____ Data taken from ____

NATIONAL ASSOCIATION OF INVESTORS CORPORATION

NAIC®

INVESTMENT EDUCATION FOR INDIVIDUALS AND CLUBS SINCE 1951

Stock Selection Guide

The most widely used aid to good investment judgment

Company _____ Date_____

Prepared by _____ Data taken from ____

Where traded _____ Major product/service ____

CAPITALIZATION   Authorized   Outstanding

Preferred

Common

Debt   Potential Dilution

1 VISUAL ANALYSIS of Sales, Earnings and Price

RECENT QUARTERLY FIGURES

	SALES	EARNINGS PER SHARE
Latest Quarter		
Year Ago Quarter		
Percentage Change		

See Chapters 8, 9 and 10 of Investors Manual for complete instructions. Use this Guide as working section of NAIC Stock Selection Guide & Report.

19 86 19 87 19 88 19 89 19 90 19 91 19 92 19 93 19 94 19 95

(1) Historical Sales Growth _____ %
(2) Estimated Future Sales Growth _____ %
(3) Historical Earnings Per Share Growth _____ %
(4) Estimated Future Earnings Per Share Growth _____ %

Earnings-per-share figures are taken from the stock report and plotted along with the sales figures for Motorola.

Figure 8-15
Plotting High and Low Prices

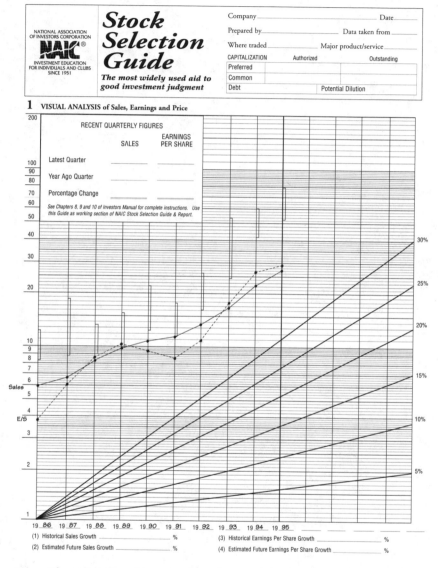

The stock's high and low prices for each year are plotted as bars on the graph.

CHAPTER 9

THE NAIC STOCK SELECTION GUIDE AND REPORT: PAGE 2

*P*age 2 of the Stock Selection Guide contains Sections 2 through 5.

The figures for Section 2, Evaluating Management, are calculated for you in some reports; in other cases you will have to calculate them yourself. Line A, Percent Pre-tax Profit on Sales, is figured by dividing net income before taxes by sales and expressing the result as a percentage. Value Line does not give you net income before taxes, but it does have figures that permit you to calculate it. First take the income tax rate, 37 percent for 1995, and express it as a decimal, 0.37. Subtract that figure from 1.00 (1.00 − 0.37 = 0.63). Value Line shows net profit as $1.935 billion for 1995. Dividing that by 0.63 gives $3.071 billion. Dividing this by sales of $27,050 million, we get 11.35 or 11.4, corrected to the first place. We repeat that process for each year. Figure 9-1 shows the completed section.

Value Line calls equity "net worth" and has calculated that figure for us. Place those yearly figures in the correct columns in Line B of Section 2. You will find that these figures may vary between different services and the company's annual report. That is because different accountants make different adjustments to the earnings figures before they make their final calculation for pre-tax profits. Accountants also calculate earnings on equity in different ways. For instance, some base it on beginning equity and others on ending equity. Some base it on the average of beginning and ending equity. The differences are not usually important, but it makes good sense to take all of your

Figure 9-1
Evaluating Management

2 EVALUATING MANAGEMENT   Company ___Motorola Inc.___

	1986	1987	1988	1989	1990	1991	19 92	1993	19 94	1995	LAST 5 YEAR AVG.	TREND UP	TREND DOWN
A % Pre-tax Profit on Sales (Net Before Taxes ÷ Sales)	4.5	6.2	7.4	7.4	6.1	5.4	6.0	9.0	11.0	11.4	8.6	↑	
B % Earned on Equity (E/S ÷ Book Value)	7.0	10.2	13.2	14.0	11.7	9.8	11.2	15.9	17.2	17.5	14.3	↑	

figures from the same source to make sure they have all been subjected to the same treatment.

For Section 3 you can get the present and past years' high and low prices from the newspaper. The other figures can be taken from the Value Line report or are calculated. The first line is for figures five years ago, and each succeeding line is for the next year. The high and low prices are the same ones we used to plot the price bars in Section 1. Earnings-per-share values come from line 3 of the Value Line table of figures.

The high and low price/earnings ratios are not given by Value Line but are easily computed by doing the calculations indicated in the column heading. Dividends per share are shown on line 4 of the Value Line table. Percent payout can be calculated based on the directions in the column heading, or you can use the figures in the Value Line table under the heading "% All Dividends to Net Profit." The differences will normally be minor.

In columns B, D, E, and G we add up the figures for the five years and put the totals on line 6. We divide these totals by 5 to give us five-year averages. Line 8, average price/earnings ratio, is used to enter the average of the high and low averages on line 7 in columns D and E. The current P/E (line 9) is found by dividing the current price by the last year's earnings (line 5 in column C). If we are doing our study in the latter half of the company's fiscal year, it is helpful to base the current P/E on the coming year's estimated earnings as shown in the Value Line report. As we were writing this book, Motorola's actual figures for 1995 became available, and, as shown in Figure 9-2, we have used the actual figures in place of Value Line's estimates.

In Section 4, part A, the average high P/E is taken from Section 3, line 7, column D unless we decide to adjust it, which we have done as we will explain later. The estimated high earnings per share for five years in the future can be determined in two ways. One is by looking at where the trend line for earnings per share five years in the future crosses our year 2000 line. We read that on the graph in Section 1 as $6.10.

Figure 9-2
Price/Earnings History

3 PRICE-EARNINGS HISTORY as an indicator of the future

This shows how stock prices have fluctuated with earnings and dividends. It is a building block for translating earnings into future stock prices.

PRESENT PRICE __56 ¼__   HIGH THIS YEAR __82.500__   LOW THIS YEAR __51.500__

Year	A PRICE HIGH	B PRICE LOW	C Earnings Per Share	D Price Earnings Ratio HIGH A ÷ C	E Price Earnings Ratio LOW B ÷ C	F Dividend Per Share	G % Payout F ÷ C X 100	H % High Yield F ÷ B X 100
1 1991	17.8	11.4	0.86	20.7	13.3	.19	22.1	1.7
2 1992	26.6	16.1	1.08	24.6	14.9	.20	18.5	1.2
3 1993	53.8	24.4	1.78	30.2	13.7	.22	12.4	0.9
4 1994	61.1	42.1	2.65	23.1	15.9	.31	11.7	0.7
5 1995	82.1	51.5	2.93	28.0	17.8	.40	12.5	0.8
6 TOTAL		145.5		126.6	75.6		77.2	
7 AVERAGE		29.1		25.3	15.1		15.4	
8 AVERAGE PRICE EARNINGS RATIO		20.2		9 CURRENT PRICE EARNINGS RATIO			19.2	

'96(E)3.68   15.3

The other method for estimating earnings per share five years into the future is called the *preferred procedure.* It starts with estimated sales rather than earnings per share. It is assumed that sales estimates are ordinarily more reliable than earnings-per-share estimates. Also, the other elements in the estimate, tax rates and profit margins, are determined by the estimator based on reasons the estimator has selected. The calculations are shown in the upper right-hand corner of the graph in Section 1 (see Figure 10-1 in the next chapter for the completed Stock Selection Guide). Reading estimated sales on the graph from our sales trend line at the year 2000, we get $5.55 billion. For our pre-tax profit margin we go to line A of Section 2. The pre-tax profit margin has been on an upswing for the past ten years. We are looking for a time in the future when favorable conditions prevail; therefore, we pick 10 percent as the possible pre-tax profit margin at the next peak for this company. That is over the 8.6 percent average for the last five years but under the 11 percent that has been attained in the last two years. That 10 percent of the $55.5 billion in estimated sales amounts to $5.55 billion. Value Line is estimating the tax rate at 37 percent, which means that 63 percent of $5.55 billion (100 − 37 = 63) will be after-tax income. That figure divided by the 588,573,987 shares we have recorded at the top of the page gives us $5.94 for our estimated earnings per share five years in the future. These figures, $5.94 and $6.10, are close enough to give us confidence that our guesses under both procedures are reasonable.

We can use either one as we proceed. The use of the lower figure will, of course, be more conservative. If the company you are studying has convertible stock or substantial options outstanding, you would make a corresponding adjustment in the pre-tax earnings figure to cover the additional shares that might be issued.

The average low price for the next five years can be estimated in five different ways. We will discuss how to choose among them later. The first procedure is to multiply the average low P/E for the last five years by the current year's earnings per share. The theory is that a growing company will be increasing its earnings each year and probably won't sell at a lower P/E than it has in the past. The average low P/E for the last five years comes from column B, line 7.

The recent severe market low price is not necessarily the lowest price in the last five years, although we should consider that as a possibility. Here we look at the events of the past five years and ask ourselves, "Was there one year in particular when negative stock market forces were very strong and knocked most stock market prices down, or was there one year in which this particular company faced severe problems?" If we were working in 1988, we would remember that 1987 was a bad year for the stock market and would consequently use the low of that year for Part B, line (c). If there were no such year, we would use the low of the five-year period. To calculate line (d), we divide the current dividend by the highest yield figure in Section 3, column H.

To set our price zones, we take the high we projected in Section 4, Part A, 119 (118.8 rounded to the nearest full number) and subtract the possible low we chose in Part B, 44. Subtracting 44 from 119 gives us 75, the range over which we expect the stock will sell. We divide that by 3 and get 25. That enables us to produce three zones, which we name the buy, hold, and sell zones.

The upside/downside ratio is calculated by measuring the distance from the price at which we can buy the stock at this time, 56¼, to our estimated high, 119 (119 − 56¼ = 62.8). This 62.8 points is our upside potential. The risk on the downside (56¼ down to our low of 44) is 12.3 points. Dividing the upside points (62.8) by the downside points (12.3) suggests that our upside potential is 5.1 times the downside.

We expect our gain in the stock to come in two ways: from possible appreciation and from dividends. Part E of Section 4 is an indication of our possible gain from price appreciation. The source of the figures and the computations to be performed are precisely indicated. Figure 9-3 shows this section completed.

Figure 9-3
Evaluating Risk and Reward

4 EVALUATING RISK and REWARD over the next 5 years

*Assuming one recession and one business boom every 5 years, calculations are made of how **high** and how **low** the stock might sell. The upside-downside ratio is the key to evaluating risk and reward.*

A HIGH PRICE — NEXT 5 YEARS

Avg. High P/E _____20_____ (3D7) X Estimate High Earnings/Share _____5.94_____ = Forecast High Price $ _____118.8_____ (4A1)

B LOW PRICE — NEXT 5 YEARS

(a) Avg. Low P/E _____15.1_____ (3E7) X Estimated Low Earnings/Share _____2.93_____ = $ _____44.2_____

(b) Avg. Low Price of Last 5 Years = _____29.1_____ (3B7)

(c) Recent Severe Market Low Price = _____24.4_____

(d) Price Dividend Will Support   Present Divd. = _____.40_____ = _____24_____
High Yield (H) _____.017_____

Selected Estimated Low Price _____ = $ _____44.2_____ (4B1)

C ZONING

_____119_____ (4A1) High Forecast Price Minus _____44_____ (4B1) Low Forecast Price Equals _____75_____ (C) Range. 1/3 of Range = _____25_____ (4CD)

(4C2) Lower 1/3 = (4B1) _____44_____ to _____69_____ (Buy)

(4C3) Middle 1/3 = _____69_____ to _____94_____ (Maybe)

(4C4) Upper 1/3 = _____94_____ to _____119_____ (4A1) (Sell)

Present Market Price of _____56 ¹/₄_____ is in the _____Buy_____ (4C5) Range

D UP-SIDE DOWN-SIDE RATIO (Potential Gain vs. Risk of Loss)

High Price (4A1) _____119_____ Minus Present Price _____56 ¹/₄_____

Present Price _____56 ¹/₄_____ Minus Low Price (4B1) _____44_____ = _____62.8_____ / _____12.3_____ = _____113_____ (4D) To 1

E PRICE TARGET (Simple Interest)

High Price (4A1) _____119_____ / Present Market Price _____56 ¹/₄_____ = (_____2.12_____) X 100 = (_____212_____) – 100 = _____112_____ (4E) % Appreciation

Section 5 is designed to show us the percent annual return the stock will produce for us if all of the estimates we have made actually develop. In Part A we divide the current dividend, $0.40, by the current price, to get 0.007. Multiplying that figure by 100 to convert it to a percentage gives us 0.7 percent.

We expect a growing company to increase its dividend each year as its earnings grow. We calculate the average dividend per year expected over the next five years by following the extended earnings-per-share trend line to the mid-year line of the five-year period, or 1998. That point is $4.60. Section 3, column G, line 7 shows us that the company historically pays out 15.4 percent of earnings in dividends. Multiplying $4.60 by 15.4 percent suggests that the average dividend will be 71 cents. That figure divided by $56¼, the current price, indicates that this stock's average dividend return over the next five years will be 1.3 percent.

In Section 4, Part E we calculated that we could enjoy as much as 112 percent appreciation in the stock's price over the next five years. In Part C of Section 5 we divide that figure by 5 to get the percent yearly average appreciation, 22.4 percent. Adding the yearly expected appreciation, 22.4 percent,

Figure 9-4
Five-Year Potential

5 5-YEAR POTENTIAL

These calculations provide a picture of future income. They also provide a standard for comparing income and growth stocks.

A Present Full Year's Dividend $ ___.40___

Present Price of Stock $ ___56.25___ = ___.007___ X 100 = ___.7___ (5A) Present Yield or % Returned on Purchase Price

B AVERAGE YIELD OVER NEXT 5 YEARS

Avg. Earnings Per Share Next 5 Years ___4.60___ X Avg. % Payout (3G7) ___15.4%___

Present Price $ ___56.25___ = ___.71___ = ___1.3___ % (5B)

C ESTIMATED ANNUAL RETURN OVER NEXT FIVE YEARS

5 Year Appreciation Potential (4E) ___112___

5 = ___22.4___ %

Average Yield (5B) . . . .   ___1.3___ %

Total Return for 5 Years (average) (5C) . . . .   ___23.7___ %

to the expected yearly dividend income, we get an anticipated 23.7 percent. This is referred to as *total return.* See Figure 9-4 for a summary of the figures in this section.

Next let us discuss what the figures we have calculated tell us about this stock.

CHAPTER 10

WHAT THE NAIC STOCK SELECTION GUIDE AND REPORT TELLS US

VISUAL ANALYSIS

*T*he Capitalization box at the top of page 1 of the Stock Selection Guide and Report requires us to take a look at the company's capital structure. Is there an unusual amount of debit or potential dilution that should be noted here? As we gather this information by consulting a service or the company's 10K or annual report, other items may come to our attention. For Motorola, Value Line shows us that while there is $3.4 billion of debt, that is only 17 percent of the company's total capitalization, and all of the balance is common stock. Furthermore, the service indicates that the company is earning enough money each year to pay the interest on its debt fifteen times. Some of the debt is convertible into common stock, but the dilution does not look like it would be substantial. Our conclusion from these facts is that Motorola has a capital structure that should be favorable to the common shareowner. The completed Stock Selection Guide for Motorola appears in Figure 10-1.

We classify Motorola as a major company in a major industry. Ordinarily, we would expect a company of its size to have a growth rate of 5 percent to 7 or 8 percent. Companies with sales in the billions have more difficulty producing growth at a rate above that than smaller companies. A look at the trend line we have drawn through Motorola's sales figures for the past ten years gets our attention for two reasons. One is the rapid rate of growth

Figure 10-1

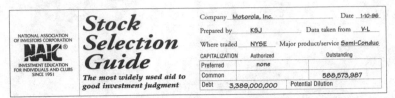

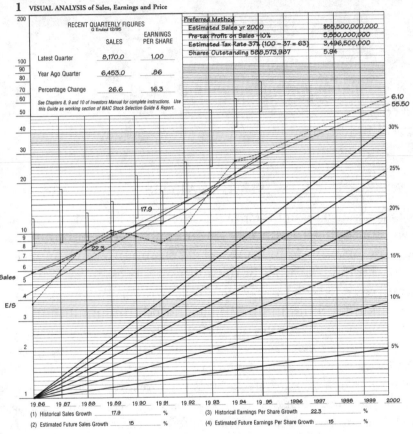

NATIONAL ASSOCIATION OF INVESTORS CORPORATION

NAIC®

INVESTMENT EDUCATION FOR INDIVIDUALS AND CLUBS SINCE 1951

Stock Selection Guide

The most widely used aid to good investment judgment

Company __Motorola, Inc.__ Date __1-10-96__

Prepared by __KSJ__ Data taken from __V-L__

Where traded __NYSE__ Major product/service __Semi-Conduc__

CAPITALIZATION	Authorized	Outstanding
Preferred	none	
Common		588,573,987
Debt	3,389,000,000	Potential Dilution

1 VISUAL ANALYSIS of Sales, Earnings and Price

RECENT QUARTERLY FIGURES
Q Ended 12/95

	SALES	EARNINGS PER SHARE
Latest Quarter	8,170.0	1.00
Year Ago Quarter	6,453.0	.86
Percentage Change	26.6	16.3

See Chapters 8, 9 and 10 of Investors Manual for complete instructions. Use this Guide as working section of NAIC Stock Selection Guide & Report.

Preferred Method
Estimated Sales yr 2000 $55,500,000,000
Pre-tax Profit on Sales 10%   5,550,000,000
Estimated Tax Rate 37% (100 – 37 = 63)   3,496,500,000
Shares Outstanding 588,573,987   5.94

(1) Historical Sales Growth __17.9__ %

(2) Estimated Future Sales Growth __15__ %

(3) Historical Earnings Per Share Growth __22.3__ %

(4) Estimated Future Earnings Per Share Growth __15__ %

Figure 10-1 (Continued)

2 EVALUATING MANAGEMENT Company __Motorola Inc.__

	19 86	19 87	19 88	19 89	19 90	19 91	19 92	19 93	19 94	19 95	LAST 5 YEAR AVG.	TREND UP	TREND DOWN
A % Pre-tax Profit on Sales (Net Before Taxes ÷ Sales)	4.5	6.2	7.4	7.4	6.1	5.4	6.0	9.0	11.0	11.4	8.6	↑	
B % Earned on Equity (E/S ÷ Book Value)	7.0	10.2	13.2	14.0	11.7	9.8	11.2	15.9	17.2	17.5	14.3	↑	

3 PRICE-EARNINGS HISTORY as an indicator of the future

This shows how stock prices have fluctuated with earnings and dividends. It is a building block for translating earnings into future stock prices.

PRESENT PRICE __56 ¼__   HIGH THIS YEAR __82.500__   LOW THIS YEAR __51.500__

	Year	A PRICE HIGH	B PRICE LOW	C Earnings Per Share	D Price Earnings Ratio HIGH A ÷ C	E Price Earnings Ratio LOW B ÷ C	F Dividend Per Share	G % Payout F ÷ C X 100	H % High Yield F ÷ B X 100
1	1991	17.8	11.4	0.86	20.7	13.3	.19	22.1	1.7
2	1992	26.6	16.1	1.08	24.6	14.9	.20	18.5	1.2
3	1993	53.8	24.4	1.78	30.2	13.7	.22	12.4	0.9
4	1994	61.1	42.1	2.65	23.1	15.9	.31	11.7	0.7
5	1995	82.1	51.5	2.93	28.0	11.8	.40	12.5	0.8
6	TOTAL		145.5		126.6	75.6		77.2	
7	AVERAGE		29.1		25.3	15.1		15.4	
8	AVERAGE PRICE EARNINGS RATIO			20.2	9 CURRENT PRICE EARNINGS RATIO	19.2			

'96(E)3.68 15.3

4 EVALUATING RISK and REWARD over the next 5 years

Assuming one recession and one business boom every 5 years, calculations are made of how **high** and how **low** the stock might sell. The upside-downside ratio is the key to evaluating risk and reward.

A HIGH PRICE — NEXT 5 YEARS
Avg. High P/E __20__ (3D7) X Estimate High Earnings/Share __5.94__ = Forecast High Price $ __118.8__ (4A1)

B LOW PRICE — NEXT 5 YEARS
(a) Avg. Low P/E __15.1__ (3E7) X Estimated Low Earnings/Share __2.93__ = $ __44.2__
(b) Avg. Low Price of Last 5 Years = __29.1__ (3B7)
(c) Recent Severe Market Low Price = __24.4__
(d) Price Dividend Will Support Present Divd. __.40__ / High Yield (H) __.017__ = __24__
Selected Estimated Low Price _____ = $ __44.2__ (4B1)

C ZONING
__119__ (4A1) High Forecast Price Minus __44__ (4B1) Low Forecast Price Equals __75__ (C) Range. 1/3 of Range = __25__ (4CD)

(4C2) Lower 1/3 = (4B1) __44__ to __69__ (Buy)
(4C3) Middle 1/3 = __69__ to __94__ (Maybe)
(4C4) Upper 1/3 = __94__ to __119__ (4A1) (Sell)

Present Market Price of __56¼__ is in the __BUY__ (4C5) Range

D UP-SIDE DOWN-SIDE RATIO (Potential Gain vs. Risk of Loss)
High Price (4A1) __119__ Minus Present Price __56¼__
Present Price __56¼__ Minus Low Price (4B1) __44__ = $\frac{62.8}{12.3}$ = __5.1__ (4D) To 1

E PRICE TARGET (Simple Interest)
$\frac{\text{High Price (4A1)} \quad 119}{\text{Present Market Price} \quad 56.25}$ = (__2.12__) X 100 = (__212__) − 100 = __112__ (4E) % Appreciation

5 5-YEAR POTENTIAL

These calculations provide a picture of future income. They also provide a standard for comparing income and growth stocks.

A Present Full Year's Dividend $ __.40__
$\frac{\text{Present Full Year's Dividend \$ .40}}{\text{Present Price of Stock \$ 56.25}}$ = __.007__ X 100 = __.7__ (5A) Present Yield or % Returned on Purchase Price

B AVERAGE YIELD OVER NEXT 5 YEARS
Avg. Earnings Per Share Next 5 Years __4.60__ X Avg. % Payout (3G7) __15.4%__ = $\frac{.71}{\text{Present Price \$} \quad 56.25}$ = __1.3__ (5B) %

C ESTIMATED ANNUAL RETURN OVER NEXT FIVE YEARS
$\frac{\text{5 Year Appreciation Potential (4E)} \quad 112}{5}$ = __22.4__ %
Average Yield (5B) . . . . __1.3__ %
Total Return for 5 Years (average) (5C) . . . . __23.7__ %

for a company its size. The second is the relative steadiness of the line for a business that is inclined to be quite cyclical.

What is the rate of growth for Motorola's sales? We plotted lines using four different methods. Refer back to pages 78 to 81 in Chapter 8. The best judgment method line we have drawn shows a growth rate of about 18 percent and the others range from 17 to 20 percent. NAIC's Tool Kit program for the Guide computes the growth rate exactly and comes up with 17.9 percent. That is the figure we have recorded at the bottom of the graph as the historical growth rate, or the rate at which we estimate the company has grown in the past ten years. Some members of the club may estimate 17 percent; others may go as high as 20 percent. The exact figure is not important. What we are deciding at this point is, has the company grown fast enough in the past ten years to make it a candidate for further study? Earlier when we were looking for a large company for our portfolio we said we would be happy with a company that had grown 5 to 8 percent. This company, at 18 percent, has a growth rate higher than we would hope to find for a small company. Motorola seems to give us the growth of a small company along with the greater strength and stability of a giant company. Motorola more than meets our test for rate of sales growth.

Next we check the earnings-per-share growth rate line. Since we are buying shares in this company and have found its sales growth rate to be satisfactory, we want to see if management is translating that growth into a similar rate of growth in earnings per share. The dotted line on the graph shows earnings-per-share growth, which has exceeded sales growth for the past five years. The slope of the line makes that very clear.

It is always a good idea to check if the growth rate in earnings per share for the last five years has been the same or better than the rate for the first five years of our study. It is clear that growth over the last five years has been very vigorous. It is difficult for a company to sustain a rate of growth as great as that which Motorola shows from 1992 through 1994. Our Tool Kit program calculates the historical growth rate at 22.3 percent. Our best judgment method estimate for the latest five years would be 25 percent or better. Obviously, Motorola meets our second test of advancing earnings per share at a rate at least as high as sales growth.

At this point we should make a judgment as to how Motorola's sales and earnings might grow over the coming five years. Experience has shown that a compounded growth rate above 15 percent a year is very difficult for a company to maintain. It is usually advisable not to project growth at a higher rate, though there are exceptions to that rule. Investors saw Wal-Mart grow at a rate in excess of 20 percent for many years. NAIC members have owned large numbers of shares in AFLAC, McDonald's, and RPM and watched them produce extraordinary rates of growth year after year. RPM has now had forty-seven straight years of increased sales and earnings per share. Nevertheless, experience dictates that we forecast a little under the rate of the past five years, especially if that rate is above 15 percent.

At this point it is a good idea to try to develop as good an understanding of the business as possible. You can do this by reading what the investment services say about the company. Your business library may have a folder of clippings of articles about the company. Your broker may have issued research reports on the company or have copies of reports others have issued. You can also call the shareholder relations department of the company; Value Line and Standard & Poor's will have the phone number in their report on the company. That department will mail you copies of the company's latest releases, its annual report, and copies of brokers' articles about it.

From these materials we learn that Motorola is a leader in the communications industry, particularly in the wireless area—cellular phones, pagers, and two-way radios. The whole world is its market, and many experts believe its growth could continue for many years.

We know there is never a guarantee that such growth will take place, but we decide to project Motorola's sales and earnings for the next five years at a compound annual rate of growth of 15 percent. There is always the question of from where we make that projection. The figures in Section 2 have some influence on that decision. However, with Motorola's record of increasing pre-tax profit margin and its current good though not excessive margin, we decide to project based on the most recent year's earnings per share.

PRE-TAX AND EQUITY MARGINS

The pre-tax profit margin is the amount of profit that a company makes on each dollar of sales before taxes. The markup on Motorola's products before taxes over the past ten years has ranged from 4½ cents to 11 cents. Compared with drug companies and a number of other businesses, that is a very modest figure. The margins in different industries vary greatly, and in time the investor learns the rate common to a particular industry and consequently recognizes margins that are outstanding. In the manufacturing industry the margins cover a wide range, 10 to 20 percent being common. In banking an operating margin above 1 percent is considered exceptional.

The interesting thing about Motorola's pre-tax profit margin is that it has increased pretty steadily over the past ten years. That indicates management's successful attention to controlling costs and increasing margins. At the same time, Motorola's margin does not seem excessive for its seemingly dominant position in the industry. Without knowing much detail about the operations, we would think that Motorola has room to maintain or increase its pre-tax margin.

Motorola's earnings on equity have followed the same pattern as its pre-tax profit margin. Earnings have been steadily increasing over the years, but are not at a level that seems impossible to sustain. If management is able to increase both sales and margins, Motorola's profit could be remarkable. The investor usually finds the greatest opportunity in companies where the percent earned on equity is above 20 percent. That's a very significant indicator of the rate at which shareowner value is increasing.

PRICE/EARNINGS HISTORY

Section 3, a record of the price/earnings history of the stock, is very important. NAIC's experience with thousands of investors shows that the great majority does a very good job of identifying high-growth companies. The most frequent error they make is paying too high a price for the stock.

The figures in Section 3 are all precise. While we emphasize that the figures in the Stock Selection Guide and Report should be adjusted to reflect changes we expect to take place, many people accept the figures as they are and make no changes. The important figures to look at in this section are the price/earnings ratios. These ratios change tremendously over a business cycle. Look at Figure I-5 on pages 10 and 11 of this book. In the seventy years spanned by that table the average price/earnings ratio on the Dow-Jones Industrials has been as low as 6.8 and as high as 25.1. When market optimism is very low, P/E ratios decline. When market optimism is high, they soar.

The first thing the investor should ask when studying a P/E is, where are we now in the long-term stock market cycle? We have enjoyed an upward-moving stock market since 1983, and at the time of this writing it is 1996. History tells us that a severe break in the upward market trend is due. Yet many factors in the world economy suggest that we could still have a number of years of market buoyancy. While the stock market is high by past standards, the excessive speculation that usually occurs before a major long-term break in the market does not seem to be present. Price/earnings ratios on the S&P 500 average 15, which is above the average for the past twenty years but not excessively high. No one ever knows what the market will do, but a good case can be made at this time that we are in a period of market enthusiasm in which average P/E ratios of 15 to 21 may prevail for some time. A number of thoughtful analysts believe that a long-term decline in the market will not occur for a number of years.

For our prediction five years into the future, our conclusion at this time is that prevailing P/E ratios are likely to continue. If we were in a period where average high ratios for the past ten years had been around 7 to 10, we would believe that an increase of 4 or 5 points would be reasonable five years forward, and would consider adjusting our projected average high P/E upward. If we judged that we were really in a period of excessive speculation and that a long-term change in the direction of the market was at hand, we would consider changing the current average high P/E to a lower figure five years out.

The P/E of a company can be affected by investor attitude toward its industry. Companies in a growth industry usually enjoy P/E ratios above the average. Also, the higher the rate of growth the company has had and the longer it has produced that growth, the higher its P/E is likely to be. Value Line periodically publishes the average P/E ratios that have prevailed in various industry classifications.

Some companies are entering a period of declining growth. When that happens, the P/E for the company will decline. A classic illustration is Wal-Mart. For many years management pushed Wal-Mart's annual sales and earnings per share ahead at 25 percent or better, and the P/E ran between 25 and 35. Then the rate of growth began to slow, and the P/E gradually dropped. The result has been that while the company is still experiencing excellent growth, its lower growth rate has led to a lower P/E and the price of the stock has changed little in several years, in spite of sizable increases in sales and earnings per share.

As we look at the P/E record of Motorola, we conclude that the company's average high P/E has been well above the market average. This, we would judge, is due to the high growth rate of sales and earnings produced by the company's management for at least the past ten years. The reports we read from management and security analysts suggest that they believe Motorola's growth is likely to continue at a high rate for at least the next five years. Our decision is to use 20, which is just below the last five years' average of the average high and low P/E ratios, as shown in Section 3, line 8, to make our five-year projection of earnings per share.

EVALUATING RISK AND REWARD

We have two estimates of what Motorola will be earning per share five years in the future. One we obtained by projecting our earnings per share trend line five years in the future at 15 percent, compounded annually, as we explained earlier. This gave us a figure of $6.10 as Motorola's potential earnings per share for the year 2000.

We obtained another estimate using what we call the preferred procedure, which is based on a projection of sales rather than earnings and the application of our estimated tax rates and profit margins. Analysts generally believe that sales can be more accurately projected than can earnings per share. Also, the separate application of a chosen tax rate and pre-tax profit margin gives you more control over your estimate. Projecting sales at 15 percent to the year 2000 results in a projection of sales at that time of $55.5 billion. Section 2, Part A shows us that the pre-tax profit margin has been increasing steadily and has been above 11 percent for the last two years. We are making an optimistic projection and so decide to use 10 percent rather than the average of the last five years, 8.6 percent. This gives us a pre-tax profit of $5.55 billion.

Value Line estimates the future tax rate at 37 percent. Since we have no ideas of our own concerning the future tax rate, we go along with Value Line. If 37 percent of profit is going to go out in taxes, we will have a balance of 63 percent left (100% − 37% = 63%) as after-tax income. That gives us $3.4965 billion, which, divided by the 588,573,987 shares outstanding, leaves us $5.94 per share according to the preferred method. That is fairly close to the $6.10 we obtained by projecting our earnings-per-share trend line. We could use either one to project our high price for the year 2000. Multiplying the average high P/E of 20 that we chose for the year 2000 by our estimated earnings for that year of $5.94 per share, we get a potential high price of $118.8, rounded to $119.

There is no guarantee that the stock will sell that high in 2000. But our judgment is that if the company grows at 15 percent, which is below the rate of 17.9 percent at which it has grown for the last ten years, and if it sells at a P/E of 20, it will reach that price.

We know that in a five-year period stocks will both go up and go down. We have estimated a possible high for our stock. The next question is, how low is this stock likely to go in the next five years? A look at the high and low prices of the past five years shows that the price has been very volatile. NAIC suggests five different ways of estimating the possible low price. Four of these are shown in Section 4, Part B of the Guide. The fifth is useful only at a certain period in the market cycle.

The first method, shown in line (a), is the same as we used in estimating the high price. We take the average low P/E for the past five years and multiply it by the earnings per share for the latest year in our study. The theory is that in a growing company, earnings will advance each year. The current year should show the lowest earnings of the coming five years and, multiplied by the average low P/E, should determine the lowest price the stock will sell at. The second method for judging the potential low price is to use the average low price for the last five years, found in Section 3, column B, line 7. The third method uses the recent severe market low, and the fourth method uses the price the dividend will support. A fifth possible low price is calculated by taking the recent high price of 82.50 and reducing it by 25 percent, which would result in 61.8.

The method of line (a) is probably the most appropriate for Motorola. This is generally the most reliable procedure for a growing company. Methods (b) and (c) are better guides for cyclical companies, where the movement up and down is dictated more by general economic conditions than by growth in the company. Method (d) is best used when the company you are looking at is bought more for yield than for growth. The idea here is that buyers looking for yield watch the price of a stock, and when it comes down to the point where the yield is as high as it has been at past low periods they come into the market and buy the stock. Their buying reverses the downward trend of the stock.

The fifth procedure is often used when the market is starting up after a long down trend. For instance, in the 1970s stock prices and price/earnings ratios moved down for a long period. The upward trend started in the 1980s. Stocks were moving to new highs and lows and moving higher each year.

Working with five years of downward-moving prices at a time when prices were moving upward resulted in forecast lows that kept investors from buying good stocks. In such periods corrections in the market seldom exceed 25 percent. Calculating a possible low in this manner and comparing it with the others can be useful under such market conditions. This method is not useful in other market conditions. Note that in Motorola's case the correction from high to low has been as much as 50 percent in one year and over 30 percent in the other years.

We chose 44.2 as our possible low price for Motorola—44 rounded to the nearest whole number.

The purpose of the zoning section, Part C, is to estimate the price ranges over which we should question whether to buy the stock, hold it, or sell it. Our goal is to double our money in the coming five years. If we buy Motorola at the current price and it reaches our projected high of 119, we will have attained that goal. Dividing the price range between our projected high and low into thirds shows us the area in which we could buy the stock and the area where we could sell and approximate our goal.

The upside/downside ratio, Part D, is another way to check whether we can currently buy the stock at a price that is favorable. Here the idea is that we want our potential on the upside to be twice our risk on the downside. This means we would like the figure in this section to be 3 to 1 or better. Again, we should keep in mind that we are working with possibilities or probabilities and not events that will precisely match our figures. In Motorola's case our upside/downside ratio at a price of 56¼ is 5.1 to 1. This suggests that the odds on the upside are better than those on the downside by 5 to 1. A buy in the present price range does not appear to be risky. This is a very-high growth stock; it is a leader in its field, and our study shows that we could double our money. We would buy. If the price were at its recent high of 82½, we would conclude that the risk is high and that a purchase should be postponed.

If we buy the stock and its price moves up into the sell zone, we should consider whether to sell. Based on the experience of NAIC investors, when you own a stock with a growth rate as high as this stock has, it is dangerous to sell it. You should consider a sale only if the growth rate comes down and there is no apparent reason to expect it to go back up in the foreseeable future. Or speculation may drive the stock to an unreasonable high. For instance, if Motorola's price suddenly moved up to 225, that would represent a P/E of 70, almost three times its normal high P/E of 24.9. Common sense suggests that price is not likely to be maintained because it is so far out of line with earnings. In such a case we might sell say 25 percent of our holdings and look for another outstanding growth company for a new opportunity.

If the price of the stock declines, it may be that we have realized enough profit from our stock and should review the prospects of our remaining shares. If the company is still judged to be a well-managed company with good growth prospects, we will continue to hold our shares.

Part E of Section 4 calculates the percent appreciation we may get from this stock if the sales and earnings growth and price action we have estimated for this stock work out as calculated. Since our goal is a 100 percent gain in five years, we are satisfied that Motorola's 112 percent meets our goal.

FIVE-YEAR POTENTIAL

Section 5 provides a further check that the combination of dividend income and appreciation projected for this stock will enable us to achieve our goal of doubling value in the coming five years. Part A is the calculation of our yield at the time of purchase. Part B is the calculation of the average annual dividend return estimated over the next five years. In Part C we add these together and see that if all goes according to our guesses, we will enjoy an annual return of 22.4 percent. We need 20 percent a year to double our value. These figures are based on an arithmetic calculation. Using compounded annual figures, the total needed to double the stock's value would be 14.9 percent each year.

REACHING A FINAL DECISION

The final set of eight questions in the Stock Selection Guide are designed to help us reach a decision based on the results we have calculated as to whether this company is the kind of investment we are looking for.

For Question 1 we review the sales and earnings-per-share record and conclude that both are growing at a rate sufficient to double our values in five years. Our decision is that this growth is likely to continue for the next five years. The company's growth seems to be based on superior research producing a superior product. We summarize our conclusions in the space provided.

Question 2 covers the three most important tests of management: Is it producing the desired rate of sales growth? Does it meet our standards for earnings growth? If so, is it earning a good rate on equity? If those answers

Figure 10-1 (Continued)

GOALS IN SELECTING A STOCK

You want to look ahead five years by **judging** Management capability and **evaluating** the Price you should pay for a stock. You should also look at **Other Considerations** and reach a **Conclusion. Your findings are registered in the table at the right and your Conclusion below.**

Novice and professional investors to varying degrees may act hastily on new products, tips, technical clues and short term factors rather than being methodical in their decisions. Thirty years of experience with this type of report tends to show that there is a RULE OF FIVE, which is this: If five companies are analyzed for their five year future, one may have unforeseeable trouble, three may be on target, and one may have unpredictable good fortune.

CONCLUSION: Motorola has a sales and earnings

per share growth record that more than meets

our goal. Its margins are good but not super.

Its price is a little high. Buy on dips.

(1) Our goal is to find a company with **able** MANAGEMENT; and (2) to buy a stock at a **good** PRICE.

	Page	Good	Average	Poor
Judging Management				
Driving Force	3	✔		
Earned on Sales	3	✔		
Earned on Equity	3	✔		
Evaluating Price				
High in 5 Years	4	✔		
Low in 5 Years	4	✔		
Upside-Downside Ratio	4		✔	
Yield Current	4			✔
Total Return	4	✔		
Other Considerations				
Industry Potentials	4			
State of Business Cycle	4			
Stock Price Trends	4			
Quality of Stock	4			
Capitalization and Finance	2			

METHOD-DATA-INSTRUCTIONS

This report organizes data presentation in a concise professional manner, avoiding among other things the agony of deciding what factors to cover. Because writing is a chore, the cross-out-method lets you report your judgments with ease. The data used comes from Value Line Reports that are available on many listed and unlisted companies. You may wish to check your 5 year "high estimate" with Value Line's estimated Target Price Range for 3 to 5 years hence. Instructions for

completing pages 3 and 4 of this report are in the *Investors Manual* obtainable from the National Association of Investors Corporation, P.O. Box 220, Royal Oak, Michigan 48068. Other sources of data are annual and quarterly reports from companies, brokers reports and visits to company annual meetings. You may learn by yourself, or with several friends, or by actually investing $20 or $50 a month through an investment club you have formed with friends.

1 WHAT DOES THE VISUAL ANALYSIS SHOW?

The trend of (sales) ~~(revenues)~~ is (up) ~~(down) (sideways)~~.

The trend of earnings per share is (up) ~~(down) (sideways)~~.

The price trend of the stock is (up) ~~(down) (sideways)~~.

If sales trend is up, the increase seems to have come from (taking a greater share of the market) ~~(mergers and acquisitions)~~ (new products or new product applications produced by research).

In my opinion, the stock should be (investigated) ~~(discarded)~~ because the trend of sales is (favorable) ~~(neutral) (unfavorable)~~; the trend of earnings per share is (favorable) ~~(neutral) (unfavorable)~~; the price is ~~(favorable)~~ (neutral) ~~(unfavorable)~~.

Also for other reasons as follows: The company's

products seem to be tops, the company

is very strong in Asia and Pacific Rim

countries and its margins have been

growing.

2 DOES THE COMPANY PASS THE THREE MANAGEMENT TESTS?

Investors lose money because of failing to test for good management. Instead they rely on outlook for the industry, new products, or a plausible story for protection and often lose.

TEST I: DRIVING FORCE OF MANAGEMENT

Management as indicated by the past record has the necessary ability to expand sales (yes) ~~(no)~~. The rate of sales expansion on the VISUAL ANALYSIS looks like ___17.9___ % annually. The rate of sales expansion is likely to be (better) ~~(same)~~ (worse) in the next five years.

TEST II: EARNED ON SALES

Management seems to have the ability to ~~(maintain)~~ (increase) profit margins (see 2A, Evaluating Management on page 2 at left). It shows the Pre-Tax Profit Margins for each of the last five years as follows in

chronological order:
___5.4___ %, ___6.0___ %, ___9.0___ %, ___11.0___ %, ___10.9___ %.

TEST III: EARNED ON EQUITY

The company has earned on invested capital from ___7.1___ % to ___17.1___ %. See 2B, Evaluating Management on page 2 at left. Earnings on equity are (above) ~~(below)~~ 10%.

I conclude from these three tests that the company has (good) ~~(average)~~ ~~(poor)~~ management and will be (stronger) ~~(same)~~ ~~(weaker)~~ in five years.

Over a period of five years, a well-managed company will generally gain ground while a poor one loses its earning power. Remember this in making your decision.

continued . . .

Figure 10-1 (Continued)

3 WHAT IS THE PRICE RANGE LIKELY TO BE FOR THE NEXT FIVE YEARS?

Complete Section 3 of the Stock Selection Guide & Report (page 2). Two considerations are important: (1) It is usually better to project sales and apply profit margins and taxes than to project earnings per share on the chart because profit margins tend to have definite upside limits; and (2) it is well to pay less attention to, or discard the much higher price-earnings ratios existing in years of low earnings. Also, avoid being misled by sales increases in early years of a new product or attributable to government or other types of contracts that may not be renewed or are due entirely to the upswing of a business cycle.

Have price-earnings (P/E) ratios for the past five years been trending (downward) (level) (upward)? Is the P/E ratio (higher) (same) (lower) than its competitors? Have the average price earnings ratios of the

past five years been influenced by years when the ratio was (unusually high) (unusually low)?

Over the next five years, the stock might be expected to reach a high price of __119__ and also a low of __44__ when the next depression comes. It now sells at __56 ¼__ , indicating (little) (average) (great) risk. Its suggested buy prices should range from __44__ to __69__ , hold from __69__ to __94__ , and sell from __94__ to __119__ .

These are the zones calculated in the Stock Selection Guide & Report (Section 4C, page 2). Be a careful buyer.

4 HOW DOES THE STOCK MEET THE THREE SAFETY TESTS OF PRICE?

Unsuccessful investment clubs and investors make two mistakes; (1) selection of poorly managed companies, (2) pay too much for stocks. The second mistake is by far the most prevalent and most damaging, and is easily corrected. Big losses have been taken in high grade stocks because they were bought mainly, "because they were moving" or sold "because they went down" —not because of price. The best results have been obtained by investors that buy carefully.

TEST I: SHOWS PROBABILITY OF GETTING OUT EVEN
The stock under review has sold at its present price in (__two__)* (none) of the last five years. The risk of loss seems (small) (average) (considerable) at the present price on the basis of price history.

* *Three of five is a good standard.*

TEST II: STACK THE ODDS IN THE INVESTORS FAVOR
The upside-downside ratio from Section 4D, page 2 of the Stock Selection Guide & Report is __5.1__ to 1. This is (favorable) (average) (unfavorable), indicating that we need to pay attention to past price history (considerably) (some) (not much).

TEST III: THESE STANDARDS HELP INVESTORS AVOID LOSS
The pay-off test is whether at least 100% appreciation is possible in five years—or in the case of cyclical stocks, 20% a year for the number of years held. Analysis shows a high price of __119__ is reasonable in __5__ years, equal to __22.4__ % a year.

In the case of cyclical stocks, comment should include the number of months the cycle has advanced and the dangers on this account.

5 WHAT ARE THE INVESTMENT CHARACTERISTICS OF THE COMPANY?

The Company is (well established) (new) and operates (internationally) (nationally) (regionally). The product line or service is (diversified) (narrow) and sold to (consumers) (manufacturers) (government). The business cycle affects sales and earnings (not much) (average). The company is (largest) (in top four) (a smaller factor) in its industry. The company and products are (well known) (average)

(not known) to the investing public. Its common stock is listed on (New York) (American) (other exchange) (unlisted) and has price records covering (five years) (only _____ years). It has (a continuous dividend record dating from __16+__) (a spotty dividend record) (no dividend record). Investment characteristics are (good) (average) (poor).

6 WHAT ARE THE CHARACTERISTICS OF THE COMPANY'S MAJOR INDUSTRY?

The __electronics__ industry is (established) (new) and has (exceptional) (average) (below-average) potential. The potential is based on (population) (product development) (science) (international expansion). Sales, profit margins and earnings per share fluctuate with the business cycle (widely—like the steel industry) (narrowly—like food) (average—like oil). Capital investment per dollar of sales in the industry is (high—like chemicals) (low—like clothing manufacture) (aver-

age—like metal products manufacturing), making it (easy) (difficult) for new competition to enter the business. Price competition between companies is (no problem) (severe) (average).

In my opinion, the major industry, everything considered, is (favorable) (average) (unfavorable). The company being analyzed will be (aided by the trend of the industry) or (will have to take business from competitors to grow).

7 WHAT ABOUT THE BUSINESS CYCLE?

About 33 months is an average business cycle, though variations from this norm are wide.

A well-managed company gains on marginal competitors in a depression or inflation as a general rule. In a period of business recovery, high grade stocks advance first, second grade stocks next, and marginal stocks last, as a general rule. Also, non-growth cyclical stocks are good purchases when business

turns up and should be sold in the later stages of the cycle because of exposure to substantial drops in price, earnings, and sometimes dividends.

The trend of business has been (up) (down) for __144+__ months. The current stage of the business cycle tends to (help) (not affect) (hurt) profits of the company. The present stage of the business cycle suggests (no concern) (caution) (daring) for the stock under review.

8 WHAT ABOUT THE STOCK MARKET AND YIELDS ON BONDS?

The price the stock is selling at is __56 ¼__ and the Dow Jones Averages are at: Industrials __4802.45__ , Transportation __1,916.17__ and Utilities __217.94__ . This provides a reference in case of review of this stock in the future.

From the Value Line, it is seen that the stock under review has performed, as compared relatively (better) (same) (below).

You may also want to comment on the behavior of bond yields and Treasury Bill rates. Yields tend to rise in the later stages of a business cycle (attracting money from the stock market) and fall when business slows and investors want safety.

Bond yields may (attract) (not affect) (discourage) investment in this stock currently are positive, we must answer the additional question, can we buy those good things at a reasonable price?

Question 3 directs us to check the P/E ratios and price zones. We conclude that Motorola's high growth rate has been recognized by the market as reflected in a high P/E. The price is in the middle of our buy zone.

It is a good idea to look at the three tests of safety concerning the price. That's what Question 4 guides us to do. If the stock has sold for a price as high as we are going to pay for it in several of the past five years, that is an indication that we can get out if something unforeseen turns up about the company suggesting that we have made a mistake and should sell. Motorola has sold at a price as high as we are going to have to pay in two of the past five years. This is favorable. Second, Motorola's upside/downside ratio is 5 to 1. The third test indicates that we could more than double our investment in five years. All three tests suggest that a buy at 56¼ is favorable at this time.

It is important to consider the market characteristics of the stock. This is the focus of Question 5. If the stock is not well known and valued by the market, its good qualities may not be recognized for a long time, and the investor will not benefit. Value Line has a sixteen-year record of Motorola. The company is older than that, but the record of the last sixteen years shows it has been an important business for all those years. It operates worldwide. Its products are sold to government, businesses, and consumers. It's a leader in its industry. It is well known to both institutional and individual investors. Its stock is listed on the New York Stock Exchange. All of these things tell us that its investment characteristics are favorable.

If the company's investment characteristics are good, we next examine the characteristics of its main industry. Question 6 prompts us in this area. Motorola is in both the electronics and communications industries, two of the biggest and fastest growing in the world. Continued growth will come from population (supplying the many still lightly industrialized nations), product development, scientific advances, and international growth. Although it is a growth business, Motorola is still affected by the business cycle. While entrepreneurs may come up with competing products, the capital needed to produce them will slow the competition. Nevertheless, competition is strong in the industry. Our conclusion is that the company is in a good industry.

For Question 7, we make an effort to determine where we are in the business and stock market cycle. Stock prices have been going up since 1983 without a lengthy, major setback. That is unusual and suggests that we shouldn't be surprised if a correction occurs. Prices could drop 25 percent or more. We would hope that they would not stay down for a lengthy period, but there have been times when a downtrend has continued for ten years or more. That suggests that our purchases should have a strong upside potential.

A long downward trend is a period of exceptional opportunity for the investor. During such periods practically every stock is an exceptional buy. But for investors such times are very difficult psychologically. The climate tends to be very pessimistic. The media features all the bad possibilities. The end of the world seems more likely than a recovery in business and the stock market. However, once the investor has gone through a down period and enjoyed the subsequent recovery, investing during a down period is much easier.

The standard Wall Street wisdom advises the investor to move out of the stock market at the peak and wait for the bottom to come back. Such logic is beyond question. The problem is that few possess the ability to pick those spots. A number of studies have been made in recent years comparing the records of individuals who try to move out of the market at peaks and back in at bottoms with the records of those who invest in good-quality stocks and move only when they decide to change one stock for another. Professors Jess H. Chua and Richard S. Woodward of the University of Calgary found that the individuals who made an effort to get in and out in response to market moves had to catch 80 percent of the moves to equal the record of the individuals who stayed in the market.

A major reason that investors are not successful in moving in and out of the market is that the major part of an up or down move ordinarily takes place in just a few days. The person out of the market misses a good part of the move while waiting to get back in, as does the individual planning on getting out. One study points out that the market from 1982 to the break in 1987 contained 1,276 trading days. If you were fully invested during all that time, your annual return would have been 26.3 percent. If you were out during the twenty days with the largest gains, your return would have been 13.1 percent. If you missed the forty days with the biggest gains, your return would have been only 4.3 percent.

Less than 4 percent of the trading days generated 80 percent of the return. The individual trying to get in and out of the market at the most profitable times faces a formidable task. It has been said that the greatest risk is not being in the market but being out of the market.

As we make a study of a company using the NAIC Stock Selection Guide and Report, it is good to keep in mind that although every stock we select has prospects of meeting our goal, not all of them will do so. Some will approximate our goal. Some will do much better, and some will be a disaster. One of NAIC's founders, and the man who developed NAIC's Stock Study Procedures, referred to the likely results as the rule of five. Out of every five stocks the investor carefully selects, one is likely to have unexpected trouble, three are likely to meet expectations, and one is likely to have unpredictable good fortune. We obtain our goal with the average.

CHAPTER 11

THE STOCK COMPARISON GUIDE

*I*nvariably, in every club, one or two people emerge who are able to sway their colleagues regardless of the merits of their case. To help your club buy the best stock, rather than voting on the best sales job, turn to the NAIC *Stock Comparison Guide.* This form should be produced during the meeting as reports are given. A giant version of the Guide that everyone can see is ideal.

To keep preconceived prejudices out of the picture, some clubs label their alternative investment opportunities not by name but by the letters A, B, and C. This strategy focuses attention exclusively on the data presented on the form.

Putting the Stock Comparison Guide to use is simple, once Stock Selection Guides have been completed on the candidate companies. Arrangement of data generally follows the same order in which findings appear in the Stock Selection Guide. One person in the club should be assigned at each meeting to prepare the Guide. This can be done as members give their reports on individual companies. After the last report is given, the club turns its attention to the Stock Comparison Guide.

Findings based on the Stock Comparison Guide will prove more meaningful if the companies under review are in similar industries. However, the comparisons made are basic to the investment potential of any stock, and as long as members keep the differences between companies in mind, the comparisons will be profitable.

DESIRABLE CHARACTERISTICS

As reports are made to the group by individual members, evaluate the data to decide whether they reflect true growth. Is growth the result of management, an accident of the industry, patent advantage, or a special skill? Keep in mind these desirable characteristics:

1. The more consistent the record of growth in sales and earnings per share, the more reliable it is as an indicator of the future.

2. A high pre-tax profit margin reflects management skill in operating efficiently, in securing a special advantage in the industry, in developing patent advantage, or in some other special area. Understanding the nature of the advantage helps you to project its likely longevity.

3. High return on stockholders' equity is another indicator of management skill and shows the rate at which share value is increasing.

4. A high rate of earnings plowback, permitting expansion financing without dilution of present stockholders' interests.

5. Established products or services of superior quality with further potential.

6. Alert, aggressive management capable of developing new products or services to broaden markets.

7. Relative independence from the business cycle and other external influences such as government regulation.

As a matter of sound practice, we recommend that all reports be heard before discussion by the membership takes place. The reports should be limited in time to permit ample time for questions and comments by the audience.

The sample Guide in Figure 11-1 features three leading companies in the electronic connector industry: AMP, Molex, and Thomas & Betts.

We first check for the company with the highest projected growth rate in sales and earnings per share. These figures are taken from the ratio chart of the corresponding Stock Selection Guides (see Figures 11-2, 11-3, and 11-4). Keep in mind that we are looking first at the historical rate of growth and then at the rate projected out five years. If we are right in our projection, it will be the most important of the two indicators. On our Stock Comparison Guide, we draw circles around the figures that are highest. The leader in both instances is Molex.

Management's ability to earn a high return on sales and on stockholders' equity are key tests. Molex boasts the best profit margin, while AMP and Thomas & Betts rank virtually even in return on equity, ahead of Molex. Molex management owns nearly half of the common shares outstanding.

Figure 11-1

Completed Stock Comparison Guide with Data for AMP, Molex, and Thomas & Betts

| NATIONAL ASSOCIATION OF INVESTORS CORPORATION **NAIC** ® INVESTMENT EDUCATION FOR INDIVIDUALS AND CLUBS SINCE 1951 | *Stock Comparison Guide* | Prepared by **F. MILLET** Date **10–9–xx** See Chapter 11 of the *Investors Manual* for complete instructions. **NAME OF COMPANY** |

GROWTH COMPARISONS (From Section 1 of the NAIC Stock Selection Guide)	AMP	MOLEX	THOMAS & BETTS		
(1) Historical % of Sales Growth	10.7	(17.2)	14.4		
(2) Projected % of Sales Growth	11	(18)	12		
(3) Historical % of Earnings Per Share Growth	11.7	(17.2)	7		
(4) Projected % of Earnings Per Share Growth	12	(18)	10		

MANAGEMENT COMPARISONS
(From Section 2 of the NAIC Stock Selection Guide)

	AMP	MOLEX	THOMAS & BETTS		
(5) % Profit Margin Before Taxes (Average for last 5 years) (2A) Trend	16.5	(19.3)	16.7		
(6) % Earned on Equity (Average for last 5 years) (2B) Trend	(16.5)	13.9	16.4		
(7) % of Common Owned by Management	—	47% Com 100% B	—		

PRICE COMPARISONS
(See Sections 3-5 of the NAIC Stock Selection Guide)

		AMP	MOLEX	THOMAS & BETTS		
(8) Estimated Total Earnings Per Share For Next 5 Years		18.18	10.45	22.05		
(9) Price Range Over Last 5 Years	High (3A) Low (3B)	71.50 26.12	28.25 11.375	67.75 33.50		
(10) Present Price		42	20¹/₂	54¹/₂		
Price Earnings Ratio Range Last 5 Years	(11) Highest (3D)	31	28.3	23.5		
	(12) Average High (3D7)	25	22¹/₂	19⁷/₈		
	(13) Average (3-8)	20¹/₂	17³/₈	17³/₈		
	(14) Average Low (3E7)	16	12¹/₈	14³/₄		
	(15) Lowest (3E)	13⁷/₈	10⁷/₈	13¹/₈		
(16) Current Price Earnings Ratio	(3-9)	15	14	16³/₈		
Estimated Price Zones	(17) Lower-Buy (4C2)	34¹/₈–52³/₄	15–25³/₄	45³/₈–66¹/₂		
	(18) Middle-Maybe (4C3)	52³/₄–71³/₄	25³/₄–36⁵/₈	66¹/₂–85³/₄		
	(19) Upper-Sell (4C4)	71³/₄–90	36⁵/₈–47¹/₂	85³/₄–106		
(20) Present Price Range	(4C5)	Buy	Buy	Buy		
(21) Upside Downside Ratio	(4D)	6.1	4.9	5.8		
(22) Current Yield	(5A)	2.9	0.1	3.9		
(23) Combined Estimated Yield	(5C)	25.9	26.5	23.3		

OTHER COMPARISONS

	AMP	MOLEX	THOMAS & BETTS		
(24) Number of Common Shares Outstanding	106,511,199	23.7 Mil 25.7 Mil A	17 Mil		
(25) Potential Dilution from Debentures, Warrants, Options		94.2 Th B 25 Mil PFD			
(26) Percent Payout (3G7)	35	1.4	59		
(27) OTHER DEBT	228.2 Mil		113.8 Mil		
(28)					
(29) Date of Source Material	6/30/9x	6/30/9x	6/30/9x		
(30) Where Traded	NYSE	OTC	NYSE		

© 1996. National Association of Investors Corporation; 711 West Thirteen Mile Road, Madison Hgts., Michigan 48071

Figure 11-2
Stock Selection Guide for AMP, Inc.

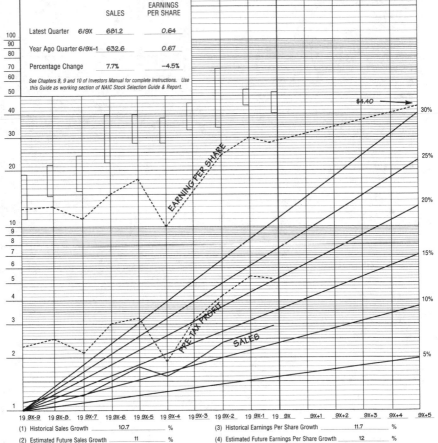

Company	AMP INC		Date JULY 199X
Prepared by	IAS		Data taken from VARIOUS
Where traded	NYSE	Major product/service	SEE TEXT

CAPITALIZATION	Authorized	Outstanding
Preferred		NONE
Common		106,511,199
Debt	$228.2 MILLION	Potential Dilution

NATIONAL ASSOCIATION OF INVESTORS CORPORATION

NAIC®

INVESTMENT EDUCATION FOR INDIVIDUALS AND CLUBS SINCE 1951

Stock Selection Guide

The most widely used aid to good investment judgment

1 VISUAL ANALYSIS of Sales, Earnings and Price

RECENT QUARTERLY FIGURES

	SALES	EARNINGS PER SHARE
Latest Quarter 6/9X	681.2	0.64
Year Ago Quarter 6/9X–1	632.6	0.67
Percentage Change	7.7%	–4.5%

See Chapters 8, 9 and 10 of Investors Manual for complete instructions. Use this Guide as working section of NAIC Stock Selection Guide & Report.

$4.40

EARNING PER SHARE

PRE-TAX PROFIT

SALES

(1) Historical Sales Growth	10.7	%	(3) Historical Earnings Per Share Growth	11.7	%
(2) Estimated Future Sales Growth	11	%	(4) Estimated Future Earnings Per Share Growth	12	%

Figure 11-2 (Continued)

2 EVALUATING MANAGEMENT

Company AMP INC. (AMP)

	19 9x-9	19 9x-8	19 9x-7	19 9x-6	19 9x-5	19 9x-4	19 9x-3	19 9x-2	19 9x-1	19 9x	LAST 5 YEAR AVG.	TREND UP	TREND DOWN
A % Pre-tax Profit on Sales (Net Before Taxes ÷ Sales)	20.0	19.5	17.2	19.3	20.0	11.8	15.2	18.6	19.8	17.0	16.5		✔
B % Earned on Equity (E/S ÷ Book Value)	22.7	20.4	16.6	20.4	21.8	10.8	14.5	18.5	21.0	17.5	16.5	✔	

3 PRICE-EARNINGS HISTORY as an indicator of the future

This shows how stock prices have fluctuated with earnings and dividends. It is a building block for translating earnings into future stock prices.

PRESENT PRICE 42 HIGH THIS YEAR 49¾ LOW THIS YEAR 40

	Year	A PRICE HIGH	B PRICE LOW	C Earnings Per Share	D Price Earnings Ratio HIGH A ÷ C	E Price Earnings Ratio LOW B ÷ C	F Dividend Per Share	G % Payout F ÷ C X 100	H % High Yield F ÷ B X 100
1	199x–4	39 ½	26 ⅛	1.87	21.1	14.0	0.64	34.2	2.4
2	199x–3	37 ⅞	27 ½	1.00	(37.9)	(27.5)	0.72	(72.0)	2.6
3	199x–2	45	32 ⅞	1.52	29.6	21.6	0.74	(48.7)	2.3
4	199x–1	71 ½	34 ⅛	2.31	31.0	14.8	0.85	36.8	2.5
5	199x	54 ¼	40 ½	2.96	18.3	13.7	1.00	33.8	2.5
6	TOTAL		161 ⅛		100.0	64.1		104.8	
7	AVERAGE		32 ¼		25.0	16.0		34.9	
8	AVERAGE PRICE EARNINGS RATIO			20.5	9 CURRENT PRICE EARNINGS RATIO			42 ÷ 2.80 = 15	

RV = 73

4 EVALUATING RISK and REWARD over the next 5 years

*Assuming one recession and one business boom every 5 years, calculations are made of how **high** and how **low** the stock might sell. The upside-downside ratio is the key to evaluating risk and reward.*

A HIGH PRICE — NEXT 5 YEARS

Avg. High P/E 20.5 (3D7) X Estimate High Earnings/Share 4.40 = Forecast High Price $ 90 (4A1)

B LOW PRICE — NEXT 5 YEARS

(a) Avg. Low P/E 16 (3E7) X Estimated Low Earnings/Share 2.60 = $ 41 ⅝

(b) Avg. Low Price of Last 5 Years = 32 ¼ (3B7)

(c) Recent Severe Market Low Price = 34 ⅛

(d) Price Dividend Will Support $\frac{\text{Present Divd.}}{\text{High Yield (H)}}$ = $\frac{1.20}{.026}$ = 46 ⅛

Selected Estimated Low Price = $ 34 ⅛ (4B1)

C ZONING

90 (4A1) High Forecast Price Minus 34 ⅛ (4B1) Low Forecast Price Equals 55 ⅞ (C) Range. 1/3 of Range = 18 ⅝ (4CD)

(4C2) Lower 1/3 = (4B1) 34 ⅛ to 52 ¾ (Buy)

(4C3) Middle 1/3 = 52 ¾ to 71 ½ (Maybe)

(4C4) Upper 1/3 = 71 ½ to 90 (4A1) (Sell)

Present Market Price of 42 is in the BUY (4C5) Range

D UP-SIDE DOWN-SIDE RATIO (Potential Gain vs. Risk of Loss)

$\frac{\text{High Price (4A1) } 90 \text{ Minus Present Price } 42}{\text{Present Price } 42 \text{ Minus Low Price (4B1) } 34\tfrac{1}{8}}$ = $\frac{48}{7\tfrac{7}{8}}$ = 6.1 (4D) To 1

E PRICE TARGET

$\frac{\text{High Price (4A1) } 90}{\text{Present Market Price } 42}$ = (2.14) X 100 = (214) − 100 = 114 (4E) % Appreciation

5 5-YEAR POTENTIAL

These calculations provide a picture of future income. They also provide a standard for comparing income and growth stocks.

A $\frac{\text{Present Full Year's Dividend \$ 1.20}}{\text{Present Price of Stock \$ 42}}$ = .029 X 100 = 2.9 (5A) Present Yield or % Returned on Purchase Price

B AVERAGE YIELD OVER NEXT 5 YEARS

Avg. Earnings Per Share Next 5 Years 3.75 X Avg. % Payout (3G7) 34.9 = $\frac{130.875}{\text{Present Price \$ 42}}$ = 3.1 (5B) %

C TOTAL RETURN

$\frac{\text{5 Year Appreciation Potential (4E) 114}}{5}$ = 22.8 %

Average Yield (5B) .... 3.1 %

Total Return for 5 Years (average) (5C) .... 25.9 %

© 1996. National Association of Investors Corporation; 711 West Thirteen Mile Road, Madison Hgts., Michigan 48071

Figure 11-3
Stock Selection Guide for Molex, Inc.

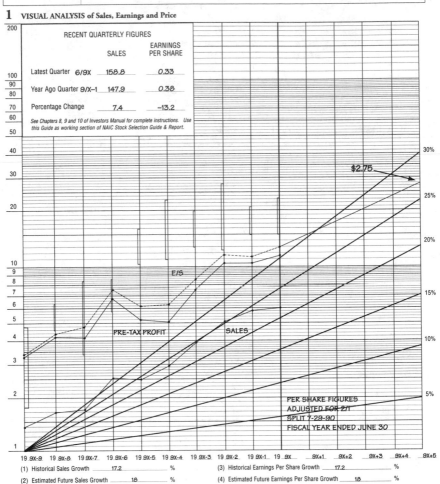

Figure 11-3 (Continued)

2 EVALUATING MANAGEMENT

Company MOLEX (MOLX)

		199x-9	199x-8	199x-7	199x-6	199x-5	199x-4	199x-3	199x-2	199x-1	199x	LAST 5 YEAR AVG.	TREND UP	TREND DOWN
A	% Pre-tax Profit on Sales (Net Before Taxes ÷ Sales)	23.7	25.4	23.8	27.8	21.0	18.4	19.6	21.1	18.3	19.3	19.3		✔
B	% Earned on Equity (E/S ÷ Book Value)	20.0	22.0	18.6	24.3	16.6	12.6	13.7	15.2	14.9	13.0	13.9		✔

3 PRICE-EARNINGS HISTORY as an indicator of the future

This shows how stock prices have fluctuated with earnings and dividends. It is a building block for translating earnings into future stock prices.

PRESENT PRICE 20 ½ HIGH THIS YEAR 24 LOW THIS YEAR 16 ⅝

	FISCAL Year	A PRICE FISCAL YEAR HIGH	B LOW	C Earnings Per Share	D Price Earnings Ratio HIGH A ÷ C	E LOW B ÷ C	F Dividend Per Share	G % Payout F ÷ C X 100	H % High Yield F ÷ B X 100
1	199x–4	22.4	11.3	0.64	(35.2)	(17.8)	0.01	1.6	0.1
2	199x–3	19 ½	12.95	0.86	28.3	(18.8)	0.015	1.7	0.1
3	199x–2	28 ¼	12 ½	1.17	24.1	10.7	0.015	1.3	0.1
4	199x–1	20 ⅞	15 ⅛	1.14	18.3	13.3	0.015	1.3	0.1
5	199x	23 ⅞	15 ⅜	1.24	19.3	12.4	0.015	1.2	0.1
6	TOTAL		65 ¼		90	36.4		7.1	
7	AVERAGE		13.05		22.5	12.1		1.4	
8	AVERAGE PRICE EARNINGS RATIO			17.3	9	CURRENT PRICE EARNINGS RATIO		20⅛ ÷ 1.43 = 14.3	

RV = 83

4 EVALUATING RISK and REWARD over the next 5 years

*Assuming one recession and one business boom every 5 years, calculations are made of how **high** and how **low** the stock might sell. The upside-downside ratio is the key to evaluating risk and reward.*

A HIGH PRICE — NEXT 5 YEARS

Avg. High P/E 17.3 (3D7) X Estimate High Earnings/Share 2.75 = Forecast High Price $ 47½ (4A1)

B LOW PRICE — NEXT 5 YEARS

(a) Avg. Low P/E 12.1 (3E7) X Estimated Low Earnings/Share 1.24 = $ 15

(b) Avg. Low Price of Last 5 Years = 13 (3B7)

(c) Recent Severe Market Low Price = 15 ⅛

(d) Price Dividend Will Support Present Divd. / High Yield (H) = .02 = NOT APPLICABLE

Selected Estimated Low Price = $ 15 (4B1)

C ZONING

47½ (4A1) High Forecast Price Minus 15 (4B1) Low Forecast Price Equals 32½ (C) Range. 1/3 of Range = 10¾ (4CD)

(4C2) Lower 1/3 = (4B1) 15 to 25 ¾ (Buy)

(4C3) Middle 1/3 = 25 ¾ to 36 ¾ (Maybe)

(4C4) Upper 1/3 = 36 ¾ to 47½ (4A1) (Sell)

Present Market Price of 20½ is in the BUY (4C5) Range

D UP-SIDE DOWN-SIDE RATIO (Potential Gain vs. Risk of Loss)

High Price (4A1) 47½ Minus Present Price 20½ / Present Price 20½ Minus Low Price (4B1) 15 = 27 / 5½ = 4.9 (4D) To 1

E PRICE TARGET

High Price (4A1) 47 ½ / Present Market Price 20 ½ = (2.32) X 100 = (232) – 100 = 132 (4E) % Appreciation

5 5-YEAR POTENTIAL

These calculations provide a picture of future income. They also provide a standard for comparing income and growth stocks.

A Present Full Year's Dividend $ .02 / Present Price of Stock $ 20½ = 0.0009756 X 100 = 0.1 (5A) Present Yield or % Returned on Purchase Price

B AVERAGE YIELD OVER NEXT 5 YEARS

Avg. Earnings Per Share Next 5 Years 2.10 X Avg. % Payout (3G7) 1.4 / Present Price $ 20½ = .029 / 20½ = 0.14 (5B) %

C TOTAL RETURN

5 Year Appreciation Potential (4E) 132 / 5 = 26.4 %

Average Yield (5B) .... .1 %

Total Return for 5 Years (average) (5C) .... 26.5 %

Figure 11-4
Stock Selection Guide for Thomas & Betts

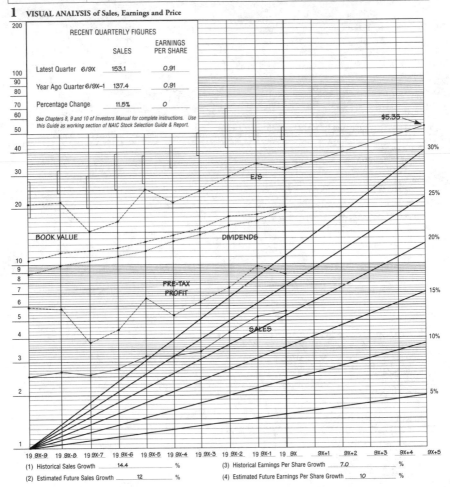

Company THOMAS & BETTS (TNB)		Date JULY 199x
Prepared by IAS		Data taken from VARIOUS
Where traded NYSE		Major product/service SEE TEXT
CAPITALIZATION	Authorized	Outstanding
Preferred		NONE
Common		17 MILLION
Debt 113.8 MILLION	Potential Dilution	

Stock Selection Guide

NATIONAL ASSOCIATION OF INVESTORS CORPORATION
NAIC®
INVESTMENT EDUCATION FOR INDIVIDUALS AND CLUBS
SINCE 1951

The most widely used aid to good investment judgment

1 VISUAL ANALYSIS of Sales, Earnings and Price

RECENT QUARTERLY FIGURES

	SALES	EARNINGS PER SHARE
Latest Quarter 6/9X	153.1	0.91
Year Ago Quarter 6/9X–1	137.4	0.91
Percentage Change	11.5%	0

See Chapters 8, 9 and 10 of Investors Manual for complete instructions. Use this Guide as working section of NAIC Stock Selection Guide & Report.

$5.35

E/S

BOOK VALUE   DIVIDENDS

PRE-TAX PROFIT

SALES

(1) Historical Sales Growth 14.4 %	(3) Historical Earnings Per Share Growth 7.0 %
(2) Estimated Future Sales Growth 12 %	(4) Estimated Future Earnings Per Share Growth 10 %

Figure 11-4 (Continued)

2 EVALUATING MANAGEMENT

Company THOMAS & BETTS (TNB)

	19 9x-9	19 9x-8	19 9x-7	19 9x-6	19 9x-5	19 9x-4	19 9x-3	19 9x-2	19 9x-1	19 9x	LAST 5 YEAR AVG.	TREND UP	TREND DOWN
A % Pre-tax Profit on Sales (Net Before Taxes ÷ Sales)	23.0	21.5	15.3	16.4	19.9	16.7	18.2	17.3	17.0	14.5	16.7		✓
B % Earned on Equity (E/S ÷ Book Value)	20.3	18.8	12.8	13.9	17.9	14.8	15.5	16.8	18.6	16.5	16.4		✓

3 PRICE-EARNINGS HISTORY as an indicator of the future

This shows how stock prices have fluctuated with earnings and dividends. It is a building block for translating earnings into future stock prices.

PRESENT PRICE 54 ¼ HIGH THIS YEAR 57 ⅜ LOW THIS YEAR 47 ⅛

	Year	A PRICE HIGH	B PRICE LOW	C Earnings Per Share	D Price Earnings Ratio HIGH A ÷ C	E Price Earnings Ratio LOW B ÷ C	F Dividend Per Share	G % Payout F ÷ C X 100	H % High Yield F ÷ B X 100
1	199x–4	43 ¼	33 ½	2.15	20.1	16.6	1.33	61.9	
2	199x–3	49 ¾	37	2.44	20.4	15.2	1.48	60.7	
3	199x–2	67 ¾	41 ½	2.88	23.5	14.4	1.64	56.9	
4	199x–1	60 ¾	45 ⅜	3.46	17.6	13.1	1.80	52.0	
5	199x	55 ¾	46	3.16	17.6	14.6	1.96	62.0	
6	TOTAL		203 ⅜		99.2	73.9		293.5	
7	AVERAGE		40.68		19.8	14.8		58.7	
8	AVERAGE PRICE EARNINGS RATIO			17.3	9	CURRENT PRICE EARNINGS RATIO		54 ¼ ÷ 3.33 = 16.3	

RV = 94

4 EVALUATING RISK and REWARD over the next 5 years

*Assuming one recession and one business boom every 5 years, calculations are made of how **high** and how **low** the stock might sell. The upside-downside ratio is the key to evaluating risk and reward.*

A HIGH PRICE — NEXT 5 YEARS

Avg. High P/E 19.8 (3D7) X Estimate High Earnings/Share 5.35 = Forecast High Price $ 106 (4A1)

B LOW PRICE — NEXT 5 YEARS

(a) Avg. Low P/E 14.8 (3E7) X Estimated Low Earnings/Share 3.16 = $ 46 ¾

(b) Avg. Low Price of Last 5 Years = 40 ⅝ (3B7)

(c) Recent Severe Market Low Price = 45 ⅜

(d) Price Dividend Will Support Present Divd. / High Yield (H) = 2.12 / .043 = 49¼

Selected Estimated Low Price = $ 45⅜ (4B1)

C ZONING

106 (4A1) High Forecast Price Minus 45 ⅜ (4B1) Low Forecast Price Equals 60 ⅝ (C) Range. 1/3 of Range = 20 ⅛ (4CD)

(4C2) Lower 1/3 = (4B1) 45 ⅜ to 66 ½ (Buy)

(4C3) Middle 1/3 = 66 ½ to 85 ⅞ (Maybe)

(4C4) Upper 1/3 = 85 ⅞ to 106 (4A1) (Sell)

Present Market Price of 54 ¼ is in the BUY (4C5) Range

D UP-SIDE DOWN-SIDE RATIO (Potential Gain vs. Risk of Loss)

High Price (4A1) 106 Minus Present Price 54¼ / Present Price 54 ¼ Minus Low Price (4B1) 45 ⅜ = 51 ¾ / 8 ⅞ = 5.8 (4D) To 1

E PRICE TARGET

High Price (4A1) 106 / Present Market Price 54 ¼ = (1.95) X 100 (195) −100 = 95 (4E) % Appreciation

5 5-YEAR POTENTIAL

These calculations provide a picture of future income. They also provide a standard for comparing income and growth stocks.

A Present Full Year's Dividend $ 2.12 / Present Price of Stock $ 54 ¼ = .039 X 100 = 3.9 (5A) Present Yield or % Returned on Purchase Price

B AVERAGE YIELD OVER NEXT 5 YEARS

Avg. Earnings Per Share Next 5 Years 4.00 X Avg. % Payout (3G7) 58.7 = 234.80 / Present Price $ 54 ¼ = 4.3 (5B) %

C TOTAL RETURN

5 Year Appreciation Potential (4E) 95 / 5 = 19 %

Average Yield (5B) .... 4.3 %

Total Return for 5 Years (average) (5C) .... 23.3 %

OBTAINING FIVE-YEAR ESTIMATED EARNINGS

The figure for item 8 of the Stock Comparison Guide, "Estimated Total Earnings per Share for the Next Five Years," comes from Section 1 of the Stock Selection Guide. Looking at the earnings-per-share trend line, add together the five figures where the projected earnings trend line intersects the time lines. The result is total estimated EPS for the next five years. The closer the current stock price is to this total, the more favorable is the price. Buying a stock for the sum of the next five years' earnings is equivalent to investing at 20 percent a year. Such a price may be difficult to find, and in some market periods probably cannot be found, but you should always keep this figure in mind. Although none of the companies approaches the target, the Molex price is most favorable in terms of the price/earnings ratio. Price/earnings ratio comparisons should be made between companies on both a current and a historical basis. P/E ratios tend to move up and down as stock prices move in major cycles.

Some stocks with a record of consistent growth tend to sell at a higher-than-average P/E ratio. If a stock is currently selling at a higher P/E than other companies in the same industry, compare it now with its own P/E five years ago and the general level of P/Es at that time. If the P/E ratios today and five years ago are comparable, the stock may still be a good long-term purchase. But keep in mind that any stock selling at an unusually high multiple is likely to suffer a sizable adjustment in a weak market if its results fail to meet the expectations of the investment community.

All of the three companies under study are at lower multiples today compared with the average for the last five years. This is shown by a comparison of the figures on line 13 with those on line 16. The lowest current P/E is offered by Molex, but those of the two competitors are comparable. All three stocks are in the "buy" range.

Item 23, "Combined Estimated Yield," comprises two figures. One is the estimated average appreciation, and the other is the average dividend yield for the next five years. The combined value is obtained from Section 5C of the Stock Selection Guide. AMP and Molex offer the highest combined estimated yields, although all three companies more than meet our goal in this respect.

The *payout,* or percent of earnings paid out as dividends, may indicate management's growth philosophy. Growth takes capital. When management retains a large share of earnings, financing expansion becomes easier. Growth financed with retained earnings usually accrues to the benefit of the share-holders. If, however, growth is financed by issuing additional stock, present holders' equity in the company will be diluted. Molex's payout is substantially lower than that of either AMP or Thomas & Betts.

Items that investors may find helpful to add to the "Other Comparisons" section are the percentage of debt to capitalization and the percent of stock held by institutions.

Some investors are interested in a stock's beta. Beta is a mathematical notation that measures a stock's volatility in comparison with the market as a whole. A beta rating of 1 indicates that the stock tends to move with the market, both up and down. Higher betas indicate greater volatility, and lower betas indicate that the stock is not influenced by overall trends as much as other issues. High betas are produced by high sales and earnings growth rates and excellent profit margins, items the investor has already covered in his or her Guide study.

INDUSTRY BACKGROUND*

Now let's take a look at how these facts and figures relate to this particular industry as a whole.

The connector manufacturing industry is large but highly fragmented, with some 600 contenders. Connector demand varies widely from quarter to quarter, putting continuing pressure on management to maximize production and distribution efficiency. Computer systems account for more than a third of connector use worldwide, with telecommunications representing another fifth. The remainder is divided among military/aerospace (15%), industrial (15%), automotive (10%), and consumer applications (5%). Of all the connector markets, only military/aerospace has a disappointing outlook.

The average selling price for connectors has declined by 3 to 5 percent a year since 1985. About 100 companies have failed. The larger competitors, as exemplified by our three entries, have responded to greater competition by improving quality and service. AMP, with about a fifth of the worldwide market, is five times larger than its nearest competitor. Since its incorporation in 1941, AMP has increased sales 100 times for an annual growth rate of 9.7 percent, comfortably outpacing gross domestic product. AMP produces

*This industry background is based on material published by David L. Babson & Co. The Stock Selection Guides were prepared by NAIC's Investor Advisory Service.

more than 100,000 different products. Foreign customers account for 60 percent of sales. The company spends more than $260 million a year on product development and improvement of its production processes.

Molex ranks second in the industry. In recent years, Molex has been the most rapidly growing. Seventy percent of its sales are foreign, and half of its revenues come from the expanding Far East market.

Thomas & Betts has been building its position in electronic connectors, historically having focused on more slowly growing electric connectors. Only 40 percent of the firm's business comes from abroad.

The companies are selling at lower multiples now because of the recession and concern over whether they can regain former growth rates. However, the strongest companies should continue to do well.

With this knowledge of the industry and the data provided on the three firms, which if any would you buy? Every investor is entitled to his or her own opinion. But remember, experience suggests that, on average, the companies with the most favorable figures are likely to do best. Our selection at this time would be Molex, based on the fact that its historical and projected sales growth rates and earnings-per-share growth rates are the highest. Also, its pre-tax profit margin is the highest. Its P/E ratio is the lowest of the three.

CHAPTER 12

THE PORTFOLIO MANAGEMENT GUIDE

As your club's portfolio grows with time, portfolio management becomes more important. The value of current deposits being invested in a new stock will pale in comparison with the total amounts invested over the years.

Many new investment club members feel that their only challenge is making a sound decision when contemplating the initial purchase of a security. The error lies in overlooking the vital importance of managing a security once it is bought. As famed financier Bernard Baruch said, "There ain't no such animal as a permanent investment." In other words, the stock you bought yesterday is not the one you hold today, because circumstances have surely changed—for better or worse.

The successful investment club reviews its portfolio at least once a year. Each stock should have the potential of reaching your goal of doubling in the next bull market. Use the Challenge Tree procedure explained in Chapter 14 to check the potential of a current holding against a possible replacement.

One strategy for investing successfully dictates that you put all of your funds into a single stock that is destined to outperform all others. The trouble with this idea is, which stock is it? No one can say for certain. Hindsight is always 20/20.

NAIC's experience suggests that for the average individual, adequate portfolio management amounts to reviewing each stock annually to confirm that it has the potential of doubling in value over the next five years (or whatever your goal for it is) and ensuring that there is good diversification both by industry and by size of company.

DIVERSIFY BY SIZE

Your club should be sure to diversify its holdings, because diversification is an important way to reduce risk. For most investors, diversification means buying stocks in a range of different industries. Investment club members have found that diversification by company size is also important. However, don't carry diversification too far. Know your club's limits, and hold only as many stocks as you can watch carefully.

Your club should organize its portfolio management program so that each holding becomes the responsibility of a single member. You may choose to have portfolio management reviews of individual stocks on an ongoing basis so that all stocks are covered once a year. It is advisable to look at your portfolio as a whole once a year and check (1) industry diversification, (2) size diversification, and (3) the ability of the total portfolio to double in value by the next market peak.

The Stock Selection Guide helps you determine the selling zone for a stock. A comparison of current price with established zones should be part of the club meeting, at least quarterly. Some clubs make this critical check at each get-together.

The *Portfolio Management Guide* (PMG) is a memory jogger. It is designed to remind you to check where each of your stocks is in relation to where your Stock Selection Guide study says it should be. The portfolio manager for a club holding should notify the club at each meeting whether the stock is in the "buy" or "sell" zone. It is unlikely that a stock with a high rate of growth would be sold unless it is substantially overpriced. Even then, only a part of the holding might be sold. Stocks with a good growth rate that are in the "buy" zone should be added to the club's list of "buy" candidates at that meeting.

FILLING IN THE FORM

Some of the figures in Section 1 of the Portfolio Management Guide, "Price/Earnings Zones," come from other sources. The figures in columns 2 and 3 are taken from line 7, columns D and E of Section 3 of the Stock Selection Guide. Column 2 represents the average high P/E for the past five years, and column 3 is the average low P/E. The headings of columns 4, 5, and 6 show how these figures are arrived at. The only logic behind the calculation of the figures in columns 4 and 5 is that experience has shown these figures to be reasonable guides. It is always important to consider the market and economic conditions that existed when those figures were developed and how they compare with current conditions.

In Section 2, "Price Zones," column 1 indicates the top of the "buy" zone. You can obtain this number from Section 4C2 of the SSG. Column 2 is used to specify the bottom of the "sell" zone, item 4C4 on the Stock Selection Guide.

Section 3 is devoted to recording earnings, prices, and price/earnings ratio computations. Column 1 lists quarterly earnings periods, and column 2 gives the earnings per share for each. You may obtain this information from the company's quarterly report or from other published reports. (See the lower left corner of the Value Line sheet under the heading "Earnings per Share.") Column 3 gives the cumulative earnings figure for the most recent four quarters. That is the sum for the quarter on this line and those on the three preceding lines. Column 4 records the specific day on which the price is recorded in column 5.

Column 6 shows the result of dividing price (column 5) by the past twelve months' earnings (column 3). Columns 7 through 12 present similar data calculated for the second and third months of the same quarter.

The Portfolio Management Guide not only disciplines club members to examine a stock's price on a regular basis, but depicts the crucial relationship over time of price to P/E ratio.

PRICE/EARNINGS JUDGMENT FACTORS

A word of caution: The Portfolio Management Guide can be dangerous to the creation of maximum profits in certain cases. In using price/earnings ratios, it is important to use judgment when analyzing the figures. Keep in mind that these ratios move up and down in long cycles just like stock prices. When there are long periods of severely depressed prices and very low stock market optimism, the price/earnings ratios on the Dow Jones averages may fall to the area of 5 to 7. This also happens during periods of very high inflation. As the market moves out of a depressed period, P/E ratios start moving up and will reach 18 to 21 on the Dow Jones averages. When you are studying a company, it is important to judge where in the cycle the economy and market are now, and estimate where they might be at the end of five years.

P/E ratios will also vary for individual companies. Generally, the higher the rate of sales and earnings-per-share growth rate, the higher the P/E ratios the company will command in the market. The length of time over which a company has maintained a good growth rate will also affect its P/E ratio. A company that has a reputation for high-quality management, a special product, or market advantage will surely be rated higher than its competitors.

Cyclical companies often sell at low P/Es when their earnings are at a peak because investors know a big dip is likely in the future. Since investors also know such companies will probably weather a recession and recover to higher earnings, the prices of such companies usually do not decline as much as earnings. As a result, such companies, as opposed to growth companies, are likely to sell at the highest P/Es when they are experiencing the greatest difficulty. The auto companies are notable for their cyclical nature.

As you gain experience and your club goes through down markets and the following recovery, your ability to recognize and judge these various factors will grow.

AN ILLUSTRATION

The accompanying Portfolio Management Guide (Figure 12-1) on Abbott Laboratories illustrates how the P/E ratio advances for a company with a high rate of growth and continuing bright prospects. Examine the "Chart of Market Prices and P/E Ratios" (Section 4).You'll see that in the four-year span under study, the market price, except for year 3, has almost always been well within the "buy" zone. The P/E ratios are another story. Over nearly the entire period under discussion, the P/Es have remained in the "hold" zone, with more of the remainder in the "sell" zone than in the "buy" zone.

Any investor selling in the second year, when the P/E first flashed "sell," would not have shared in the company's continued growth. It is often a good idea, for a current year, to consider estimated earnings, since that will give you a P/E ratio for the current year closer to its historical level.

We advise buying stocks with the expectation of seeing their value double within five years. However, you should recognize that a stock's doubling in value is not a sell indicator. Reevaluate the situation when your goal is reached. Are future gains likely? If so, then continue to hold. Is upside potential limited in comparison with downside risk? If this seems to be the case, consider selling. At that point, go through the same evaluation as you would for a new prospective company.

Remember that many, many companies advance significantly in price. Media General Financial Services identified the 100 stocks that achieved the

Figure 12-1

Completed Portfolio Management Guide for Abbott Laboratories

NATIONAL ASSOCIATION OF INVESTORS CORPORATION **NAIC** ® INVESTMENT EDUCATION FOR INDIVIDUALS AND CLUBS SINCE 1951	*Portfolio Management Guide*	See Chapter 12 of the *Investors Manual* for instructions on the use of this guide.

Company _____ ABBOTT LABORATORIES _____ Prepared by _____ I.A.S. _____

1 PRICE EARNINGS ZONES   Refer to Section 3, columns D and E, line 7, of your Stock Selection Guide study of this company for the information in columns 2 and 3 below.

1	2	3	4	5	6
YEAR	Average Price Earnings Ratios for Previous Five Years		Sum of Cols. 2 and 3	Column 4 divided by 2	Column 5 Multiplied by 1 1/2
	High	Low		Low P/E Guide Line	High P/E Guide Line
19x1	17.2	11.4	28.6	14.3	21.5
19x2	18.8	11.8	30.6	15.3	23.0
19x3	20.0	12.4	32.4	16.2	24.3
19x4	19.6	12.4	32	16.0	24.0

2 PRICE ZONES   See Section 4C of the Stock Selection Guide. 1 below is top of Buy Zone. 2 below is bottom of Sell Zone

YEAR	1. Consider Buying Below	2. Consider Selling Above
19x1	22	41
19x2	26	48
19x3	29	49
19x4	33	55

3 CUMULATIVE EARNINGS AND CURRENT PRICE-EARNINGS RATIO COMPUTATIONS

1	2	3	4	5	6	7	8	9	10	11	12
3 Months Ending	Earnings Per Share	Total Earnings for Last 4 Quarters	Date	Price	P/E Ratio at Time of Meeting	Date	Price	P/E Ratio at Time of Meeting	Date	Price	P/E Ratio at Time of Meeting
3/19x0	.183										
6/19x0	.207										
9/19x0	.19										
12/19x0	.26	.84	1/26	12¹/₂	14.9	2/27	13	15.5	3/25	14¹/₂	17.3
3/x1	.22	.88	4/27	13¹/₈	14.9	5/27	13³/₈	15.2	6/26	13⁵/₈	15.5
6/x1	.24	.91	7/26	14⁷/₈	16.3	8/27	15	16.5	9/26	14⁷/₈	16.3
9/x1	.22	.94	10/27	15	16.0	11/26	15¹/₄	16.2	12/27	16¹/₄	17.3
12/x1	.29	.97	1/27	17	17.5	2/26	17	17.5	3/27	17	17.5
3/x2	.26	1.01	4/28	20	19.8	5/27	21	20.8	6/26	27	26.7
6/x2	.285	1.06	7/27	27	25.5	8/27	26	24.5	9/26	24³/₄	23.3
9/x2	.265	1.10	10/28	22¹/₈	20.1	11/26	25	22.7	12/28	25¹/₂	23.2
12/x2	.35	1.16	1/27	28	24.1	2/26	31¹/₈	26.8	3/27	33¹/₄	28.6
3/x3	.31	1.21	4/27	32¹/₄	26.9	5/28	30¹/₄	25	6/25	33	27.3
6/x3	.34	1.27	7/28	32	25.2	8/28	33	26	9/26	32⁵/₈	25.7
9/x3	.32	1.32	10/28	30¹/₂	23.1	11/27	25	18.9	12/29	24¹/₈	18.3
12/x3	.42	1.39	1/28	25	18.0	2/26	26¹/₄	18.9	3/29	26¹/₈	18.8
3/x4	.38	1.46	4/27	25	17.1	5/27	23¹/₈	15.8	6/27	24³/₄	17.0
6/x4	.41	1.53	7/29	23	15.0	8/28	23¹/₈	15.1	9/27	23⁷/₈	15.6
9/x4	.38	1.59	10/28	23⁷/₈	15.0	11/27	23¹/₂	14.8	12/29	23	14.5
12/x4	.50	1.67	1/28	23¹/₄	13.9	2/26	26	15.6	3/28	27¹/₂	16.5

Figure 12-1 (Continued)

Company _____ ABBOTT LABORATORIES

4 CHART OF MARKET PRICES AND PRICE-EARNINGS RATIO

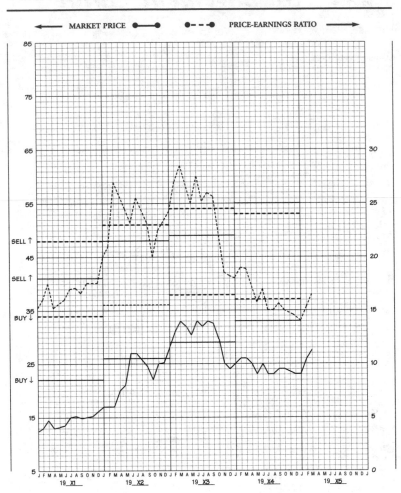

greatest price appreciation in the decade of the 1980s. The advances ranged from 9,637 percent for the leader to 1,184 percent for the bottom entry.

We advocate that you buy and hold high-growth stocks and make additional purchases when the price dips. Whenever the growth rate of the company under scrutiny is 10 percent or higher, use the Portfolio Management Guide for deciding whether to purchase on dips, not whether to sell on peaks. We counsel against selling at apparent peaks and buying back after a decline in price. Very few investors can profit from such speculation, especially for high-growth stocks.

NAIC suggests that investors look at their portfolio as a total entity once a year. The club's total portfolio should be displayed showing the current price, estimated five-year low, and estimated five-year high for each stock, and with columns showing each stock's size and industry classification. Such a display might look like the one in Figure 12-2.

The purpose of the review is threefold: (1) to check the diversification of the portfolio by industry, (2) to check the diversification by size, and (3) to confirm growth potential. In one set of columns in Figure 12-2 we have listed the annual revenues of each company (M is millions, B is billions) and then classified it A for very large, B for medium, and C for small. This division comes out as follows:

A		B		C	
Abbott Labs	$14,218	Becton-Dick	$10,462	Allied Group	$15,975
Amoco	16,937	Century Tele.	13,281	Kuhlman	7,647
Colgate-Palm.	12,818	Dynatech	14,875	Linear Tech.	4,525
		Synovus Fin.	13,050	Medic Comp.	8,000
	$43,973		$51,668		$36,147

A first look at the above table suggests that we are well off of our rough goal of $33,500 each in A and C and $67,000 in B (one-quarter, one-quarter, and one-half of total value). C at $36,147 is OK, but we are high on A. However, the wide difference in the size of companies between the bottom end of A and the upper end of B suggests that this is not of concern. We believe our holdings at the small aggressive end are about right.

In the right-hand column of Figure 12-2 we list the business of each company as described on the Value Line sheet. We have no industry in mind that we want to concentrate on, and we believe we have a good spread between different industries.

Our more detailed study comes when we look at the columns for the five-year high and low. Our current value is $133,940, and our estimated high at the next market peak is $272,717. That shows we should be able to

Figure 12-2
Example of Club Portfolio Display

Stock	No. of Shares	Current Price	Current Value	5-Year High Price	5-Year High Value	5-Year Low Price	5-Year Low Value	Size Sales	Size Class	Industry
Abbot Labs	350	40.625	$14,218	60	$21,000	26	$9,100	10	BA	Health care
Allied Group	450	35.500	15,975	75	33,750	22	9,900	300	MC	Insurance
Amoco	250	67.750	16,937	83	20,750	56	14,000	27	BA	Petro—largest
Becton-Dick	150	69.75	10,462	95	14,250	51	7,650	2.7	BB	Medical Mfg.
Century Tele.	425	31.25	13,281	78	33,150	22	9,350	0.5	BB	Tel.
Colgate-Palm.	175	73.25	12,818	125	21,875	53	9,275	7.5	BA	Household prod.
Dynatech	1,000	14.875	14,875	46	46,000	12	12,000	0.47	BB	Communications
Kuhlman	665	11.5	7,647	26	17,290	9	5,985	0.24	BC	Elect. Mfg.
Linear Tech.	100	45.25	4,525	114	11,400	27	2,700	200	MC	Comp. Products
Medic Comp.	125	64	8,000	128	16,000	27	3,375	10.7	MC	Mgt. Systems
Synovus Fin.	450	29	13,050	78	35,100	21	9,450	6	BB	Fin. Service
Cash			2,152		2,152		2,152			
Total			$133,940		$272,717		$94,937			

meet our goal of doubling; our portfolio doesn't need adjustment for that purpose. Our risk on the downside is $39,000 or 29 percent. When we look at individual stocks, we are pretty well satisfied with our group A stocks. As giants they have a better-than-average growth rate and should add stability in a recessionary period.

In group B we have some disagreement in the club about continuing to hold Becton-Dickinson since our study does not indicate that the upside potential we would like is there. Some members argue that our Stock Selection Guide study of this holding should provide for a higher growth rate and P/E ratio and consequently argue to hold it. Others feel that the high we have on record is accurate and that we should sell the stock. The club's decision is to restudy the stock over the next couple of meetings. We also have members who feel the estimated high for Dynatech is unrealistic, and our decision is to restudy it also.

Members should update the information in Figure 12-2 and bring it to the meeting regularly over the following year.

STAY IN THE MARKET

Getting in and out of the stock market is very dangerous. Studies have shown that individuals who invest in good-quality stocks of companies with a fairly steady increase in sales and earnings levels do better than the investor who moves from one group of stocks to another and in and out of stocks. There are very few investors who are willing to jeopardize all that they have earned for such speculation. One of the reasons that the "switcher" has difficulty succeeding is that when the market changes directions and starts up, the upward movement takes place so quickly that many investors miss the opportunity.

For instance, a study by Delaware Funds showed that in the ten up markets following 1970, 39 percent to 75 percent of the increases came within a two-week to three-month period.

John J. Curran, writing in *Fortune,* pointed out that while stocks provided a return of 17.6 percent through the decade of the 1980s, the greater part of the gain took place on just 40 of the 2,528 days the stock market was open during that period. If you were out of the market on those days, your average gain would have been only 4 percent a year.

CHAPTER 13

PORTFOLIO EVALUATION REVIEW TECHNIQUE

The Portfolio Evaluation Review Technique (PERT) is a system of portfolio management that shows you how to monitor either stocks you hold or stocks that you might consider for possible future purchase. It should not be thought of as a trading or timing tool.

The PERT process parallels the evaluation technique used with the NAIC Stock Selection Guide. The logic for using PERT is very similar to that for using the Guide:

1. It documents the decision-making process as you select growth stocks.

2. It helps you decide whether a company is well managed.

3. It helps you decide whether a stock is a good value.

PERT gives you the tools to decide whether the growth, profitability, and value that first attracted you to the stock are still valid today. It consists of three parts: Worksheet B, Worksheet A, and the form itself.

WORKSHEET B

PERT Worksheet B records the past fundamental stock data in exactly the same way as Section 3 of the Stock Selection Guide. The Worksheet is completed for each stock in the club's portfolio. The following data are recorded for each of the past five years:

1. High and low price range (columns C and D).

2. Earnings per share (column B).

3. Dividends per share (column J).

131

After completing these steps, make the following calculations for each year for which data were recorded. This is essentially the same information as in Section 3 of the SSG. An example using Abbott Laboratories is illustrated (Figure 13-1).

1. High and low price/earnings ratio for each year (columns E and F).
2. Five-year average for the high, low, and average P/E ratio (columns G, H, and I).
3. Percent payout of dividends compared to earnings per share for each year, and the average for the past five years (columns K and L).
4. The highest dividend yield for each year (column M).

PERT Worksheet B reproduces data and calculations from the Stock Selection Guide and adds data from the most recent fiscal year. As each year's earnings data are reported, the earnings and dividend data are added for the new year. Look in the newspaper or *Barron's* at the end of each fiscal year to find the fiscal-year price range. S&P and Value Line do not report price range data by fiscal year. If you are following a company whose fiscal year does not coincide with the calendar year, you have to do a bit of searching for fiscal-year price range data. There are two sources:

1. The company's annual report gives the fiscal-year price range by quarter for the last two years. (The last four annual reports include this information.) Be sure to adjust price data for subsequent splits and stock dividends.
2. A reasonably good approximation can be found by picking the high and low figures from a chart displaying monthly or weekly price ranges as vertical bars.

The logic for using fiscal-year price range data is related to the way the market works. Investors push the trading price of a stock up and down in anticipation of reported earnings. The closer the time relationship between price trading data and reporting of earnings, the better the correlation for future use.

The accompanying example of PERT Worksheet B illustrates the process. We have adjusted all prices, earnings per share, and dividends for the effect of a 2-for-1 stock split on May 31, 1990. The second 2-for-1 stock split

Figure 13-1
PERT Worksheet B for Abbott Laboratories

NATIONAL ASSOCIATION
OF INVESTORS CORPORATION ®
INVESTMENT EDUCATION
FOR INDIVIDUALS AND CLUBS
SINCE 1951

PERT Worksheet—B

Company __ABBOTT LABS__ Symbol __ABT__

| YEAR | EPS | PRICE RANGE | | P/E RATIO | | 5 YEAR AVERAGE P/E RATIO | | | DIV/ SHARE | % PAYOUT | | % HIGH YIELD |
		HIGH	LOW	HIGH	LOW	HIGH	AVG	LOW		THIS YEAR	5 YEAR AVERAGE	
1981	0.50	8.125	5.875	16.3	11.8				0.18	36.0		3.1
1982	0.59	10.250	6.250	17.4	10.6				0.21	35.6		3.4
1983	0.72	13.250	9.000	18.4	12.5				0.25	34.7		2.8
1984	0.84	12.200	9.200	14.5	11.0				0.30	35.7		3.3
1985	0.97	18.000	10.000	18.6	10.3	17.0	14.1	11.2	0.35	36.1	35.6	3.5
1986	1.16	27.500	15.750	23.7	13.6	18.5	15.0	11.6	0.42	36.2	35.7	2.7
1987	1.39	33.500	20.000	24.1	14.4	19.8	16.1	12.3	0.50	36.0	35.7	2.5
1988	1.67	26.200	21.375	15.7	12.8	19.3	15.9	12.4	0.60	35.9	36.0	2.8
1989	1.93	35.200	23.125	18.2	12.0	20.1	16.3	12.6	0.70	36.3	36.1	3.0
1990	2.22	46.375	31.250	20.9	14.1	20.5	16.9	13.4	0.84	37.8	36.4	2.7
1991	2.55	69.750	39.250	27.4	15.4	21.3	17.5	13.7	0.96	37.6	36.7	2.4
1992												
1993												
1994												
1995												
1996												
A	B	C	D	E	F	G	H	I	J	K	L	M

on May 29, 1992, it not yet factored into the data, but will be recognized later in PERT Worksheet A and the PERT Report for the monthly meeting.

The columns in PERT Worksheet B are:

A   Year

B   Earnings per share

C   High price for the fiscal year

D   Low price for the fiscal year

E   Calculated high price/earnings ratio (column C divided by column B)

F   Calculated low price/earnings ratio (column D divided by column B)

G   Five-year average high P/E ratio (add up the last five years of calculated high P/E ratios in column E and divide by 5)

H   Five-year average P/E ratio (add the five-year average high P/E ratio and the five-year average low P/E ratio and divide by 2)

I   Five-year average low P/E ratio (add the last five years of calculated low P/E ratios in column F and divide by 5)

J   Dividend per share

K   Percent payout (calculated by dividing dividend per share by earnings per share and multiplying by 100; on a calculator, enter dividend amount, press "divide," enter earnings per share, and press the "%" key)

L   Five-year average percent payout (add up the last five years of calculations in column K and divide by 5)

M   Percent high yield for the year (divide the dividend per share by the low price and multiply by 100; if you're using a simple calculator, enter dividend, press "divide," enter the year's low price, and press the "%" key)

It is not necessary to adjust prior years' per-share data for stock splits and dividends because the per-share calculations of price/earnings ratio, yield, and payout are not affected.

WORKSHEET A

When you used the NAIC Stock Selection Guide to help pick the right growth stock, you made certain decisions and observations about:

1. Compound annual growth rate of sales, pre-tax profits, and earnings per share.

2. Pre-tax profit margins as a percent of sales, and income tax rates as a percent of pre-tax profits.

These decisions, made by the market as a whole, affect perceptions of a stock, its future price/earnings ratio, and, thus, the future price action. Future growth is usually financed by retained earnings invested in the business. Unless profit margins and sales growth are maintained, the growth of earnings per share will slow. If the only factor in growth of earnings per share is a reduced income tax rate, sooner or later growth will come to a halt. Earnings-per-share growth basically depends on sales growth and profit margins.

By displaying these data on PERT Worksheet A (Figure 13-2), you develop a clear picture of what is happening—both favorably and unfavorably—with the stock's market value. It also gives a comparison between the assumptions you made for the future in the Stock Selection Guide and what is actually happening. If the actual results deviate significantly from the assumptions made when the stock was purchased, you need to find out why. Either some fundamental factors have shifted radically, calling for you to reevaluate your position in the stock, or your original analysis was flawed—in which case you need to find out why and how it happened in order to avoid repeating the mistake in the future.

Don't forget that the decision to buy is not the end of the investment process. Portfolio management is just as critical. PERT Worksheet A is a valuable tool for following through to ensure success.

Utilizing Worksheet A

Let's take a closer look at PERT Worksheet A—where the data come from, how they are recorded, what calculations are necessary, and how to interpret the data.

The Worksheet is divided into two sections. The quarterly data are recorded on the left. The last twelve months' data are recorded on the right side as the sum of the data for the prior four quarters. Look for information on the company's four quarters in the quarterly reports, annual reports, and financial public relations releases. Financial public relations releases are published prior to the shareholders' reports and are then reported in financial newspapers as corporate earnings. These reports are useful, especially for pre-tax profit information, because they are the earliest source of data. The

Figure 13-2
PERT Worksheet A for Abbott Laboratories

NATIONAL ASSOCIATION OF INVESTORS CORPORATION
INVESTMENT EDUCATION FOR INDIVIDUALS AND CLUBS SINCE 1951

PERT Worksheet—A

Company __ABBOTT LABORATORIES__

PERIOD	EPS $		EPS % CHANGE	PRE-TAX PROFIT $ MIL	% SALES	% CHANGE	SALES $ MIL	% CHANGE	INCOME TAX RATE	EPS $		PRE-TAX PROFIT $ MIL	% SALES	SALES MIL	INCOME TAX $ MIL	% RATE	EPS % CHANGE	PRE-TAX PROFIT % CHANGE	SALES % CHANGE
				QUARTERLY DATA								LAST 12 MONTHS DATA							
12-86	.70			243.3	22.9		1,063.2	11.4			2.32	818.7	21.5	3,807.6	278.2	34.0			
3-87	.62		19.2	229.8	20.9	12.1	1,003.8	16.0			2.42	841.4	21.3	3,945.9					
6-87	.68		19.3	229.8	21.7	13.5	1,059.5	13.0	32.5		2.53	868.6	21.4	4,067					
9-87	.64		20.8	216.0	19.8	16.2	1,091	16.0	32.5		2.64	898.7	21.3	4,217.6					
12-87	.84		20.0	281.5	22.8	15.7	1,234	16.1	32.5		2.78	937.1	21.4	4,388	304.5	32.5	19.8	14.5	15.2
3-88	.76		22.6	243.2	20.5	22.8	1,118	18.3			2.92	970.6	21.2	4,572					
6-88	.82		20.6	261.9	21.3	14.0	1,230	16.1	29.2		3.06	1,002.7	21.1	4,743					
9-88	.76		18.8	238.3	19.7	10.3	1,212	11.2	29.3		3.18	1,025.0	21.1	4,865					
12-88	.99		17.9	312.1	23.9	10.9	1,306	5.8	27.7		3.33	1,055.5	21.4	4,937	303.5	28.8	19.8	12.6	12.5
3-89	.88		15.8	274.6	21.1	13.0	1,295.5	9.0			3.45	1,087.2	21.6	5,044					
6-89	.95		15.9	295.2	22.5	12.7	1,318.5	7.2	28.0		3.58	1,120.5	21.6	5,133					
9-89	.88		15.2	272.6	20.8	14.4	1,310.3	8.1	28.0		3.70	1,154.9	22.1	5,230.6					
12-89	1.14		15.9	351.4	24.1	12.6	1,455.4	11.4	28.0		3.85	1,194.2	22.2	5,379.7	334.4	28.0	15.6	13.1	9.0
3-90	.51	1.02	14.6	314.6	21.9	14.4	1,438.4	11.0	28.5		3.99	1,233.9	22.3	5,522.6					
6-90	.55	1.10	14.6	335.9	22.3	13.8	1,503.3	14.0	28.5		4.13	1,274.6	22.3	5,707.5					
9-90	.51	1.02	15.9	308.9	20.5	13.3	1,506.7	15.0	28.5	2.14	4.27	1,310.9	22.2	5,904					
12-90	.65		14.0	391.3	22.9	11.3	1,710.1	17.3	28.5	2.22		1,305.5	21.9	6,159	385.0	28.5	15.3	13.1	14.5
3-91	.59		15.7	360.4	21.8	14.6	1,653.6	15.0	29.5	2.30		1,396.5	21.9	6,374.2					
6-91	.63		14.5	330.6	22.6	13.3	1,692.9	11.9	29.5	2.38		1,441.1	22.0	6,553.8					
9-91	.59		15.7	336.6	21.6	15.5	1,653.7	9.8	29.5	2.46		1,489.0	22.2	6,701					
12-91	.74		13.8	446.4	23.7	14.1	1,886.3	10.3	29.5	2.55		1,544.2	22.5	6,876	455.5	29.5	14.9	14.3	11.6
3-92	.69		16.9	408.6	21.8	13.4	1,877.9	13.6	28.0	2.66		1,592.4	22.4	7,100					
	A	B	C	D	E	F	G	H	I	J	K	L	M	N	O	P	Q	R	S	T

accompanying example using Abbott Laboratories will illustrate where we found the data as well as how we make the computations.

Column A is used to identify the quarterly figures in columns B and C.

Columns B and C are both for listing the quarterly EPS data. Start recording in one column. When a split occurs, start using the second column. For example, Abbott Labs declared a 2-for-1 split effective May 31, 1990. The $1.02 EPS for the quarter ending March 1990 in column C is converted to the after-split amount of $0.51 in column B.

Column D is for the calculation of the percentage change in EPS compared with the same period a year earlier. The $0.69 EPS reported for the quarter ended March 1992 is 16.9 percent greater than the $0.59 per share reported a year earlier.

Column E lists quarterly pre-tax profits in millions of dollars. For example, Abbott Laboratories' recorded earnings before taxes were $408.6 million for the first quarter of 1992 (line 25). Not all companies report their final fiscal quarterly pre-tax profit. It can easily be calculated by adding up profits for the first three quarters and subtracting the sum from the fiscal-year-ending pre-tax profit. Fiscal-year-end data are provided in the annual report.

Column F shows pre-tax profit as percent of sales or revenues. The $408.6 million in earnings before taxes is 21.8 percent of the $1,877.9 million in quarterly sales (recorded in Column H, line 25). A glance down the column since the last quarter of 1986 indicates that pre-tax profit is holding fairly steady at about 20 to 23 percent of sales.

Column G is similar to column D. It is used for the calculation of the percent change in pre-tax profit from one quarter compared to the same quarter a year earlier. The March 1992 pre-tax profit of Abbott Labs of $408.6 million in column E, line 25, is 13.4 percent greater than the $360.4 million for March 1991 recorded in column E, line 21. Unless pre-tax profit margins are maintained and show a percentage growth similar to expected levels, EPS growth will falter, and the price of the stock may sink.

Column H shows quarterly sales in millions of dollars.

Column I is the percent change of sales or revenues from column H compared with the same quarter a year earlier. For the March quarter of 1992, the $1,877.9 million in sales (column H, line 25) is 13.6 percent greater than the $1,653.6 in sales for the March quarter of 1991 (column H, line 21). The 13.6 percent is recorded in column I, line 25. A glance down column I shows quarterly sales generally rising about as expected.

Column J gives the calculated income tax rate for the quarter. This is an estimate since final adjustments are made at year end as the books are audited and the income tax calculated. On the quarterly and annual income statement, the income tax provision is usually presented on the line just below pre-tax income or pre-tax profits. Some companies do not actually spell out the dollar amount of income taxes. In such cases, it can be calculated as the difference between pre-tax income and net income. For the March quarter of 1992, the 28.0 percent income tax rate for Abbott in column J, line 25, corresponds to the estimated income taxes of $114.4 million as a percent of pre-tax income (column E, line 25). We obtained estimated taxes from the quarterly income statement.

Last Twelve Months' Data

Quarterly results tend to be erratic. It's better to review long-term trends—recognizing, of course, that quarterly results are part of those larger trends. Occasionally, the data from a particular quarter or two will be so different from what you expected that a "red flag" is raised and you might want to sell.

PERT, like the Stock Selection Guide, is not a short-term trading tool. PERT provides guidance to you as a long-term investor. The sum of the figures for the prior four quarters provides the data for the *last twelve months,* or *trailing twelve months.*

Column K or L shows the sum of the last four quarters of EPS from column B or C. The calculation is most conveniently made as the difference between the most recent quarterly EPS and the EPS a year ago, added to the fiscal-year-ending EPS. For example, $0.69 for the quarter of March 1992, less $0.59 for the quarter of March 1991, is $0.10. This $0.10 is added to year-end EPS of $2.55 (column L, line 24) and recorded as $2.65 in column L, line 25. Differences between second-quarter or third-quarter data are treated in a similar fashion.

Column M, pre-tax profit, gives the sum of the last four quarters. As we did with earnings per share, we can go back to column E and take the 12-91 pre-tax profit (446.4) and subtract the figure for the quarter one year ago (391.3). We add this difference, 55.1, to the full-year earnings for the previous quarter, 1,489, to get 1,544.1.

Column N lists pre-tax profits as a percent of sales. The calculation is the same as for the quarterly figures in column F, but uses data from column O, sales, and column P, income tax.

Data for column O can be taken from company or service reports. Alternatively, figures for the last four quarters from column H can be added and the sum entered here.

The total income tax, column P, comes from the company's annual report.

The income tax rate in column Q is calculated as the amount in column P, income taxes in millions of dollars, divided by pre-tax profits, column M.

Column R indicates the percent change represented by the most recent twelve-month EPS compared to the twelve-month EPS a year earlier. The EPS of $2.55 in column L, line 24, is 14.9 percent greater (column R, line 24) than the EPS of $2.22 a year earlier (column L, line 20) ($2.55 − $2.22 = $0.33); ($0.33 ÷ $2.22 = 14.9 percent). The figures for percent change over the past twelve months in columns R, S, and T are computed using data in column K or L, column M, and column O. For example, sales of $6,876 million (column O, line 24) were $717 million, or 11.6 percent, greater than the sales of $6,159 million a year earlier (column O, line 20) (717 ÷ 6,159 = 11.6 percent), so this percentage is recorded in column T, line 24.

Use of PERT Worksheet A Data

Look for favorable and unfavorable trends in percent changes. Watch income tax rates. A falling income tax rate (columns J and Q) can postpone declining EPS and may be covering other dangerous trends. Eventually, EPS growth will slow if sales growth stalls or pre-tax profit margins decline.

When you are considering purchasing additional shares of a stock, look at PERT Worksheet A data and make certain all is well. If the P/E ratio looks like a real bargain, it may be because of a deterioration of growth or profit margins. If so, the purchase may not turn out to be a bargain unless the declines were caused by a recession. If management has restored profitability following adverse economic forces in the past, it is more likely to do so in the future.

If a fundamental change in the industry impacts growth or profitability, be skeptical about a recovery. For example:

- The introduction of diagnosis-related groups (DRGs) for Medicare reimbursement of medical expenses depressed hospital profits.
- The end of the cold war has left several large defense companies with much lower government orders, forcing them to shift major markets.

- The development of the personal computer and the very rapid decline in price in relation to performance reduced demand for mainframe computers. Manufacturers of mainframe computers saw their profit margins erode, sales growth slow, and EPS growth decline and become erratic.

The last twelve months' data for EPS, pre-tax profits, and sales or revenues should be plotted on a giant NAIC Stock Selection Guide. First, plot the last ten years' data exactly as you did when you prepared the SSG for evaluation of the stock. For follow-up purposes, plot the trailing twelve months' data as they become available. The data for the first three months are plotted one quarter of the distance between the line for the last fiscal year and the line for the next fiscal year. The data for the twelve months ending in mid–fiscal year are plotted halfway between the lines for the last full fiscal year and the next fiscal year. Each month, record the price of the stock as a small mark. Use different colors for EPS, pre-tax profits, sales, and stock price so club members can easily see the data.

Compare the actual trend with the trend you anticipated at the time you used the Stock Selection Guide to analyze the stock. When deciding whether to buy, hold, or sell, look at the trend as well as valuation factors in the monthly PERT Report.

PERT REPORT

Portfolio Evaluation Review Technique is a logical extension of the NAIC Stock Selection Guide. It is used for portfolio management. The idea is to review at each monthly meeting all your stocks' present fundamentals, looking at the same factors as you did using the Stock Selection Guide when the stocks were purchased. The PERT Report utilizes the data collected on Worksheets A and B. The Report is used in conjunction with a giant Stock Selection Guide that displays the trailing twelve months' data for:

Sales

EPS

Pre-tax profits

The giant SSG helps you to visually analyze the stock and clearly see trends. This section, including the accompanying illustration (Figure 13-3), explains the PERT Report.

While the PERT Report is very adaptable to a computer spreadsheet, it may easily be prepared manually using a hand calculator that computes:

Percent change

Percent

Periodic interest rate per compounding period

The PERT Report helps you determine whether the stock:

1. Retained the same growth and profitability characteristics you assumed when the stock was originally purchased.
2. Should be considered a buy, hold, or sell based on fundamentals of value.

The PERT report incorporates a number of valuation characteristics that suggest which stocks will have the highest capital gains if the following estimates are correct:

Growth rate of EPS

Future high P/E ratio

Future low-price risk

EPS approximately twelve months in the future

The accompanying PERT Report (Figure 13-3) illustrates the concept.

Column H, percent change of EPS, reports what is happening to EPS growth on the most recent quarterly basis. However, beware of making investment decisions using short-term data.

Column J, percent change of sales, tells you the recent quarterly sales growth. If sales are meeting growth expectations, are earnings per share also following through? Or is a deceleration in sales growth responsible for a shortfall of EPS?

Column L, pre-tax profits as a percent of sales, shows what is occurring in terms of profitability on a short-term basis. If profit margins are up, they should translate into EPS growth greater than sales growth. If profit margins have declined, this may explain a deceleration in EPS growth. In any event, find out the reason for a change in profit margins.

Column M, percent change of pre-tax profits, reports the percent change in the dollar amount of quarterly results. Don't consider a big jump a plus if there has been an acquisition. If part of the company has been disposed of, understand that the percent change will go down. Find out why the change

Figure 13-3   Sample PERT Report

NATIONAL ASSOCIATION OF INVESTORS CORPORATION ®
INVESTMENT EDUCATION FOR INDIVIDUALS AND CLUBS SINCE 1951

PERT

Portfolio Evaluation Review Technique

Date

Row	DIV	COMPANY	% YLD	EST EPS	QTR END	EPS $	% CHG	SALES MIL $	% CHG	PRE-TAX MIL $	% SALES	% CHG	TRAIL 12MO EPS $	% CHG	CUR P/E	PRICE	RV	P/E HI	AVG	LOW	EST GR RATE EPS	P/E AS % GR	US/DS	% COMPD ANN RET	EST 5YR LOW	HIGH
11	0.60	ABBOTT LABS	2.0	3.18	3/92	0.69	17	1,877.9	13.6	408.6	21.8	13.4%	1.33	15.2	18.9	30.000	108%	21.3	17.5	13.7	15%	126	3.0	16.6	40.25	118.467
12					3/91	0.59		1,653.6		360.4	21.8		1.15													
14	2.76	BRISTOL-MYERS SQUIBB	4.2	4.62	3/92	1.06	13	2,783.4	2	751.0	27.0	7%	4.07	16.6	14.3	66.000	82%	20.6	17.4	14.3	14%	102	10.0	19.5	56.500	160.742
15					3/91	0.34		2,735.0		704.0	25.7		3.49													
17	0.56	DEAN FOODS	2.1	1.85	2/92	0.33	-19	566.3	9	23.9	4.2	-21%	1.72	-1.1	14.4	26.625	92%	18.4	15.7	12.9	11%	131	3.8	14.2	20.000	51.675
18					2/91	0.41		521.1		30.1	5.8		1.74													
20	2.20	GENL ELECT.	2.8	5.96	3/92	1.23	7	13,525	1	1,058	7.8	6%	5.18	28.2	13.0	77.250	98%	15.9	13.2	10.6	11%	118	3.1	13.2	56.000	143.858
21					3/91	1.15		13,333		999	7.5		4.04													
23	0.48	MACNEAL SCHWENDLER	4.3	0.25	4/92	0.26	8	14.72	0	4.73	32.1	7%	0.14	-85.6	44.5	11.125	342%	16.3	13.0	9.7	7%	636	-1.3	-13.6	6.500	5.341
24					4/91	0.24		14.70		4.44	30.2		0.97													
26	2.70	MARSH & McLENNAN	3.5	4.56	3/92	1.41	8	766.8	3	175.4	22.8	4%	4.28	2.6	17.0	77.500	106%	18.9	16.1	13.2	8%	212	4.7	8.6	69.000	117.252
27					3/91	1.31		744.1		168.1	22.6		4.17													
29	0.40	LIZ CLAIBORNE	1.2	3.07	3/92	0.74	3	566.9	11	98.1	17.6	1%	2.63	9.6	11.0	33.875	78%	18.9	14.2	9.5	13%	85	10.8	22.8	28.250	94.605
30					3/91	0.72		502.0		96.9	19.3		2.40													

Column labels: B · C · D · E · F · G · H · I · J · K · L · M · N · O · P · Q · R · S · T · U · V · W · X · Y · Z · AA · AB has occurred by studying management comments in the quarterly report. Do the reasons ring true?

Column O, percent change of trailing twelve months' EPS, looks at the annual rate of growth of EPS over the past year. How does this compare with your estimate of the future growth rate in column V, which probably came from your Stock Selection Guide? In a recession, expect growth results to be subpar.

Column R, relative value, starts to get into the valuation criteria. Relative value (RV) is the current P/E ratio (based on estimated EPS for the next twelve months, in column E) as a percent of the historical average P/E ratio (column T). You make money in a stock from a combination of P/E ratio expansion (to the average high P/E ratio) and EPS growth.

An RV of 100 percent or less indicates the stock may be reasonably priced. As the RV moves above 100 percent, the probability of a price gain, from a P/E ratio expansion, becomes remote. This figure is only as reliable as your estimate of the next twelve months' EPS (column E) and your record of the average P/E ratio (column T).

Relative value is computed as the current P/E ratio (column P) as a percent of the average P/E ratio (column T). The current P/E ratio is computed by dividing current price (column Q) by the next twelve months' estimated EPS (column E). The price/earnings ratio as a percent of the growth rate (column X) may be one of the less useful computations. It is determined by computing the current P/E ratio (column P) as a percent of the growth rate of EPS (column V). The data in column V come from your NAIC Stock Selection Guide analysis. Double-check your estimate with other sources since this is a key statistic in other calculations. Be wary of being either too optimistic or too pessimistic.

Another source for EPS growth is the monthly *Standard & Poor's Earnings Guide*. This and *Nelson's Earnings Outlook* are good sources of current and next-fiscal-year EPS estimates. The odds of a gain should be 3:1 for the investor.

The numbers in column X give you a feel as to how much you are paying in terms of the P/E ratio for growth. The lower the number, the better the value. However, be aware that superior-quality stocks are characterized by high P/E ratios. Column Y, upside/downside ratio, is a familiar term from the Stock Selection Guide. It is a measure of the risk of an investment based on current price (column Q), estimated growth rate (column V), estimated EPS twelve months in the future (column E), and estimated five-year low price (column AA).

The upside potential is the difference between the estimated high price (column AB) and the current price (column Q). The downside risk is the difference between the present price (column Q) and the estimated low price (column AA).

The upside/downside ratio is the upside potential (column AB less column Q) divided by the downside risk (column Q less column AA). When buying, insist on an upside/downside ratio of 3 to 1 or greater. When the upside/downside ratio has reached 1 to 1 or less, check two calculations:

1. Is the current P/E ratio (column P) greater than the average high P/E ratio (column S)? If it is, the possibility of a P/E ratio expansion becomes remote. Be sure your EPS estimate for the next twelve months (column E) is realistic and your record of the average high P/E ratio (column S) is correct.

2. Check to see if your estimate of the future low price (column AA) is realistic. If your estimate is too low, it will produce a depressed upside/downside ratio. Look at the lows during a market drop in the past year or so. Also check by multiplying the low P/E ratio (column U) by the last twelve months' EPS (the upper line in column N). If earnings per share are declining, try to determine how low they might sink based on previous declines in profit margins.

Resist the error of selling high-quality stocks because they appear overpriced by the upside/downside ratio. Check your records in PERT Worksheet B. The P/E ratio may be rising.

Column Z, percent compound annual rate of return, is very useful for determining optimistic investment potential. Calculating the compound annual rate of return is the way professional investors measure investment performance. That's the number you see mutual funds dealers brag about or not mention, depending on results. With a pocket financial calculator, such as a Texas Instruments BA-55 or BA-35, first compute the estimated high EPS five years in the future. Input present value (PV) from column E, estimated EPS one year in the future. Input percent growth of EPS from column V (%i). Input the number of periods (N on the calculator) as 4 (because estimated EPS is already one year in the future). Then press CPT (for compute) and FV (for future value). The result will be EPS five years in the future if the estimated EPS and growth rate are correct.

Next, multiply the estimated EPS five years in the future by the average high P/E ratio to determine the estimated high price five years in the future. Record the result in column AB. If you have a recent NAIC Stock Selection Guide, you can obtain the estimated high price from that source.

Next, calculate estimated percent compound annual rate of return. Input the high price from column AB as future value (FV). Input the present price (column Q) as PV. Input the number of periods (N) as 5. Then compute percent return by pressing CPT and %i. This is the compound annual rate of return from expected price action. To that add percent dividend yield (column D). The result is the percentage of compound annual rate of total return from the combination of price action and dividends. Record this result in column Z.

The quarterly data are assembled on PERT Worksheet A first from newspaper reports and then from quarterly and annual reports. If you come to the end of the year and the company has not supplied the final-quarter pretax profit data, just subtract data for the previous three quarters from the annual figures to obtain the figures for the fourth quarter.

Maintain a giant NAIC Stock Selection Guide for each stock. Plot trailing twelve months' data to provide a visual analysis for comparing actual trend results with your expectations. First-quarter trailing data are plotted one fourth of the way from the end of the vertical line representing the last fiscal year toward the vertical line representing the next fiscal year. The trailing twelve months' data for the third quarter are plotted three quarters of the distance between the vertical lines representing the last fiscal year and the next fiscal year. Data are plotted on a fiscal-year basis since some companies do not use a calendar year as their fiscal year.

CHAPTER 14

THE CHALLENGE TREE

The *Challenge Tree* is a systematic approach to improving the performance of your portfolio. It shows you how to compare the merits of one stock against another. Even if you are a relatively inexperienced investor, you can use Challenge Tree guidelines to avoid some of the hazards of buying and selling stocks.

The Challenge Tree utilizes a five-year estimate of a stock's future price range—long enough to include the business cycle extremes of boom (bull market) and recession (bear market). The Challenge Tree guides you to companies with good management that should earn more and be worth more in the coming five years. It also guides you in comparing the prices of stocks and directing your attention to possible substantial price appreciation opportunities.

The *Rule of Five* is an investment theory for intelligent portfolio management. The rule holds that of every five stocks owned over a five-year period, one will encounter difficulty unforeseen by the investor, three will perform more or less according to expectations, and one will far exceed the standard set for it. With the Challenge Tree, you will be able to upgrade your portfolio as any disappointing results become apparent.

The Challenge Tree uses the five-year upside/downside ratio and quality considerations to enhance your portfolio's defensive strength. The two major indicators for purchase are:

1. A stock selling in the lowest third of its estimated five-year price range and showing potential for 100 percent appreciation during that time.

2. A stock offering sound reasons to expect substantial price appreciation in the next six to eighteen months.

These indicators help you to focus clearly on goals and enable you to turn aside "story" stocks and other speculative hazards in favor of solid information.

ASSEMBLING DATA

First, the NAIC Stock Selection Guide should be completed for the two stocks being considered for purchase or sale (Figures 14-1 and 14-2). If you already have NAIC Portfolio Management Guide or PERT records on the companies, all the better.

Next, transfer your information to the *Challenge Tree Comparative Form* (Figure 14-3). The gain to five-year high and loss to five-year low are calculated for each stock as follows:

$$\% \text{ Gain} = \frac{\text{Five-year high price} - \text{Present price}}{\text{Present price}}$$

$$\% \text{ Loss} = \frac{\text{Present price} - \text{Five-year low price}}{\text{Present price}}$$

Questions in Figure 14-3 under the "6 to 18 Month Upside Action" heading should be answered using single words. However, there is room for brief comments if necessary.

MAKING DECISIONS

The challenger stock must be of equal or higher quality. Both *Standard & Poor's Stock Guide* and Value Line are reliable sources of quality ratings. The Challenge Tree form, Figure 14-3, calls for the S&P rating. If another service is used, indicate that on the form.

Here's the Challenge Tree reasoning: Suppose you purchased a stock based on the estimate that its value would double in five years. It is now in the middle third of its range, having posted a 33 to 66 percent gain. This stock appears to have realized 50 percent of its potential gain in the past six

Figure 14-1

Stock Selection Guide for Weis Markets

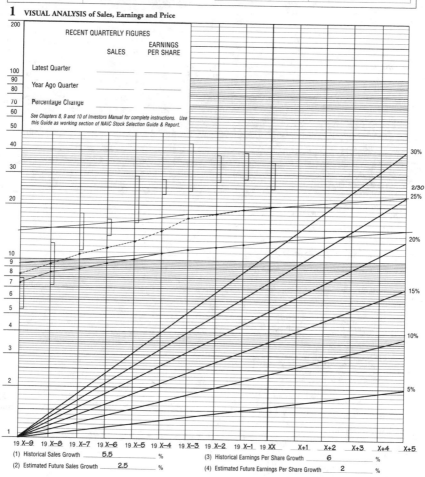

Stock
Selection
Guide

*The most widely used aid to
good investment judgment*

Company **WEIS MARKETS**		Date **FEB 2, 19XX**
Prepared by **RBT**		Data taken from **S&P-VL**
Where traded **NYSE**	Major product/service **SUPERMKT**	
CAPITALIZATION	Authorized	Outstanding
Preferred	–0–	
Common	44.453 Mil	
Debt	–0–	Potential Dilution

1   VISUAL ANALYSIS of Sales, Earnings and Price

RECENT QUARTERLY FIGURES

	SALES	EARNINGS PER SHARE
Latest Quarter		
Year Ago Quarter		
Percentage Change		

See Chapters 8, 9 and 10 of Investors Manual for complete instructions. Use this Guide as working section of NAIC Stock Selection Guide & Report.

19 X–9   19 X–8   19 X–7   19 X–6   19 X–5   19 X–4   19 X–3   19 X–2   19 X–1   19 XX   X+1   X+2   X+3   X+4   X+5

(1) Historical Sales Growth _____**5.5**_____ %

(2) Estimated Future Sales Growth _____**2.5**_____ %

(3) Historical Earnings Per Share Growth _____**6**_____ %

(4) Estimated Future Earnings Per Share Growth _____**2**_____ %

Figure 14-1 (Continued)
Stock Selection Guide for Weis Markets

2 EVALUATING MANAGEMENT

Company WEIS MARKETS

	19X-9	19X-8	19X-7	19X-6	19X-5	19X-4	19X-3	19X-2	19X-1	19XX	LAST 5 YEAR AVG.	TREND UP	TREND DOWN
A % Pre-tax Profit on Sales (Net Before Taxes ÷ Sales)	9.5	10.2	10.8	10.7	10.9	11.1	11.6	10.9	10.8	10.4	11.0		✔
B % Earned on Equity (E/S ÷ Book Value)	19.2	18.9	18.9	18.2	17.5	16.9	17.7	17.2	16.1	14.8	16.5		✔

3 PRICE-EARNINGS HISTORY as an indicator of the future

This shows how stock prices have fluctuated with earnings and dividends. It is a building block for translating earnings into future stock prices.

PRESENT PRICE 29 HIGH THIS YEAR 34 3/8 LOW THIS YEAR 24 1/4

	Year	A PRICE HIGH	B PRICE LOW	C Earnings Per Share	D Price Earnings Ratio HIGH A ÷ C	E Price Earnings Ratio LOW B ÷ C	F Dividend Per Share	G % Payout F ÷ C X 100	H % High Yield F ÷ B X 100
1	19X-4	27 7/8	22 1/8	1.42	20	16	.36	25	1.6
2	19X-3	41 5/8	23 7/8	1.66	25	14	.434	26	1.8
3	19X-2	37	27	1.82	20	15	.500	27	1.9
4	19X-1	37 1/2	28 1/8	1.91	20	15	.560	29	2.0
5	19XX	34 3/8	24 1/4	1.93	18	13	.600	31	2.5
6	TOTAL		125.375		103	73	.64	138	
7	AVERAGE		25		20.6	14.6		28	
8	AVERAGE PRICE EARNINGS RATIO			17.6	9 CURRENT PRICE EARNINGS RATIO				15

4 EVALUATING RISK and REWARD over the next 5 years

Assuming one recession and one business boom every 5 years, calculations are made of how ***high*** *and how* ***low*** *the stock might sell. The upside-downside ratio is the key to evaluating risk and reward.*

A HIGH PRICE — NEXT 5 YEARS
Avg. High P/E 17.6 (3D7) X Estimate High Earnings/Share 2.30 = Forecast High Price $ 40.50 (4A1)

B LOW PRICE — NEXT 5 YEARS
(a) Avg. Low P/E 14.6 (3E7) X Estimated Low Earnings/Share 1.93 = $ 28

(b) Avg. Low Price of Last 5 Years = 25 (3B7)

(c) Recent Severe Market Low Price = 24 1/4

(d) Price Dividend Will Support Present Divd. / High Yield (H) = .64 / .025 = 25.6

Selected Estimated Low Price = $ 24 1/4 (4B1)

C ZONING
40.50 (4A1) High Forecast Price Minus 24 1/4 (4B1) Low Forecast Price Equals 16.25 (C) Range. 1/3 of Range = 5.50 (4CD)

(4C2) Lower 1/3 = (4B1) 24 1/4 to 29.75 (Buy)
(4C3) Middle 1/3 = 29.75 to 35.25 (Maybe)
(4C4) Upper 1/3 = 35.25 to 40.50 (4A1) (Sell)

Present Market Price of 29 is in the BUY (4C5) Range

D UP-SIDE DOWN-SIDE RATIO (Potential Gain vs. Risk of Loss)

High Price (4A1) 40.50 Minus Present Price 29
—————————————————— = 11.50 / 4.75 = 2.4 (4D) To 1
Present Price 29 Minus Low Price (4B1) 24.25

E PRICE TARGET

High Price (4A1) 40.50 / Present Market Price 29 = (1.40) X 100 = (140) − 100 = 40 (4E) % Appreciation

5 5-YEAR POTENTIAL

These calculations provide a picture of future income. They also provide a standard for comparing income and growth stocks.

A Present Full Year's Dividend $ .64 / Present Price of Stock $ 29 = .022 X 100 = 2.2 (5A) Present Yield or % Returned on Purchase Price

B AVERAGE YIELD OVER NEXT 5 YEARS
Avg. Earnings Per Share Next 5 Years 2.18 X Avg. % Payout (3G7) .28 = .61 / Present Price $ 29 = 2.1 (5B) %

C TOTAL RETURN
5 Year Appreciation Potential (4E) / 5 = 8 %
Average Yield (5B) . . . . 2.1 %
Total Return for 5 Years (average) (5C) . . . . 3.36 %

© 1996. National Association of Investors Corporation; 711 West Thirteen Mile Road, Madison Hgts., Michigan 48071

Figure 14-2

Stock Selection Guide for First Financial Management Corporation

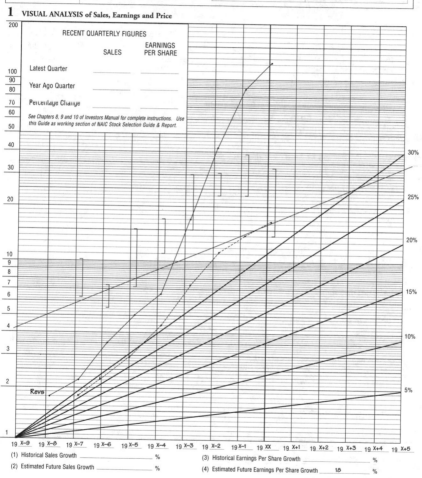

NATIONAL ASSOCIATION OF INVESTORS CORPORATION **NAIC** ® INVESTMENT EDUCATION FOR INDIVIDUALS AND CLUBS SINCE 1951	*Stock Selection Guide* *The most widely used aid to good investment judgment*

Company **FIRST FINANCIAL MGT**　　　Date **APR 5, 19XX**

Prepared by **FSW**　　　　Data taken from **VL & S&P**

Where traded **NYSE**　　　Major product/service **FIN. SERV.**

CAPITALIZATION	Authorized	Outstanding
Preferred	–0–	
Common	36.853 Mil	
Debt	773.86 Mil	Potential Dilution

1 VISUAL ANALYSIS of Sales, Earnings and Price

RECENT QUARTERLY FIGURES

	SALES	EARNINGS PER SHARE
Latest Quarter		
Year Ago Quarter		
Percentage Change		

See Chapters 8, 9 and 10 of Investors Manual for complete instructions. Use this Guide as working section of NAIC Stock Selection Guide & Report.

Revs

| 19 X-9 | 19 X-8 | 19 X-7 | 19 X-6 | 19 X-5 | 19 X-4 | 19 X-3 | 19 X-2 | 19 X-1 | 19 XX | 19 X+1 | 19 X+2 | 19 X+3 | 19 X+4 | 19 X+5 |

(1) Historical Sales Growth _____ %

(2) Estimated Future Sales Growth _____ %

(3) Historical Earnings Per Share Growth _____ %

(4) Estimated Future Earnings Per Share Growth __18__ %

Figure 14-2 (Continued)
Stock Selection Guide for First Financial Management Corporation

2 EVALUATING MANAGEMENT

Company FIRST FINANCIAL MGMT. CORP.

	19 X–9	19 X–8	19 X–7	19 X–6	19 X–5	19 X–4	19 X–3	19 X–2	19 X–1	19 XX	LAST 5 YEAR AVG.	TREND UP	TREND DOWN
A % Pre-tax Profit on Sales (Net Before Taxes ÷ Sales)			13.0	11.4	11.5	13.2	11.0	11.8	10.7	9.4			
B % Earned on Equity (E/S ÷ Book Value)			13.5	16.4	10.3	14.1	5.2	10.5	10.8	11.7			

3 PRICE-EARNINGS HISTORY as an indicator of the future

This shows how stock prices have fluctuated with earnings and dividends. It is a building block for translating earnings into future stock prices.

PRESENT PRICE 21 HIGH THIS YEAR 33 3/4 LOW THIS YEAR 14 1/4

	Year	A PRICE HIGH	B PRICE LOW	C Earnings Per Share	D Price Earnings Ratio HIGH A ÷ C	E Price Earnings Ratio LOW B ÷ C	F Dividend Per Share	G % Payout F ÷ C X 100	H % High Yield F ÷ B X 100
1	19X–4	17 5/8	11	.44	40	25			
2	19X–3	30 1/4	15	.74	40	20			
3	19X–2	31 7/8	23 1/8	1.15	28	20			
4	19X–1	39	23 3/8	1.43	27	16	.098	4	
5	19XX	33 3/4	14 1/8	1.67	20	8	.10	4	
6	TOTAL		86.625						
7	AVERAGE		17.3						
8	AVERAGE PRICE EARNINGS RATIO				9 CURRENT PRICE EARNINGS RATIO				

4 EVALUATING RISK and REWARD over the next 5 years

*Assuming one recession and one business boom every 5 years, calculations are made of how **high** and how **low** the stock might sell. The upside-downside ratio is the key to evaluating risk and reward.*

A HIGH PRICE — NEXT 5 YEARS
Avg. High P/E 18 (3D7) X Estimate High Earnings/Share 3.35 = Forecast High Price $ 60 (4A1)

B LOW PRICE — NEXT 5 YEARS
(a) Avg. Low P/E 10 (3E7) X Estimated Low Earnings/Share 1.67 = $ 17–
(b) Avg. Low Price of Last 5 Years = 17 3/8 (3B7)
(c) Recent Severe Market Low Price = 14 1/8
(d) Price Dividend Will Support Present Divd. / High Yield (H) = – / – = –
Selected Estimated Low Price = $ 14 1/8 (4B1)

C ZONING
60 (4A1) High Forecast Price Minus 14 1/8 (4B1) Low Forecast Price Equals 45 7/8 (C) Range. 1/3 of Range = 15 1/4 (4CD)

(4C2) Lower 1/3 = (4B1) 14 1/8 to 29 3/8 (Buy)
(4C3) Middle 1/3 = 29 3/8 to 44 5/8 (Maybe)
(4C4) Upper 1/3 = 44 5/8 to 60 (4A1) (Sell)

Present Market Price of 21 is in the BUY (4C5) Range

D UP-SIDE DOWN-SIDE RATIO (Potential Gain vs. Risk of Loss)
High Price (4A1) 60 Minus Present Price 21 / Present Price 21 Minus Low Price (4B1) 14 1/8 = 39 / 6 7/8 = 5.7 (4D) To 1

E PRICE TARGET
High Price (4A1) 60 / Present Market Price 21 = (2.86) X 100 = (286) – 100 = 186 (4E) % Appreciation

5 5-YEAR POTENTIAL

These calculations provide a picture of future income. They also provide a standard for comparing income and growth stocks.

A Present Full Year's Dividend $ – / Present Price of Stock $ – = – X 100 = – (5A) Present Yield or % Returned on Purchase Price

B AVERAGE YIELD OVER NEXT 5 YEARS
Avg. Earnings Per Share Next 5 Years X Avg. % Payout (3G7) – = – / Present Price $ = – (5B) %

C TOTAL RETURN
5 Year Appreciation Potential (4E) – / 5 = – %
Average Yield (5B) . . . . – %
Total Return for 5 Years (average) (5C) . . . . – %

© 1996. National Association of Investors Corporation; 711 West Thirteen Mile Road, Madison Hgts., Michigan 48071

Figure 14-3
Challenge Tree Form Comparing Weis Markets and First Financial
Management Corporation

NATIONAL ASSOCIATION
OF INVESTORS CORPORATION

NAIC®

INVESTMENT EDUCATION
FOR INDIVIDUALS AND CLUBS
SINCE 1951

Challenge Tree Comparative Form

Date   FEB. 10, 19XX

	COMPANY HELD	CHALLENGING COMPANY
	WEIS MARKETS	FIRST FINANCIAL MGT. CO.
Current Price	29	21
Estimated 5 Year High	40.50	60
Estimated 5 Year Low	24.25	14 ⅛
Gain to 5 Year High	11.50 – 40%	39 – 185%
Loss to 5 Year Low	4.75 – 16%	6 ⅞ – 33%
5 Year Upside-Downside Ratio	2.4	5.7
Lower Price Range	24.25 – 29.75	14 ⅛ – 29 ⅜
Middle Price Range	29.75 – 35.25	29 ⅜ – 44 ⅞
Upper Price Range	35.25 – 40.50	44 ⅞ – 60
S & P Quality Rating	A+	B+
Value Line Timeliness Rating	4	3
6 to 18 Months Upside Action	NEUTRAL	GOOD
Earnings Advancing	DOWN LIKELY	YES
Business Cycle Upswing	DOWN TO NEUTRAL	NEUTRAL
Industry Outlook	VERY COMPETITIVE	GOOD
Upside-Downside Outlook	FAIR	GOOD
Growth Stock Potential	POOR	VERY GOOD
Technical Base Forming	NO	YES
New Products Coming In	MORE COMPETITION	PURCHASES

JUDGING MANAGEMENT	Good	Average	Poor	Good	Average	Poor
Driving Force:						
Rate of Sales Gain			✔	✔		
Rate of Earnings Per Share Gain			✔	✔		
Earned on Sales		✔		✔		
Earned on Equity		✔			✔	
Evaluating Price:						
High in 5 Years		✔		✔		
Low in 5 Years		✔		✔		
Upside-Downside Ratio			✔	✔		
Current Yield		✔				✔
Total Return			✔	✔		
Other Considerations:						
Industry Potentials			✔	✔		
State of Business Cycle		✔		✔		
Stock Price Trends			✔		✔	
Quality of Stock	✔				✔	
Capitalization and Finance	✔				✔	

The Investor first prepares an NAIC Selection Guide and Report on the challenged and challenging companies. That information is then recorded above for comparison purposes.

to eighteen months. Its upside/downside ratio has dropped from 3 to 1 when you purchased it to 1 to 1. The upside gain, because of the stock's rise, has deteriorated from 100 percent to 50 percent.

If you can identify a replacement stock of equal or higher quality, a 3-to-1 upside/downside ratio, and 100 percent appreciation potential, buy it. You'll find that your investment results will improve over the years as you continue to use this technique.

On occasion, the stock market cycle will come to a point where you can no longer locate a 3-to-1 upside/downside ratio and 100 percent appreciation potential in addition to equal or higher quality. When this occurs, consider buying short-term bonds as up to 20 percent of the most speculative part of your portfolio. These will provide income while your club waits for a major stock market correction, after which stocks will again be attractive. At the onset of a new upward movement, you may consider several challengers of lesser quality. As the market advances, you should also enhance the quality of your holdings.

ERRORS TO AVOID

Avoid these two common errors:

1. Do not hold lesser-quality stocks as a bull market winds down, or your results will be erratic. Only stronger companies survive the depths of the downturn that follows a boom. By raising quality with each Challenge Tree exercise, you increase your chances for better results.

2. Do not assume that simply because a company has doubled in value, it cannot continue to appreciate. Superior growth companies do. Why settle for a 50 to 100 percent profit when holding growth stocks for a longer period could mean a gain of 200 percent, 500 percent, or even more?

Determining whether a particular company has further potential requires going beyond the figures. You should be thoroughly familiar with the company from your reading of corporate messages and the business press and be able to make an informed decision as to the company's prospects for the next several years.

THE CHALLENGE TREE AT WORK

An actual Challenge Tree experience illustrates how the procedure works and the results that can be achieved. An investor with $450 made her initial stock purchase in 1957, buying 25 shares of Hoover Ball & Bearing at $18. These shares were sold the following year at $30.875, returning $755.96. The investor then bought 50 shares of Copeland at $13.50 with $675 of the money she made.

A year later Copeland was sold at $23.25. Within a week, she purchased 50 shares of Delta for $26, an investment of $1,300. In 1962 she sold 30 shares of Delta for $53.375, receiving $1,601.25. She then bought 100 shares of American Metal Products at $14, spending $1,400.

In 1965 her Metal Products stock was selling for $25 and her Delta holdings had grown to 70 shares with splits, selling at $17.25. Her portfolio totaled $5,057.50. She had received dividends totaling $686.43 since the inception of her program, and in just eight years the original $450 had grown to $8,243.93.

By 1983 this investor had a portfolio of 462 Delta, 60 Fruehauf, 239 Occidental, and 249 Asarco, with a total value of $37,031. In addition, she had received dividends totaling $12,978.

Not all Challenge Tree experiences will be this profitable, but this procedure represents an opportunity to significantly improve your financial progress as an investor. The purpose of the Challenge Tree is to provide you with a proven, consistent method for analyzing your holdings and making informed decisions.

APPLYING CHALLENGE TREE TO TWO STOCKS

Let's apply the Challenge Tree to two actual stocks. A club has owned Weis Markets, Inc. for more than ten years. It was first bought at a price, after stock splits, of 8¾. In the past year the stock has sold as high as 34¼ and as low as 24¾. The Stock Selection Guide shows that the rate of sales growth in the past three years has dropped to under 3 percent. Earnings-per-share growth has dropped even more, and management has indicated that the current year's earnings will be down. This is also shown by declines in the pre-tax percent earned on sales and in earnings on equity.

The challenging company is First Financial Management Corporation. A club member was attracted to this stock when he noticed that over the past year its price declined from 39 to a low of 14¼, yet revenues were growing very rapidly and earnings per share were increasing at 18 percent. In spite of its rapid rate of growth, the company sold at a price/earnings ratio of 16. The investor read reports by S&P, Value Line, and several security analysts. The reports concluded that the corporation was being considered as a bank by the market and was subject to the same suspicion and distrust that all banks were experiencing at that time. Actually, the main business of the corporation is processing credit reports and credit cards for banks and financial companies. It's very different from a bank.

A review of the Stock Selection Guide for Weis Markets makes it clear that sales growth has slowed substantially in recent years. Earnings-per-share growth has also recently slowed. Some of this resulted from a lower tax rate. The investor who also keeps an NAIC PERT form on his or her stocks would have noted that the decline in sales growth started in 1987. The profit margins were maintained, and the reduction in the tax rate enabled earnings per share to continue to advance. The Stock Selection Guide on Weis also shows the slowing growth rate is causing a reduced P/E ratio both at the high and the low prices.

The challenging company has caught our attention for two reasons: the very high rate of growth and the substantial decline in price in spite of the fact that the company has continued to increase earnings per share.

DISCUSS THE REASONING

After filling in the Challenge Tree form, the club member goes over the figures and conclusions with the other members to see if they agree with the conclusion. The price and gain figures come from the Stock Selection Guide, and the members agree that Weis's growth rate has slowed and that First Financial has an exceptional rate of growth. All agree that a conservative projection of a 15 percent compound annual growth rate five years into the future is reasonable.

The club discussed the quality ratings of the two companies a great deal and almost decided to drop the challenging company because of its lesser quality. The members finally agreed that the quality rating of the challenger was not bad in view of its brief history and very rapid growth. Then the club looked at the current stock market cycle. It concluded that the market was in a minor decline and probably had two to three years to go in the current major upward cycle. Therefore, holding a stock with the challenger's quality rating did not pose a problem at this time.

In the next six to eighteen months, Weis will face both a continued weak business period and competition from two new chains in its market. Conversely, First Financial seems likely to continue its advance. In terms of the "Driving Force" items listed on the Challenge Tree form, First Financial is strongly ahead of Weis. The same is true of the "Evaluating Price" items.

Among other considerations, it is clear that Weis is ahead in quality and financial condition, but the members decided the First Financial's growth potential outweighed these two items. Therefore, the club decided to sell its shares of Weis and use the proceeds to buy First Financial.

CHAPTER 15

DECIDING WHEN TO SELL

*F*amed investor Warren Buffett has a theory on the best time to sell: "Never." This may be an extreme position, but without question, amateur investors are more likely to sell too soon than to hold their stocks too long.

How likely is it that a decision to sell will prove profitable? Consider that with each sell action you must make not one, but two, right decisions. First, you must decide to sell stock A. Then, you must find its replacement. And stock B must offer less downside risk and greater upside potential than its predecessor in order to justify the action.

CONSIDER COSTS

The decision is not limited to share price. You can't forget commission, either. A low estimate of the commission involved is 2 percent to buy and another 2 percent to sell. Plus you must add the additional federal and state taxes you and your fellow club members will have to pay on your profits, further eroding your "gross" profit. You may be startled to learn that, on average, after both commissions and taxes are taken into account, a new stock must register a 37 percent gain before you even begin to make money!

REASONS TO SELL

What are legitimate reasons for selling stocks? Certainly, one is to reap the rewards of years of successful investing and withdraw funds for a new house, a child's education, or other major expense. The other is to improve your portfolio.

You should sell:

1. Because of an adverse management change. New management is not necessarily good management. It might be difficult for you to assess the ability of brand new management, but you can consider the opinion of investment professionals, who are probably familiar with the individuals' track records.

2. Because of declining profit margins. This is a leading indicator of corporate problems. Keep in mind the Wall Street saying "There is no such thing as one bad quarter." The company may be in for a year or more of depressed earnings.

3. Because of a deteriorating corporate financial condition. If a company has taken on too much debt, it may face serious trouble meeting interest and principal payments in a slowing economy. Keep up to date on changes in the company's capitalization, and check the impact of leverage, as you learned to do in Chapter 4.

4. Because competition is affecting profits. Nobody has a monopoly on a good idea. When others see the potential for a product or service and enter the business, price cutting, earnings erosion, and even bankruptcy may follow. Although the company's earnings may continue to advance, they could decline in P/E ratio if the EPS growth rate slackens.

   Don't follow the crowd and chase "in" industries. Think for yourself, and look at the ability of management, not the glamour of the business.

   An example: RPM is a specialty chemical company making adhesives and coatings. "Not a very exciting business," you might think. Perhaps not, but RPM has chalked up increases in sales and earnings for 47 straight years! And we all know that price is related to earnings.

5. Because of dependence on a single product. In the 1960s, Brunswick Corporation was viewed as a growth stock. When the automatic bowling pin machine was introduced, bowling lanes throughout the country and abroad made sure to buy it. However, once every bowling facility had the equipment, the growth slowed. This was product growth, contrasted with the growth that stems from good management. At Minnesota Mining and Manufacturing, the company has traditionally

garnered a quarter of its sales from products not on the market five years before. Such a company will probably show slower growth than that of a shooting star, but the growth is longer-lasting.

6. Because a stock's quality will change as economic circumstances change. The quality of a stock comprises many factors. To name a few: size, financial condition, consumer acceptance, market share, effectiveness of research, and depth of management. But say raw materials triple in price. The stock's quality attributes are still good, but the changed economic situation has changed its quality as well.

7. Because securities that have proven to be cyclical and that have a recent history of low growth should be sold when the economy peaks. Buy cyclicals during the trough when P/E ratios are relatively high and the market is predicting their earnings recovery. Don't buy when the multiples are relatively low and the stocks seem to be a bargain, as this indicates that earnings are headed for a decline.

8. Because it's important to maintain balance by company size in your portfolio. Remember our recommendation: Keep 25 percent of your holdings in companies with $2 billion or more in sales, 25 percent in small companies with sales under $400 million and with rapid growth rates, and 50 percent in medium-sized companies.

SELLING DON'TS

Set these rules for yourself concerning selling:

1. Don't sell just because the price hasn't moved. One of the cardinal requirements for successful investing is patience. Don't concentrate on price as a trader would; rather, focus on the fundamentals as a long-term investor should. If the basics remain attractive, over time you need not worry about price.

2. Don't sell because of a paper loss. You might think it's smart to sell out when a decline in price of 10 or 20 percent is posted. But a stock well worth keeping can go down that far in a declining market.

3. Don't sell because of a paper profit. You might be tempted to sell when a stock doubles, yet many stocks post gains of 2,000 percent, 3,000 percent, or even more over a ten-year span. Think how much you'd miss out on if you sold in the first year! Again, concentrate on the study of

fundamentals. As long as the stock meets the criteria you have established, hold on to it.

4. Don't sell on temporary bad news. A perfect example is Metromedia, which once enjoyed an earnings gain of 40 percent in a quarter when newspapers in two of its major markets—New York and Los Angeles—were on strike. Advertisers flocked to Metromedia's TV stations, and management pointed out that earnings probably would be less in the same quarter a year hence. Sure enough, they were. And the price of the stock fell sharply, even after management's caveat. But, as management had also predicted, earnings resumed their upward trend, and so did the stock price.

5. Don't sell just to take action. This is sometimes appealing if you feel frustrated that something isn't happening quickly enough. Be patient and wait out the market.

6. Don't sell a stock that has fallen so far that your remaining downside risk is minimal compared to the upside potential.

If you are unsure about whether to sell, why not hedge your decision? Sell part of the holding and keep the rest. You'll be diversifying your portfolio, which can be especially important if a single issue has become too large a part of your holdings. In a small portfolio (under $100,000 in size), a single issue should not account for more than 20 percent of total value. In a large portfolio (at least $100,000 in size), no single holding should represent more than 10 percent of the total value.

To sum up, selling may be the most difficult decision you face as an investor. Take full advantage of the Portfolio Management Guide and PERT. If sales and earnings gains continue to meet or exceed your minimum requirement, and if the pre-tax profit margin is rising, consider selling only if the price multiple exceeds one and a half times the historical average high price/earnings ratio. And even then, you may find reasons why you should continue to hold the stock. Don't sell too quickly—remember Warren Buffett.

WINNING WITH AN INVESTMENT CLUB

CHAPTER 16

STARTING A CLUB

*W*hen you form an investment club, your first task is to identify prospective members. You'll probably find plenty of people intrigued by the idea of pooling money together to invest.

WHAT TO LOOK FOR

There are three elements to the successful start-up club. Only when those elements come together are you assured of success.

First, the venture must be an enjoyable social activity as well as an educational and money-making program. You'll want to attract people who are compatible and able to function as a team. You are embarking on an activity that could last a lifetime; your fellow adventurers should wear well.

The second requirement is to ensure that all members are committed to the same investment philosophy. The single most frequent cause of early dissolution of investment clubs is conflicting investment philosophies. A club cannot exist if it's divided between long-term investors who want to follow NAIC principles, and others who are determined to act as traders, moving in and out of the market. For many inexperienced first-timers, the allure of fast profits and active trading is irresistible. Successful investment clubs adhere to the more conservative point of view that wealth building is a slow process, particularly in the beginning years. The popular conception of investing is that you frequently buy and sell. Many prospects have that idea. It is important that the club make clear to all prospects that its policy is to buy carefully and then hold.

Third, the club will thrive best when members are committed to active participation. The reality is that some members are not willing to contribute more than their monthly dues; they gladly leave to others the work of investigating prospective purchases and sales. (Of course, as a result, these inactive individuals learn little or nothing about investing.) Almost every club has a few of these members. You need to make sure you have enough energetic, dedicated people that the investigative requirements can be managed by them. In time most club members build their own security accounts outside of the club. The monthly club meeting is a valuable source of ideas for these members.

Remember, an investment club works so well because the work is shared by several people. Research takes time and, by splitting it up, you benefit from the shared responsibility of membership.

WHERE TO LOOK

Make up a list of people to approach. Consider friends from every facet of your life: neighbors, members of your church, or those you know from civic and charitable organizations. If you know someone who works as a volunteer and takes that responsibility seriously, you have a most attractive prospect. You will probably want to invite co-workers to your meeting, but don't limit the range of possibilities to this or any other single group. The most successful clubs are made up of individuals from a variety of backgrounds and experience. As a general rule, try to limit the number of individuals from any one place of employment to no more than half the total membership.

Don't feel obligated to include an accountant and an attorney; most clubs succeed without either. Above all, don't seek out a financial expert, whether a registered representative, an investment analyst, or a long-time successful investor. Other members will tend to lean on such an individual and will know no more after years of membership than they did upon joining. Furthermore, the collective judgment of a number of reasonable people can be much sounder than the opinion of a single source, however knowledgeable that individual might be.

Travel time to meetings limits the geography of your search, so your club should be localized. Think about where you will be meeting, and who could reach the site(s) in an hour or less.

In the final analysis, investment club members need only be individuals willing to work to gain knowledge, with an above-average desire to learn for themselves about the world of securities. Members should also regard their investment program as a life-long process. Investing experience is not a requirement for success, as hundreds of high-performance NAIC clubs can attest.

HOW MANY MEMBERS?

Ideally, a club should be big enough for members to divide the work without it becoming burdensome for any individual, yet small enough to give everyone a sense of direct involvement and personal interest. For most clubs, this number averages fifteen. Another advantage of holding the count to around fifteen is that meetings can remain informal and not become so unwieldy that decisions are difficult to reach. What's more, if membership exceeds fifteen, the number of appropriate meeting places will be limited.

Whatever your target total, seek out three or four extra people, because inevitably some portion of your prospective membership will decide not to join. So if you're looking for fifteen and twenty people express interest, chances are you'll be right on target.

Invite everyone who's interested to an exploratory meeting to learn more, and be sure to get enough information folders from NAIC to pass out to every prospect, so that all will have a better idea of what lies ahead. Don't seek a final commitment from anyone until afterward.

BEFORE THE MEETING

Send a reminder to each of the prospects, enclosing reprints of the Introduction and Chapter 1 of this book. Also include a copy of the suggested Club Operating Agreement, Chapter 17.

Ask each person to review the materials prior to attending, and to come prepared with questions and comments as well as possible names for the club.

Arrange for an experienced investment club member to attend your initial session. If this is impractical, try to attend an existing club's meeting as an observer, to gain useful background and get answers to any questions you may have. If there is an NAIC Council in your area, attend a meeting to make contact with experienced club members.

AT THE MEETING

First, briefly go over the materials furnished to the prospects. Explain what the benefits of joining an investment club are, what will be expected of members, and how the group will be organized. Remind each person that the club is not a get-rich-quick operation. Emphasize that the time to decide whether or not one belongs in a club is before joining.

Next, ask for questions. When all inquiries have been satisfied, ask for a show of hands to determine how many people are interested in joining the group. If most are interested, proceed with the organization, and consider the Club Operating Agreement. (Most clubs form as a partnership; Chapter 17 spells out the many points to be considered in setting up the organization.) To save time, propose that the club adopt NAIC's agreement for a six-month trial period. After that, proposed changes should be considered by the membership. Operating procedures could be adopted in the same way.

Pick the time and place for monthly meetings, and establish the date of the next get-together, when initial deposits will be made. Decide on the amount to be collected from each member, being sure that the sum is not excessive for anyone. Emphasize that this is risk capital. Although members should have every expectation of making money, they should also be prepared to suffer losses without experiencing hardship. Ideally, members should not expect to withdraw money from a beginning club for several years. Of course, every individual does have the right to close out his or her account at any time, but hopefully members will join with the expectation that monthly deposits will be left at work in investments for the foreseeable future.

Your members should be aware of a few market realities. It often takes time—months or even years—before investments become profitable. Remember that it takes a considerable rise in value to cover commissions and taxes. And if a prolonged market downturn occurs—presenting an extended opportunity to buy stocks at bargain prices—members won't be able to liquidate their holdings at a profit until the downturn ends.

Typically, members contribute $20 to $50 monthly. Although it's not absolutely necessary, you might consider allowing exceptionally high contributions for the first year of operation. After that time, some members might want to contribute more than others, and some may need to withdraw a portion of their funds. These variations may be handled quite easily under NAIC's recommended bookkeeping procedures. The method not only permits the receipt of varying deposits, but allows for withdrawals as well.

Flexibility is important, because people have different requirements, and no one can predict the future.

New members can be added at any time without being asked to match the financial commitment of long-time members. The accounting system maintains the correct representation of members' equity in accord with deposits and withdrawals over time. Thus, you will be in a position to attract interested individuals on a continuing basis as vacancies occur.

Discuss the idea of working with a broker. Traditionally, investment clubs have depended on good advice from brokers who agree with the club membership's basic philosophy. Today, some clubs do not believe they need advice beyond the research efforts of members, and use discount brokers for placement of orders. Discount brokerage firms offer no advice, but will place buy and sell orders for lower fees than traditional full-service firms. We recommend that you and your fellow club members explore all of your options together and decide which course is best for you. If you are all inexperienced, you might think about using a full-service brokerage firm for at least the first year or two, reviewing your options again when you've gained more experience.

In selecting a broker, you—as the organizer—should seek recommendations in advance from established clubs or experienced individual investors. If you decide to use a full-service broker, be sure to find a broker who is compatible and receptive to your club's overall investment philosophy, and is willing to conduct business within your guidelines. Some brokers may try to get you to speculate and take more chances than you wish to take.

You might end up with several broker prospects, and you'll want to call or visit more than one broker before the initial meeting so you can make recommendations to the group.

Before signing a broker-club agreement, review Chapter 18, "Working with a Broker."

SELECT CLUB OFFICERS

Most clubs form as a partnership to minimize taxes and to give themselves maximum operating and reporting efficiency. The presiding partner is responsible for setting the time and place for meetings, appointing committees, presiding at meetings, and overseeing the activities of the club. The assistant presiding partner not only takes the place of the presiding partner when the latter is unable to serve, but usually also leads the investment education program.

The recording partner keeps minutes of proceedings and notifies members of the time and place of meetings. Typically, the recording partner assumes responsibility for notifying absent members of club actions by mailing copies of minutes.

The financial partner maintains the club's financial records and places buy and sell orders with the broker. Record keeping includes an accounting of club receipts and disbursements and calculation of each member's share of interest in the club. The financial partner also prepares a monthly liquidating statement and files an annual informational tax return with the federal government. Your financial partner should obtain NAIC's club accounting kit and should follow the instructions carefully from the outset of your operations to ensure that records are both complete and accurate. The kit will make the entire financial reporting job much easier.

RECORD KEEPING ALTERNATIVES

NAIC offers computer programs for club record keeping. Another alternative is to contact one of the many experienced investment club members who keep records for a modest fee. These services are advertised in *Better Investing* Magazine. Some clubs feel that the task of keeping records is simply too big for one person, and that it's preferable to pay someone else to do it.

With officers identified, you will want to come up with a name for your group. Pick a first as well as a second choice, in case another club is already doing business under your first-choice name and is using the same broker you want to work with.

Clubs select names denoting geographic location, business affiliation, or the purpose of the group. Others pick names "just for fun." Here are some examples: Money Mad Matrons, Tuesday Tycoons, Engine 63 (a group of firemen), Gamma Gals (sorority sisters), Money Tree, and Bowlers' Investment Club. Use your imagination, but try to be accurate. A group of Chicago women called themselves the "Gold Coast Clippers," thinking they'd be clipping coupons. Only later did they discover that delightful task is reserved for bondholders!

Consider affiliation with NAIC. Membership in this national group could be the single most important step your club takes. Share with members the contents of the brochure "Benefits of Belonging to the National Association of Investors Corporation." Of course, NAIC membership is voluntary, and you may use any or all of the available services as you choose. However, bear in mind that NAIC materials have guided the growth of thousands of clubs over the past four decades. Make all of your members aware of the materials available from NAIC. Some will use them more than others and possibly contribute more to the club's success.

As head of the educational effort, the assistant presiding partner is responsible for exposing other members to the contents of NAIC's stock selection and portfolio management information. Ideally, he or she delegates members to report on different portions of the material. This background will prove useful to members as they assume responsibility for reporting on prospective buys or monitoring securities already purchased. NAIC also has a video that portrays the operation of a model club meeting.

ORGANIZE YOUR STUDY PROGRAM

NAIC offers the "Investment Club Monthly Study Program," a series of twelve lessons that teach stock study tools to club members. Using these lessons at your next twelve meetings will help your members understand NAIC's stock study procedures. These are provided upon request and at no cost to affiliated clubs. Simply write NAIC, give your membership number, and ask for the "Monthly Study Program."

The assistant presiding partner should outline what will be expected from each member during the first year. The success of the club depends on the willingness of its members to contribute their time and talent, as well as money.

In advance of the first monthly meeting, the assistant presiding partner delegates a member to prepare a report on a corporation on the NAIC Stock Check List (see Chapter 7), while another member is asked to evaluate the same security using the Stock Selection Guide (see Chapters 8–10). Solicit ideas from the group about companies to look into as possible purchases, but also be prepared with ideas of your own. Launch the club properly. Acting on a hot tip is *not* the way to begin. Whenever a member mentions a hot tip, ask him or her to prepare a Stock Selection Guide on the company for consideration at the next meeting. (See Chapter 2, "Finding Companies to Study.")

Stock selection is complex, and it takes practice to master the technique. In the beginning, every term will be unfamiliar and every instruction difficult to follow. That's true of any new body of knowledge. However, climbing this learning curve is important because the skill you will develop is valuable.

One new member wrote to NAIC headquarters in despair recently, proclaiming in her letter that "It is 4 a.m. and I just finished my first 'ten minute' analysis!" (now called the Visual Analysis). She wrote back a month later and said that her time per company was down to thirty minutes.

You might be able to find an experienced club member to help you master NAIC tools, or you may be able to obtain help from a regional Council in your area. If both of these alternatives fail, you should read over the information in Chapters 7–10 of this book, which are devoted to the Stock Check List and Stock Selection Guide. You'll be pleasantly surprised at how quickly you can become comfortable with these tools as you progress. For extra help with the Stock Selection Guide, NAIC has developed a videotape and a home study course that you can purchase.

With so much accomplished at the organizational meeting, your new club will be off to a fast start. At your first regular meeting, you will hear one or more reports on a prospective buy and make your first investment decision as a group. You might decide to purchase a security right away, or wait until the next stock study is presented. Remember, don't rush or feel pressured to make an immediate decision; the market will still be there when you're through studying. Whether you buy at once or decide to hold off until the next meeting, you are on the proper path to knowledgeable investing.

CHAPTER 17

THE CLUB AGREEMENT

*E*very investment club needs to define a shared investment philosophy. However, it also needs a set of operating rules, acceptable to all members, that complies with all regulatory and tax requirements.

The Mutual Investment Club of Detroit is one of America's oldest investment clubs. The agreement used by this landmark club works because of its simplicity. It is also designed in response to the members' needs. A review of this club's agreement will give you some excellent ideas for formulating your own agreement. This chapter illustrates the historical experience of one club, and should not be considered as legal or tax advice. You are encouraged to consult with your own legal and tax advisers.

In choosing between two possible forms—corporation or partnership—Mutual looked for answers to these five questions:

1. *Taxes.* Under which type of organization would members pay the least in taxes from the time money was first earned until it was received by individual members?

2. *Personal liability.* Which type would minimize members' financial risk?

3. *Transfer of securities.* With which form can securities be transferred with the least need for supporting resolutions?

4. *Organizational costs.* Which type would minimize the cost of setting up the club?

5. *Maintenance costs.* From the standpoint of both time and money, which type would be more economical over the life of the club?

TAXES

In 1960, the Treasury Department issued a ruling (which remains effective as of the date of this publication) that clubs are taxable as partnerships rather than corporations unless they have four or more of the following characteristics:

1. A group of associates.
2. A common objective to carry on a business and divide the resulting gains.
3. Continuity of life.
4. Centralization of management.
5. Limited liability.
6. Free transfer of interests.

The Treasury Department ruled that investment clubs have the first two characteristics, but generally do not have the remaining four. The application of these characteristics to a particular club requires legal interpretation and consultation with an attorney.

Mutual reviewed partnership tax law and found that a partnership as a whole would not have to pay any taxes, but that individual partners would be responsible for reporting their own shares of the club's annual income on their personal tax returns. Each partner would owe no further tax on that previously reported income if and when he or she elected to withdraw from the club or the club disbanded.

Mutual saw that even with some of the advantages of being a corporation, only a partnership avoided paying two taxes on the same income (a corporate-level tax on the corporation's earnings and an individual income tax on the distribution of corporate earnings as dividends to the shareholders). They concluded that their tax bills would be less if the club operated as a partnership rather than as a corporation.

Most clubs don't seriously consider trying to get S corporation status. This is a form of corporation that enjoys corporate advantages but is taxed as a partnership. It applies only on the federal level. States continue to tax S corporations as corporations.

The S corporation designation is available only if your club meets these requirements:

1. You have no more than thirty-five shareholders.

2. All shareholders are individuals (as opposed to other partnerships or corporations).

3. All shareholders are residents of the same state, and all are legal residents of the United States.

4. You have only one class of stock.

Once you elect to be taxed as an S corporation, there is a time limit on when you can reverse your decision.

PERSONAL LIABILITY

Under the corporate form, personal liability is usually limited to each member's investment in the club—in other words, you cannot be sued for more than the value of your shares. In Mutual's case, no obvious personal liability limitation existed under the partnership form, and some members feared they would be liable for the personal debts of other partners. However, the club's attorney advised that personal liability would be restricted to acts of a partner performed within the scope of his or her authority and in the course of conducting partnership business. In addition, the individuals of virtually all investment clubs could be held liable for the wrongful actions of the club's agents committed while conducting club business. However, an investment club conducts only one business activity, buying and selling securities, and has only one party in its transactions, its broker. You should consult with an attorney to determine the scope of each partner's personal liability.

In addition to consulting with their attorney, Mutual members were reassured about personal liability by the 1958 study published by the *University of Pennsylvania Law Review.* In this study, research stretching back to the turn of this century uncovered no individual involved in a lawsuit stemming from investment club membership. However, this same article anticipates litigation as the investment club movement grows. To date, NAIC is unaware of any such litigation.

TRANSFER OF SECURITIES

NAIC worked with the Securities Transfer Association to make operating investment clubs more convenient. This led to the establishment of Rule 3.0610. This rule permits clubs operating as partnerships to transfer securities directly into and out of the club's name with the signature of only one partner. Normally, there is no need for any supporting papers. If your brokerage firm asks for supporting papers or for all partners' signatures for transactions, refer them to the above rule number.

Endorsement of your security certificates should read: "ABC Investment Club, a partnership, Jane Anymember, partner."

You reduce the chances of any member misusing club funds by circulating the brokerage firm's monthly statement at every club meeting. Be sure you verify that each month's payments have been deposited to the account, that no unauthorized disbursements have been made, and that securities ordered have been purchased. Set a policy that the financial partner is to circulate the broker's most recent monthly statement to all members at each monthly meeting.

ORGANIZATIONAL COSTS

The Mutual Investment Club of Detroit learned that as a Michigan corporation, it would have to pay a fairly large registration fee to the state. As a partnership, Mutual was required merely to register with the county under the Michigan Assumed Names Act and pay a $10 fee. Registration forms for corporations were lengthy and complicated. The partnership form, in contrast, required only a list of partners' names and addresses.

This information made the partnership alternative even more attractive. Check with your state's licensing board, Department of Corporations, Department of Revenue, or similar regulatory agency to find out the degree of complexity involved in establishing your club either as a corporation or partnership.

MAINTENANCE COSTS

Mutual discovered that as a corporation it would need to file an annual report with the state and pay a franchise fee based on its capital and surplus. As a partnership it merely had to renew its registration under the Michigan Assumed

Names Act every five years. Again, find out beforehand what reporting requirements apply to each type of organization.

The club also asked its attorney about Securities and Exchange Commission (SEC) and state securities commission registration requirements, and learned that there were no filing requirements to be met in either case. However, some states consider an investment club membership to be a security, and certain steps are required for exemption from registration under the state securities laws.

Currently, at least three states (Wisconsin, Illinois, and New Mexico) impose securities filing requirements. You should check the security filing requirements in your state. In Wisconsin, for example, an exemption is granted for clubs organized as general partnerships. Limited partnerships and corporations starting with fifteen or fewer members are also exempt. In Illinois, clubs qualify for an exemption if membership never exceeds seventy, no more than thirty-five members join within a twelve-month period, and sales do not total more than $100,000 within a twelve-month period. General solicitation and advertising for members is not allowed, and new members must be reported within thirty days. This report is the only action required of clubs operating in Illinois that use the Partnership Agreement shown in this chapter. In New Mexico, clubs adopting the Agreement are usually eligible for exemption (be sure to check for yourself, as rules can change). Request a copy of Section 58-13B-27 NMSA 1978, and then file a letter responding to Section questions and request an exemption. The SEC has stated that a club with twenty-five or fewer members would be assumed not to be in violation of any of its rules requiring registration.

Each club is responsible for knowing about and complying with any federal, state, or local regulations pertaining to investment clubs. You should consult an attorney for guidance. In any event, the agreement developed by Mutual may prove helpful in your decision-making process. However, it is only an example and should not be considered legal or tax advice. Copies of the Agreement have been given to the SEC, the fifty state security commissions, the Internal Revenue Service, the Securities Transfer Association, and the major securities industry exchanges and associations. None of these agencies express an opinion on the Agreement.

Now, let's look at the agreement itself (Figure 17-1).

Figure 17-1

Partnership of the Mutual Investment Club of Detroit

Partnership Agreement
of
The Mutual Investment Club of Detroit

THIS AGREEMENT OF PARTNERSHIP, effective as of____(date)____, by and between the undersigned, to wit:

(Name of all partners)

NOW, THEREFORE, IT IS AGREED:

1. **Formation.** The undersigned hereby form a General Partnership in accordance with and subject to the laws of the State of Michigan.

2. **Name.** The name of the partnership shall be Mutual Investment Club of Detroit.

3. **Term.** The partnership shall begin on____(date)____and shall continue until December 31 of the same year and thereafter from year to year unless earlier terminated as hereinafter provided.

4. **Purpose.** The only purpose of the partnership is to invest the assets of the partnership solely in stocks, bonds, and other securities ("securities") for the education and benefit of the partners.

5. **Meetings.** Periodic meetings shall be held as determined by the partnership.

6. **Capital Contributions.** The partners may make capital contributions to the partnership on the date of each periodic meeting in such amounts as the partnership shall determine, provided, however, that no partner's capital account shall exceed twenty percent (20%) of the capital accounts of all the partners.

7. **Value of the Partnership.** The current value of the assets of the partnership, less the current value of the liabilities of the partnership (hereinafter referred to as "value of the partnership") shall be determined as of a regularly scheduled date and time ("valuation date") preceding the date of each periodic meeting determined by the Club.

8. **Capital Accounts.** A capital account shall be maintained in the name of each partner. Any increase or decrease in the value of the partnership on any valuation date shall be credited or debited, respectively, to each partner's capital account in proportion to the sum of all partner capital accounts on that date. Any other method of valuating each partner's capital account may be substituted for this method, provided the substituted method results in exactly the same valuation as previously provided herein. Each partner's capital contribution to, or capital withdrawal from, the partnership, shall be credited, or debited, respectively, to that partner's capital account.

9. **Management.** Each partner shall participate in the management and conduct of the affairs of the partnership in proportion to the value of his capital account. Except as otherwise determined, all decisions shall be made by the partners whose capital accounts total a majority of the value of the capital accounts of all the partners.

10. **Sharing of Profits and Losses.** Net profits and losses of the partnership shall inure to, and be borne by, the partners in proportion to the value of each of their capital accounts.

11. **Books of Accounts.** Books of account of the transactions of the partnership shall be kept and at all times be available and open to inspection and examination by any partner.

12. **Annual Accounting.** Each calendar year, a full and complete account of the condition of the partnership shall be made to the partners.

Drawing up an agreement like this one will provide your club with a written statement of your procedures and processes.

Figure 17-1 (Continued)

13. **Bank Account.**   The partnership may select a bank for the purpose of opening a bank account. Funds in the bank account shall be withdrawn by checks signed by any partner designated by the partnership.

14. **Broker Account.**   None of the partners of this partnership shall be a broker. However, the partnership may select a broker and enter into such agreements with the broker as required for the purchase or sale of securities. Securities owned by the partnership shall be held in the partnership name unless another name shall be designated by the partnership.

Any corporation or transfer agent called upon to transfer any securities to or from the name of the partnership shall be entitled to rely on instructions or assignments signed by any partner without inquiry as to the authority of the person(s) signing such instructions or assignments, or as to the validity of any transfer to or from the name of the partnership.

At the time of a transfer of securities, the corporation or transfer agent is entitled to assume (1) that the partnership is still in existence, and (2) that this Agreement is in full force and effect and has not been amended unless the corporation or transfer agent has received written notice to the contrary.

15. **No Compensation.**   No partner shall be compensated for services rendered to the partnership, except reimbursement for expenses.

16. **Additional Partners.**   Additional partners may be admitted at any time, upon the unanimous consent of all the partners, so long as the number of partners does not exceed twenty-five (25).

16A. **Transfers to a Trust.**   A partner may, after giving written notice to the other partners, transfer his interest in the partnership to a revocable living trust of which he is the grantor and sole trustee.

16B. **Removal of a Partner.**   Any partner may be removed by agreement of the partners whose capital accounts total a majority of the value of all partners' capital accounts. Written notice of a meeting where removal of a partner is to be considered shall include a specific reference to this matter. The removal shall become effective upon payment of the value of the removed partner's capital account, which shall be in accordance with the provisions on full withdrawal of a partner noted in paragraphs 18 and 20. The vote action shall be treated as receipt of request for withdrawal.

17. **Termination of Partnership.**   The partnership may be terminated by agreement of the partners whose capital accounts total a majority in value of the capital accounts of all the partners. Written notice of the meeting where termination of the partnership is to be considered shall include a specific reference to this matter. The partnership shall terminate upon a majority vote of all partners' capital accounts. Written notice of the decision to terminate the partnership shall be given to all the partners. Payment shall then be made of all the liabilities of the partnership and a final distribution of the remaining assets either in cash or in kind, shall promptly be made to the partners or their personal representatives in proportion to each partner's capital account.

18. **Voluntary Withdrawal (Partial or Full) of a Partner.**   Any partner may withdraw a part or all of the value of his capital account in the partnership and the partnership shall continue as a taxable entity. The partner withdrawing a portion or all of the value of his capital account shall give notice of such intention in writing to the Secretary. Written notice shall be deemed to be received as of the first meeting of the partnership at which it is presented. If written notice is received between meetings it will be treated as received at the first following meeting.

In making payment, the value of the partnership as set forth in the valuation statement prepared for the first meeting following the meeting at which written notice is received from a partner requesting a partial or full withdrawal, will be used to determine the value of the partner's capital account.

The partnership shall pay the partner who is withdrawing a portion or all of the value of his capital account in the partnership in accordance with paragraph 20 of this Agreement.

Figure 17-1 (Continued)

19. **Death or Incapacity of a Partner.** In the event of the death or incapacity of a partner (or the death or incapacity of the grantor and sole trustee of a revocable living trust, if such trust is a partner pursuant to Paragraph 16A hereof), receipt of notice of such an event shall be treated as notice of full withdrawal.

20. **Terms of Payment.** In the case of a partial withdrawal, payment may be made in cash or securities of the partnership or a mix of each at the option of the partner making the partial withdrawal. In the case of a full withdrawal, payment may be made in cash or securities or a mix of each at the option of the remaining partners. In either case, where securities are to be distributed, the remaining partners select the securities.

Where cash is transferred, the partnership shall transfer to the partner (or other appropriate entity) withdrawing a portion of all of his interest in the partnership, an amount equal to the lesser of (i) ninety-seven percent (97%) of the value of the capital account in the partnership being withdrawn or (ii) the value of the capital account being withdrawn, less the actual cost to the partnership of selling securities to obtain cash to meet the withdrawal. The amount being withdrawn shall be paid within 10 days after the valuation date used in determining the withdrawal amount.

If a partner withdrawing a portion or all of the value of his capital account in the partnership desires an immediate payment in cash, the partnership at its earliest convenience may pay eighty percent (80%) of the estimated value of his capital account and settle the balance in accordance with the valuation and payment procedures set forth in paragraphs 18 and 20.

When securities are transferred, the partnership shall select securities to transfer equal to the value of the capital account or a portion of the capital account being withdrawn (i.e. without a reduction for broker commissions). Securities shall be transferred as of the date of the club's valuation statement prepared to determine the value of that partner's capital account in the partnership. The Club's broker shall be advised that ownership of the securities has been transferred to the partner as of the valuation date used for the withdrawal.

21. **Forbidden Acts.** No partner shall:

(a) Have the right or authority to bind or obligate the partnership to any extent whatsoever with regard to any matter outside the scope of the partnership purpose.

(b) Except as provided in paragraph 16A, without the unanimous consent of all the other partners, assign, transfer, pledge, mortgage or sell all or part of his interest in the partnership to any other partner or other person whomsoever, or enter into any agreement as the result of which any person or persons not a partner shall become interested with him in the partnership.

(c) Purchase an investment for the partnership where less than the full purchase price is paid for same.

(d) Use the partnership name, credit or property for other than partnership purposes.

(e) Do any act detrimental to the interests of the partnership or which would make it impossible to carry on the purpose of the partnership.

This Agreement of Partnership shall be binding upon the respective heirs, executors, trustees, administrators and personal representatives of the partners.

The partners have caused the Agreement of Partnership to be executed on the dates indicated below, effective as of the date indicated above.

Name: _____   Name: _____

Dated: _____   Dated: _____

Name: _____   Name: _____

Dated: _____   Dated: _____

COMMENTARY ON THE PARTNERSHIP AGREEMENT OF THE MUTUAL INVESTMENT CLUB OF DETROIT

Paragraphs 1, 2, and 3. Self-explanatory.

Paragraph 4. The purpose of the club is strictly limited. An important reason for such limitations is to reduce the actual or apparent authority of any partner.

Paragraph 5. Most clubs meet regularly, such as on the first business day of each month or the third Thursday. Regularity makes it possible for members to plan schedules and avoid conflicting engagements.

Paragraph 6. Since dollar cost averaging is one of the basic investment principles followed by NAIC clubs, most partners make a regular capital contribution at each meeting. In the majority of new clubs, partners normally deposit the same amount. In older clubs, partners frequently deposit varying amounts. For the convenience of the treasurer, a valuation unit of $10 is selected, and partner deposits are usually required to be made in multiples of $10 to facilitate bookkeeping.

Many clubs start out under the assumption that the membership will remain constant and all members will continue to contribute the same amount. However, change is inevitable. From the outset, you should use a recording system flexible enough to provide for varying capital contributions. New members will be easier to attract if only a modest regular monthly payment is suggested or required. On the other hand, some clubs are concerned that one particular partner might become a majority owner. Commonly, clubs provide that no partner may add to his or her capital account beyond a certain percentage of the total (often 20%).

Paragraph 7. The assets of an investment club constantly fluctuate. New capital coming into the club must be valued in proportion to the value of the partnership at the time of deposit. Otherwise, the new funds would immediately acquire a value greater or less than existing funds, depending on the club's current worth. To help determine the value of new deposits, a Valuation Statement is prepared for each meeting. To provide adequate time for compiling this statement, a cutoff date well in advance of the meeting date (e.g., ten days, last business day of the previous month, etc.) should be determined. Calculations are made effective as of that date. The Valuation Statement is detailed in Chapter 21 of this book.

Paragraph 8. Self-explanatory.

Paragraph 9. Most clubs provide that members will have a voice in the club's operation in proportion to their financial commitment. Generally, the members with the greatest financial interest have been members longer, and they have more experience. An investment club is a business and, like other businesses, seems to function best when decision-making power relates to risk capital employed.

Paragraph 10. Under current federal tax law, if the partnership earnings and losses are distributed on other than a pro rata basis, serious tax consequences could result. For detailed procedures for determining and reporting profits and losses, see Chapter 22.

Paragraph 11. NAIC offers accounting help to clubs in both text and software forms.

Paragraph 12. See Chapter 22 for a more detailed discussion.

Paragraph 13. Many clubs do not have a bank account but deposit all funds with the broker and usually invest the available funds each month. Some clubs have the financial partner maintain a separate personal account for the club.

Paragraph 14. Initially, the Mutual Investment Club of Detroit did not allow a broker to be a member of the club, but it has since changed this policy. The club may handle its relationship with a broker in one of several ways. Refer to Chapter 18 for a detailed description of these procedures and a listing of the advantages and drawbacks of each.

Clubs generally restrict broker contact to one member, who calls for suggestions about stocks to study, and transmits buy and sell orders.

Paragraph 15. Self-explanatory.

Paragraph 16. In the experience of NAIC, the strongest clubs have between ten and twenty members.

Paragraph 16A. Placing investment club equity in a revocable living trust provides two primary advantages to members choosing this option: Probate expenses are avoided and the assets in the trust are immediately available for use as designated in the trust document.

Paragraph 16B. Sometimes a member loses interest in the club, consistently missing meetings and not doing his or her share of the work. Such a member will often just resign, so this paragraph's provision is seldom used.

Paragraph 17. Self-explanatory.

Paragraph 18. See Internal Revenue Code, Section 708 for further information on the continuation of a partnership as a taxable entity.

Paragraph 19. Same procedure as in paragraph 18 and paragraph 20. The remaining partners should exercise care to ensure that the deceased or incapacitated partner's account is paid in cash or stock to the proper claimant. Many clubs provide for the deposit of the deceased or incapacitated partner's funds in a separate bank account in cash, or to a brokerage account in stock, until advice is received as to ownership. An attorney can be consulted if there is any doubt about to whom payment should be made.

Paragraph 20. When a partner withdraws only part of the value of his capital account in the partnership, the partner has the choice of whether to receive cash or securities or a mix of the two.

Most partners seeking a partial withdrawal will choose to receive cash rather than securities since the tax consequences will usually be more favorable that way (see the following paragraph for further explanation). If cash is requested, the partnership must sell enough securities to satisfy the request and allocate any capital gain to all the partners in the current year. The partner withdrawing a portion of the capital account then reduces his or her tax basis by the amount of the cash distribution. If the partner has used up his or her tax basis, the distribution is then considered taxable income.

If the partner in a partial withdrawal chooses to receive securities, the club transfers securities of its choosing with a current value equal to the value being withdrawn. Any subsequent sale is at the discretion and expense of that partner. If the partner receives securities, under current federal tax law the partner withdrawing a portion of the value of his capital account is subject to federal income tax on the difference between the partnership's tax basis in the securities withdrawn and the value of the securities, but only upon the partially withdrawing partner's subsequent sale of the securities on the open market.

When a partner requests full withdrawal of the entire value of his or her capital account in the partnership, the remaining members have the choice of satisfying the request in cash or securities or a mix of the two. If they choose to transfer cash, they must decide which securities to sell, divide any capital gain among all the partners, and then transfer the cash. The withdrawing partner recognizes a pro rata share of taxable income before the distribution. After the distribution, the withdrawing partner allocates his or her tax basis to the securities received in proportion to their value. Tax between the tax basis distributed on their receipt and the eventual sale is payable at the time of sale.

For the most benefit to remaining members, payment should be made by transferring securities with a substantial paper profit to the withdrawing partner. Currently, the Internal Revenue Code does not classify such a transfer as a taxable transaction, so the remaining members do not incur taxable income as they would if the securities were sold and cash paid to the withdrawing partner. The withdrawing partner will not have a taxable transaction if the securities are held, but once they are sold, he or she will have to recognize a taxable capital gain of the difference between the net selling price of the securities and his or her tax basis in the partnership.

Transferring securities allows your club to postpone taxes on securities with capital gains while not increasing the tax liability of the withdrawing partner. Prior to the withdrawal date, that partner might consider opening an account with the same broker who handles the club's account. The securities can then be transferred and sold in the member's account on the same day, ensuring that he or she receives the current price. See Chapter 7 of NAIC's *Accounting Manual* for a discussion of the advantages of transferring stock to a partner making a full withdrawal.

Transaction costs (mainly broker commissions) may run as high as 10 percent in smaller clubs, while in larger clubs they may amount to only 3 percent or even less. When cash is distributed in a partial withdrawal, brokerage commissions as incurred (or 3%, whichever is the larger amount) are charged to the partially withdrawing partner, and the net proceeds are then distributed to that partner. Because securities fluctuate in value, the date used to determine the partner's capital account value should be set after the date of sale of securities used to satisfy the partner's request.

Paragraph 21. Self-explanatory.

The Partnership Agreement adopted by the Mutual Investment Club was a broad agreement designed to facilitate the club's general operation. To cover the detailed operation of the club, motions were passed by the partners from time to time. Following are the first minutes of the Mutual Investment Club. (Each club should discuss detailed operating procedures with its attorney in the light of its own needs and desires.)

OPERATING PROCEDURE
MUTUAL INVESTMENT CLUB

Duties of Partners

Annually, at the first meeting in February, partners shall elect the following positions and assign duties as described below by a majority vote;

1. *President.* The President's duty is to preside over meetings, set meeting dates and locations, appoint committees and see that resolutions passed by the partnership are carried out.

2. *Vice-President.* The Vice-President takes the place of the President when the President is absent or incapacitated. The Vice-President shall assign companies to report on at Club meetings to each partner and shall be responsible for insuring that the Club's study program is properly carried out.

3. *Secretary.* The Secretary's duty is to keep a record of the actions authorized by the partners and notify partners of meetings and other activities.

4. *Treasurer.* The Treasurer's duty is to keep a record of the Club's receipts and disbursements and partners' interests in the Club. The Treasurer will give partners receipts for payments, place the buy and sell orders authorized by the partners with the Club's broker, and prepare the Club's monthly Valuation Statement. He will see that the needed tax information is compiled and file the necessary reports.

Guests

Partners may invite guests to any meeting of the Club as long as advance clearance is obtained from the host of the meeting. When consideration is given to adding partners to the Club under paragraph 16 of the Club's partnership agreement, anyone considered shall have been a guest for at least two prior meetings.

Meetings

The Club shall hold a meeting on the second Tuesday of each month at a place designated by the Club. Written notice of each meeting shall be given to each partner by the Secretary at least one week before the meeting. Special meetings may be called by the President upon similar notice to the other partners.

Procedure

The monthly valuation statement shall be effective as of a regularly scheduled date and time preceding each monthly meeting.

In maintaining the records of each partner's capital account in the Club, the unit value method as outlined in Chapter 21 of this manual will be used.

Additional deposits in the Club may be made by members in multiples of $10.

The Vice-President shall contact investment counsel immediately preceding the monthly meeting and secure investment counsel's suggestions on new companies to consider, and any comments on stocks owned by the Club. He shall report this information at the meeting. The Vice-President shall appoint at least two partners at each meeting to prepare a report on the NAIC Stock Selection Guide on a security for presentation to the partnership at the following meeting. The Vice-President shall remind each person assigned to prepare an NAIC Stock Selection Guide of his assignment one week before the meeting.

Buy and/or sell action may be taken after a period of discussion by the members, and when voted by a simple majority of the members' interests.

End of motion.

AN ALTERNATIVE AGREEMENT

With the creation of the Individual Retirement Account (IRA) (a federal income tax planning vehicle to defer tax on income), the Mutual Investment Club of Detroit sought a means of allowing members to invest their IRAs in the club. To accommodate IRA requirements, Mutual had to arrange for an approved IRA custodian (bank or trust company) to become a member of the club. Further regulations required that member to be a limited partner. Mutual became a limited partnership in 1982 after more than forty years of operating with its original agreement.

The trustee of an IRA account (typically a bank) may only be a limited partner, and therefore has no voice in the management of the club. In a limited partnership, a general partner may own no more than 20 percent of all the general partnership units, while both limited and general partners are unrestricted in their ownership of limited partnership units.

When a partner wishes to establish an IRA account in the club, and the other members agree to it, the partnership agreement should be altered as shown in Figure 17-2.

If a member has an IRA or Keogh account in the club, he or she typically maintains a general partner account also. During the year members usually make deposits only to their general partner accounts. Since the trustee of the IRA or Keogh account probably charges a fee for each transaction, members try to limit the number of transactions they make in IRA or Keogh accounts. Some accumulate cash and make only one IRA or Keogh deposit per year. Others make deposits into their general partner account and transfer funds to the IRA or Keogh account annually.

If your club runs into problems in finding a bank to handle the trustee account, NAIC can put you in touch with a financial institution to perform the task. You may also consider using a regular or discount brokerage firm that provides this service (usually for a small annual fee).

Until recently it was very difficult to buy stock for your IRA account through a dividend reinvestment plan or NAIC's low-cost investment program. NAIC now has a simple low-cost way to make such purchases. Members will receive details upon request

IRA or Keogh accumulations can become substantial over time. One general partner of the Mutual Investment Club of Detroit Limited Partnership has invested $2,000 into his IRA limited partner account in the club every year since 1982. As of early 1992, his total IRA deposits of $22,000 had grown to $43,800, an average annual increase of more than 12 percent. If he manages to sustain this rate of growth, his IRA account will be worth $124,879 by the year 2000. His contributions by then will total $36,000.

As of early 1992, this same member's account included $9,534 in dividends and realized capital gains. If the Mutual Investment Club of Detroit had not become a limited partnership and therefore provided members the benefit of IRA or Keogh accounts, those dividends and capital gains would have been subject to federal income tax at that time and would not have still been in the account building future value.

Figure 17-2

Limited Partnership Agreement for the Mutual Investment Club of Detroit

Limited Partnership Agreement
of
Mutual Investment Club of Detroit Limited Partnership

THIS AGREEMENT OF LIMITED PARTNERSHIP, effective_____ (Date)_____ , by and between the undersigned as General Partners, to:

(Names of General Partners)

and_____ (Name)_____ Bank, Trustee of the Individual Retirement Trust Accounts, Master Trust agreement.

(If the Club is a new partnership, it would begin at paragraph 1, below. If it is a Club converting from a general to a limited partnership, it should include wording appropriate to the law of its own State similar to the following, through "NOW THEREFORE, IT IS AGREED.")

WHEREAS, the Mutual Investment Club of Detroit has been in existence as a general partnership for over forty-six (46) years and has executed numerous partnership agreements based upon various changes in partners, but such partnership has continued as one tax entity since its formation; and

WHEREAS, the partners of the Mutual Investment Club of Detroit desire to organize such partnership as a limited partnership as such term is defined by the Michigan Revised Uniform Limited Partnership Act, MCL 449.1101 *et seq.* and, therefore, the partners desire and hereby do cancel the previous partnership agreement but continue as the same tax entity.

NOW, THEREFORE, IT IS AGREED:

1. **Formation.** The undersigned hereby form a Limited Partnership (the "partnership") in, and in accordance with the laws of the State of Michigan. All partners shall be general partners except those admitted to serve as Trustees of IRA or Keogh Accounts on behalf of the general partners with such trustees to be referred to as "limited partners."

2. **Name.** The name of the partnership shall be: Mutual Investment Club of Detroit Limited Partnership.

(Paragraphs 3 through 5 of the preceding agreement would be unchanged.)

6. **Capital Contributions.** The partners may make capital contributions to the partnership on the date of each periodic meeting in such amounts as the partnership shall determine, provided, however, that no general partner's capital account shall exceed twenty percent (20%) of the capital accounts of all the general partners.

(Paragraphs 7 and 8 of the preceding agreement would be unchanged)

9. **Management.** Each general partner shall participate in the management and conduct of the affairs of the partnership in proportion to the value of his capital account. Except as otherwise determined, all decisions shall be made by the general partners whose capital accounts total a majority of the value of the capital accounts of all the general partners.

(Paragraphs 10 through 15 of the preceding agreement would be unchanged.)

16. **Additional Partners.** Additional partners may be admitted at any time, upon the unanimous consent of all the general partners, so long as the number of general partners does not exceed twenty (20).

By creating a limited partnership, club members are able to invest their IRAs and defer taxable income.

Figure 17-2 (Continued)

16A. **Transfers to a Trust.**   A general partner may, after giving written notice to the other general partners, transfer his interest in the partnership to a revocable living trust of which he is the grantor and sole trustee.

16B. **Removal of a Partner.**   Any partner may be removed by agreement of the general partners whose capital accounts total a majority of the value of all partners' capital accounts. Written notice of a meeting where removal of a partner is to be considered shall include a specific reference to this matter. The removal shall become effective upon payment of the value of the removed partner's capital account, which shall be in accordance with the provisions of full withdrawal of a partner noted in paragraphs 18 and 20.

16C. **Limited Partners.**   If any general partner establishes an IRA (under section 408 of the Internal Revenue Code), or Keogh, the trustee of such account may be admitted to the Partnership as a limited partner. No limited partner shall have the obligation or the right to participate in the management of the Partnership or in Partnership decisions, and shall have no liability with respect to partnership obligations, and the provisions of this Agreement relating specifically to General Partners shall not apply to Limited Partners. No general partner may own more than 20% of the value of all the general partners' capital accounts. Both general and limited partners are unrestricted in their purchase of limited partnership units. Unless otherwise required by law, Limited Partners shall not be counted as partners in applying the limitation on the number of partners allowed under this Agreement. Limited partners shall not have the power to grant the right to become a limited partner to an assignee of any part of the partnership interest.

17.   **Termination of Partnership.**   The partnership may be terminated by agreement of the general partners whose capital accounts total a majority in value of the capital accounts of all the general partners. Written notice of the meeting where termination of the partnership is to be considered shall include a specific reference to this matter. The partnership shall terminate upon a majority vote of all general partners' capital accounts. Written notice of the decision to terminate the partnership shall be given to all the general partners. Payment shall then be made of all the liabilities of the general partnership and a final distribution of the remaining assets, either in cash or in kind, shall promptly be made to the general partners or their personal representatives in proportion to each general partner's capital account.

(Paragraph 18 of the preceding agreement would be unchanged.)

19.   **Death or Incapacity of a General Partner.**   In the event of the death or incapacity of a general partner (or the death or incapacity of the grantor and sole trustee of a revocable living trust, if such trust is a general partner pursuant of Paragraph 16A hereof), receipt of notice of such an event shall be treated as notice of full withdrawal.

(Continue with the preceding agreement to paragraph 21B and at the end add:) No limited partner shall have the power to assign, transfer, pledge, mortgage or sell all or part of his interest in the partnership.

(After paragraph 21e continue:)

This Agreement of Limited Partnership hereby declared and shall be binding upon the respective heirs, executors, trustees, administrators and personal representatives of the parties.

The parties have caused this Agreement of Limited Partnership to be executed on the dates indicated below, effective on the date indicated above.

General Partners

Name:_____   Name:_____

Dated:_____   Dated:_____

Limited Partners

Name:_____   Name:_____

Dated:_____   Dated:_____

CHAPTER 18

WORKING WITH A BROKER

Picking the right broker is not always an easy task. You need to go about your search the same way you would if you were looking for an attorney, accountant, real estate agent, or other professional. Many factors contribute to your choice, but compatibility is the most important feature.

For new clubs, the cost factor looms particularly large. Even if costs are not a big concern, experienced investors inevitably end up working with a discount brokerage rather than a full-service firm, because they don't need the advice and, more to the point, they don't *want* to be pressured into decisions. Commission-based brokers often call their clients (including investment clubs) and promote a particular security—regardless of whether it would be a good purchase for the club or not.

As a first essential step, you need to find a broker who knows how clubs work and who is willing to advise you, rather than trying to push you into buying the brokerage firm's stock of the day.

Next, consider cost. Minimum commissions are often the same for both major discount and full-service brokers. Once you begin investing in larger blocks, the discounts become more significant.

An alternative is the "deep-discount" brokerage firm. The price gap between the deep-discounters and the rest of the brokerage business is widening. A survey by Mercer, Inc. lists 30 firms offering the lowest commissions on a number of different trades and is available for $34.95 from the firm at 80 Fifth Avenue, New York, NY 10011. What you need to know is this: If you are looking for modest commissions and don't care about brokerage advice, get comparisons from several brokerage firms and select the one offering the best bargain rates. Also look for firms offering flexible services, such as custodial accounts for IRAs.

Keep in mind two other avenues for keeping the costs of investing as low as possible. The first is to take advantage of a special program offered by several major full-service brokers. It's not advertised; you must ask whether it's available at a particular firm. Here's how it works: You mail in your money and your market order, and the order is executed at market opening the day after receipt. The firm's commission is prorated over the number of shares executed on behalf of program participants. As a result, it's impossible to know in advance what your exact cost will be. No service is offered with the program; you interact with a clerk, not a broker.

The second way to limit transaction costs is with NAIC's own Low-Cost Investment Plan, a boon to clubs with monthly receipts under $500. NAIC has joined the dividend reinvestment program of a number of corporations. You forward your money to an escrow agent in care of NAIC for investment in a particular company or companies. Once your first purchase of a certain stock has been made, you send future payments directly to the corporation's dividend reinvestment agent. NAIC's plan permits clubs to save as much as 10 percent in commissions the first year, an amount sufficient to spell the difference between profit and loss in many cases.

Here's the record of a four-year-old club that initially invested exclusively through NAIC's Low-Cost Investment Plan (Figure 18-1). As of early 1996, the group held twenty-two different securities. The club has been profitable since its beginning.

Figure 18-1
Harvestors Investment Club

Date	Cumulative Total Paid in by Members	Cumulative Total Value of Club	Total Paid out to Withdrawing Members
1-31-88	$ 460.00	$ 460.00	—
1-31-89	9,105.00	9,300.15	$ 604.69
1-31-90	17,365.00	18,831.46	2,103.93
1-31-91	27,510.00	29,591.12	3,264.34
1-31-92	37,795.00	52,402.43	8,326.26
1-31-93	18,193.63	88,893.36	11,000.00
1-31-94	21,489.13	109,957.86	5,670.57
1-31-95	17,599.07	158,790.41	16,354.52
1-31-96	28,338.49	168,843.57	18,642.66

In the fourth or fifth year of operation, a club may wish to move to a full-service broker to gain another perspective on the market, as well as to broaden investment choices. On the other hand, you might become more confident in your club's ability to make good decisions without the advice of a broker, and confirm your desire to remain with a deep-discount firm.

Whether you select a full-service or a discount firm, there are some procedures you will always have to follow. All members of the club have to sign an agreement when your account is opened. The agreement varies from firm to firm, but in all cases authorization must be given to the designated individuals to place buy and sell orders.

FULL-SERVICE BROKERS

If you select a full-service broker, remember the most essential and necessary element in the relationship: The broker *must* understand your investment philosophy and help you to achieve your goals. If the broker tries to force decisions on you, the relationship won't work.

As part of the relationship, your broker should be willing to provide your club with extra services not necessary for individual customers: custody of securities, dividend collection, and forwarding of stockholder notices. Some brokers want a service charge for these extras. The broker probably also expects that several, and possibly all, of your members will eventually open personal accounts with him or her.

Respect the broker's objectives. Remember, the broker is in business to make money. During the hours the market is open, brokers are consumed with placing buy and sell orders or soliciting such orders from customers. Ask if there is a particular time, either early morning or late afternoon, that is the best time to talk.

Also, out of respect for the broker's requirements, don't expect him or her to deal with more than one individual—usually the financial partner—on behalf of the club. About twenty-four hours before the club meeting, ask the broker for any recent information on stocks in your club's portfolio, as well as the stocks being studied for possible purchase.

Do not ask the broker what stock to buy; that is your club's decision. (However, once your decision has been made, you may wish to ask your broker's opinion before placing your order. If he or she has valid objections, you should listen carefully and then poll club members before proceeding.)

Information gained from your broker in advance of the meeting should be recorded and shared with club members before any investment actions are taken. As soon as possible after the meeting, the club's contact person should place the authorized order with the broker. Don't hesitate to call during trading hours with a buy or sell order. That is the best time. However, if you want to talk at length with your broker, wait until after hours and try to schedule such discussions in advance.

When your club has selected a stock to study, ask the broker for copies of Standard & Poor's or Value Line sheets.

REQUESTING MATERIAL

Be fair in requesting material from the full-service broker; help him or her minimize the expense of handling your account. There is no need to order more than the two to four Standard & Poor's sheets required for next month's reports. Ones you need later should be ordered when the material is current. Mail your sheet order request to your broker, and enclose a self-addressed stamped envelope.

You should never call the broker for prices; these are listed in *The Wall Street Journal* and other financial publications, as well as in the financial section of your local newspaper. Some computer services provide instant on-line prices.

Once you have made a purchase, your financial officer should transmit *one* check to your broker, having deposited members' payments in his personal account or the club's bank account. Be prompt; payment must reach the broker within three business days following issuance of the buy order. The broker is subject to a fine if he or she fails to require on-time payment. If you don't meet the deadline, your broker could be required to place your club on a restricted list and possibly be forced to collect funds from you in advance of accepting your orders.

Don't ask your broker to attend all your meetings; you are in business to learn by doing, not to defer to the opinions of others you consider to be more knowledgeable than yourself. Invite the broker to your annual meeting only. The broker should be asked to give you suggestions on your study program for the months ahead. However, remember that you started your club to make your own decisions with your fellow members. The broker should be asked only to comment generally, and should not be expected to assume responsibility for your investing success. That's your task.

REGISTRATION OF SECURITIES

The most practical form of registration currently available for your stock certificates is known as "street name." Under this form of registration, the broker establishes an account in the club's name, or in the name of an agent or agents specified by the club. Every month as the club purchases securities, they are registered in the broker's name or "street" form. He will submit to the club a monthly statement itemizing transactions and listing securities in the club's account. However, you won't receive stock certificates. This is the most convenient form of registration, because you won't have to safeguard certificates or pay to have them stored.

Dividend payments are sent directly to the broker and credited to your club account. Stockholder notices received by the broker, such as annual and quarterly reports and proxy statements, should be forwarded to you promptly.

Your club can receive annual and quarterly reports directly from corporate investor relations departments if you send a written request. Explain that your shares are held in street name, and that you will advise the company when you sell and ask to be removed from the mailing list.

When securities are held in street name, you are not allowed to participate in a corporation's dividend reinvestment program. To do so, you will have to ask your broker to deliver securities in the club's own name. When securities are registered in street name, you cannot physically hold your own stock certificates. However, the industry is moving toward electronic record keeping in the interest of cost reduction, and stock certificates are becoming arcane. The SEC has lent its support to this effort. Recently, a major brokerage firm began imposing a fee on clients who request that securities be registered and shipped to them in certificate form. The charge is $15 per certificate; when a single order is placed, the fee is capped at $30. This policy may accelerate the trend away from the use of stock certificates.

A new stock registration form is now awaiting an SEC go-ahead. It is referred to as the IRO (Individual Registration Option) and offers advantages to individuals and corporations. Under IRO the club's securities are registered in the club's name directly with the corporation. Certificates may be obtained at no cost from the corporation, and securities in IRO are eligible for dividend reinvestment plans. Securities can be released to the broker with a phone call. Corporation reports are mailed on time directly to the owner. Since the securities are directly registered with the corporation, no danger exists from the possible bankruptcy of the broker holding your securities in street form.

CHAPTER 19

CONDUCTING THE MONTHLY MEETING

*T*he monthly meeting is the focal point of club activity. Your group is a business and should be run like one, with the social aspects a necessary and important side element. Clubs that hold well-run, organized meetings consistently enjoy superior investment results—and that's not just coincidence. Success results from skillful organization and planning. NAIC has a video which shows how a model club meeting would be conducted. Contact NAIC with your request to show it to your group.

The presiding partner prepares club get-togethers and ensures that each meeting is run effectively. Members should come away from the meeting with a sense that the time they spend at club meetings is well spent. Participants should be allowed to express themselves without being pressured; the presiding partner should encourage open discussion and thoughtful consideration of all issues, while making sure business moves along at a good clip.

The meeting should be only as long as necessary to thoroughly cover all essential business. No one enjoys exhausting, long meetings. Except under the most unusual circumstances, two hours should be sufficient for taking care of business at the monthly meeting.

START PROMPTLY

The presiding partner should call the meeting to order at the appointed hour. Don't keep everyone waiting for a few stragglers. Reward the majority of your members for being there on time.

The presiding partner presents the agenda, including a list of specific items of old or new business that are to be covered. After reading the minutes of the last meeting, the financial partner presents each member with a copy of the club's current valuation statement and reviews highlights of his or her discussions with the club's broker. Any important comments concerning securities the club already owns or is considering for purchase should be explained and passed along to the members. Any stocks the broker has suggested will be identified and assigned to particular members for study, assuming the club wants to follow up on the recommendation.

The assistant presiding partner next calls upon each member following a stock in the club's portfolio to circulate any information he or she has gathered, including whether the Portfolio Management Guide shows that the stock is a candidate for purchase, holding, or sale.

Then members who have researched possible stocks to purchase present their findings. Each report should be prepared manually or by computer on a Stock Selection Guide (or, in the case of new clubs, a Stock Check List). Copies of the form should be distributed so that all members have a chance to review the analysis.

LET EVERYONE SEE

One option is to use a presentation-size Guide, if the Club has the capability of displaying it so that all can see. Remember, it's virtually impossible to assimilate all these figures unless the listener is also able to see them. If all members have equal access to the financial data, full discussion and better decision making will follow. As the members give their stock selection reports, an officer should record key data on each possible purchase on a giant Stock Comparison Guide. As an alternative, information can be collected in advance of the meeting and copies of a Stock Comparison Guide prepared for distribution to each member. If you do this, the Guide should not be made available until the reports are completed. Otherwise, some members won't listen carefully to the reports and will instead base their decision strictly on the data before them.

When all the different stock reports have been summarized on the form, other members are allowed to propose stocks previously studied but never purchased. However, original reports should be updated to include current data. At this point, the club is ready to make a decision on the best stock to purchase. It's helpful for the investment program leader to indicate which of the prospects ranks highest on the basis of each of the statistics. This emphasis helps members avoid the trap of buying the best report rather than the best stock.

Discourage members from making decisions for the wrong reasons. For example, some members of new clubs are intent on buying as many shares as possible, so they'll gravitate to the lowest-price stocks. In terms of value, low-price stocks could be expensive while higher-price stocks may offer considerably more for your money. Members should take into account not only new securities, but also previously considered securities.

VOTING

After a motion is made, the club is ready to vote. If the motion fails, additional motions are permitted until the club comes to a decision. Occasionally the club may take more than one action—buying two different securities for example, or buying one and selling one.

The important point is that the club should not consider any security that does not have an accompanying report. This minimizes the possibility of selecting stock based on emotion rather than reason and succumbing to "hot tips."

The presiding partner next opens the meeting to discussions of old and new business. During this time, the club's contact with NAIC should announce conventions, local Council meetings, and other items of interest. Also any annual reports received from NAIC should be passed along to the investment program head.

The assistant presiding partner then asks for suggestions for new companies or industries to be considered at the next meeting and makes assignments for the following month's stock study presentations. Each month, NAIC's *Better Investing* magazine features a stock to study. Many clubs automatically include this security in their review. The stock to study is not a recommendation, but NAIC's selection committee takes care to pick companies that have the prospect of doubling in five years.

It's not mandatory to act immediately; you can study the stock the following month. Sound company fundamentals are the key to investment success, not picking for price movement. So don't be too concerned about the precise timing of your decision.

After a year of operation, the club should update the Stock Selection Guides on securities in the portfolio and possibly look at fewer new companies as the club devotes more time to current holdings. As more and more funds go into the existing portfolio, it may be wise to spend time reviewing the entire portfolio. See the last section of Chapter 12 for a suggested procedure for an annual review of the total portfolio.

ENJOY THE MEETING

Once the formal business is concluded, club members can turn their attention to having a little fun—enjoying refreshments, talking informally, and getting to know each other better. Relaxing before going home helps you to end each meeting on a friendly basis.

You should welcome guests to your meetings, including prospective members as well as people who might want to form a club of their own. Some clubs appoint a Membership Committee responsible for identifying and attracting qualified people to the club. Both business and personal factors cause members to leave the group. Without replacements, the club will ultimately wither and die. If there's a waiting list of prospects, well and good; however, few clubs enjoy such a luxury. The best plan is to encourage people to attend more than one meeting, so they know the extent and type of effort required. This will also help current members and prospective members get to know each other and find out if they are compatible.

One person on the Membership Committee should be assigned to help each newly elected member become familiar with club procedures and tasks. The group suffers along with the newcomer who is left to fend for himself. Encourage new members to ask questions and make it easy for them to get answers.

New members should be encouraged to attend the classes your nearest NAIC Council has on the use of NAIC's stock study procedures. Your club may have one member who will spend time helping a new member complete an NAIC Stock Selection Guide and Report. Even in the most lively group, meetings tend to fall into a routine. As part of your collective goal to expand your investment knowledge, consider finding interesting guest speakers to address your club. Assign one club member the primary responsibility of enlisting a speaker every third or fourth meeting. Consider economists from local universities, financial writers in your area, bank executives, financial planners, stock market employees, and regulators, among others. Once you begin thinking about the range of prospective interesting speakers, you will probably be able to come up with an endless supply.

CHAPTER 20

KEEPING INTEREST HIGH

Keeping members interested may be the most challenging part of forming a club—perhaps even more difficult than earning a profit from your investments.

At the outset, everyone will be filled with enthusiasm. However, over time, particularly in a declining market, members' interest may flag. If you allow the club to dissolve at this crucial point, the potential to achieve long-term gains will vanish. In contrast, if club members can be persuaded to continue even during long down periods, you are virtually certain to purchase stocks at bargain prices and profit handsomely when prices move upward again.

Fortunately, there are countless ways to rekindle the spirit of members until the amount invested becomes large enough that everyone's attention remains focused. Involve all of the members; after you get to know everyone, you will know who is best suited for outside activities, such as a field trip or party. Your outside activities do not have to be related to investing, although a field trip to a financial institution such as a stock exchange could be very interesting.

EDUCATIONAL PROGRAMS

The most knowledgeable members are usually also the most committed to the club's continuing success. Look for every possible opportunity to increase the knowledge of all your club members. Encourage members to take night classes conducted by your local NAIC council, read newly published investment trade books, subscribe to market-oriented magazines, and seek out informative guest speakers to address meetings.

Invite each member to regularly read at least one business publication. *The Wall Street Journal, Barron's, Business Week, Forbes,* and *Fortune,* as well as NAIC's own magazine, *Better Investing,* are all good resources. NAIC recommends that everyone in your club read *Better Investing* as a matter of routine. Such features as "A Stock to Study" and "The Repair Shop" are invaluable educational tools for investment clubs.

Some clubs name a club economist who reports regularly but briefly to the membership on economic trends. If possible, the economist should be someone who will benefit professionally from the research—a purchasing agent or sales/marketing executive, for example. The economist should monitor the impact of economic trends on specific industries and companies, focusing on companies that the club either owns stock in or is considering.

For example, your club economist could develop up to eight reports on industries or companies worthy of consideration as potential investments. He or she may discuss the international and national economic outlook on a quarterly basis. Sources of data for the economist range from business publications of general interest to the monthly newsletters on economic matters published by leading banks. Government publications such as the Department of Commerce's *Survey of Current Business* are also useful.

NAIC RESOURCES

Many clubs set aside a fifteen- or twenty-minute period in every meeting for instruction. This book offers a wealth of material appropriate for mini-lessons; the chapters on investment philosophy, the Stock Selection Guide, and portfolio management can keep you busy for months. Appendix D, "Sources of Further Information," can serve as a springboard for volunteers to prepare and present commentaries on subjects of special interest to them.

One or more members should plan to attend the annual National Investors Congress of NAIC. This meeting offers all investment clubs a great forum to exchange ideas; it also provides you the chance to meet with many other investment club organizers and members. Conversations with fellow investment club members from across the country are always one of the more pleasant and instructive side benefits of attendance. The Congress is always held in a major city, so attendance can also serve as a vacation for you and your family. For club members who are computer-oriented, the annual CompuFest will provide a host of ideas.

You may also think about entering your club's investing record in NAIC's Annual Performance Survey. (See each year's May edition of *Better Investing*.) After you have been notified of your ranking, compare your portfolio with those of the winning clubs. If you use a computer, you can project what your continued deposits plus compounded earnings will be worth five, ten, fifteen, or even twenty years ahead.

NAIC COUNCILS

If an NAIC Council operates in your area, we encourage you and your fellow members to attend the annual Investors Fair. This event includes presentations from four or five companies of different sizes. You will have the chance to talk one-on-one with corporate officials in companies whose stock you might consider buying.

Each January issue of *Better Investing* lists all Investors Fairs for the year. You may wish to attend not only the fair in your own community, but all other fairs within your state or close by. One member might enjoy the assignment of attending all Council meetings and reporting back to the club. Most of the meetings are devoted to NAIC stock study and portfolio tools. New members in experienced clubs could find Council attendance particularly helpful.

You may also consider inviting a Council leader to attend one of your meetings to critique your portfolio and your procedures.

OTHER RESOURCES FOR EDUCATION

Following are some additional ideas for you and your fellow club members to improve your investment knowledge base:

Invite your broker to your annual meeting to discuss your holdings and evaluate the club's current investment opportunities.

Go on a field trip to the broker's office. Take an after-trading-hours tour of the premises to discover how your orders are processed and to become familiar with resources available in the library.

If you live in or near a city with a stock exchange, or if you can arrange a visit to one, take advantage of the visitors gallery to learn first-hand how the market works.

Arrange a visit to a local company in which you own shares, to see first-hand the people who work in supplying the company's product or service.

Designate a member to attend the annual meeting of a local company in which you have invested and to report back on management's message, business discussed and voted on, opportunities or problems brought up and reported on, and questions raised by other stockholders.

Take a field trip to your local library, and let the business department head review available references for investors.

If there is a chapter of the Financial Analysts Federation in or near your community, call and ask about upcoming meetings. You may be allowed to attend as a guest and learn meaningful information about companies of interest to your club. You will be interested in hearing the questions investment professionals pose to management.

Invite as a guest speaker an experienced member from a successful club with a significantly longer operating history than your own. Ask him or her for a critique of your portfolio.

Ask a local economist, banker, company executive, or college professor to visit your club to discuss the regional, national, and international economic outlook. Also invite a corporate representative to discuss his or her company and industry.

OTHER ACTIVITIES

Invite a friend to visit your club. If there are no openings in your club, express your willingness to help your friend get a new club launched.

Become pen-pals with an overseas investment club, either in Europe or in the Pacific Rim. Arrangements can be made through NAIC and overseas associations.

Publish an annual report, including the year-end evaluation statement; members' names, addresses, and phone numbers; and the club's operating agreement. Distribute it to families of members, friends, your broker, and any acquaintances who have expressed an interest in investment clubs.

Hold your annual meeting at a special location such as an elegant restaurant or meeting hall.

Stage one or two special events during the year, such as a Christmas party or summer picnic, and invite nonmember friends and family.

Hold an annual retreat for a day or a weekend to let members review the club's performance away from daily distractions. Establish goals for the coming year. At subsequent retreats, review the club's attainment of prior goals before setting new ones.

Initiate an investment competition for a set time period with an established sum of imaginary money. Give a prize to the member achieving the greatest profit.

Award a prize to the member who picked the most profitable investment of the year. Give another award to the member who did the most during the year to further the club's goals.

Sponsor an annual guessing game to allow members to forecast the Dow Jones averages, club results, gross domestic product, and any other statistics of interest. Reward the best guesser.

Stage a joint cocktail party with one or more other investment clubs.

Have one meeting per year for a purely social pursuit.

Consider contributing one month's contributions to a charity or toward participation in a local social event rather than investing the money. If you come up with an especially fun alternative, write to the Editor of *Better Investing*. Your idea may be featured in the magazine and benefit clubs nationwide.

As you can see, there are many ways to keep up the interest in your club. The very best way of all, of course, is to obtain superior investment results. To review, here are a few guidelines for creating a successful club:

- Follow a structured yet flexible agenda.
- Set goals, both short- and long-term, and track the club's performance toward achieving them.
- Require involvement of all members.
- Reward member participation.
- Support the continuing education of all members.
- Maintain a disciplined approach to stock study and selection and to portfolio management procedures.
- Think creatively: "How can we continue to meet the needs of our club?"
- Encourage member involvement in Council activities and national NAIC Congresses.
- Promote a spirit of enthusiasm, excitement, and enjoyment.
- Use available aids such as computers, videotapes, and overhead projectors to facilitate member participation and understanding.

CHAPTER 21

RECORD KEEPING

One of the first tasks for your newly formed club is setting up the books. You need to come up with a system to track every cash transaction and to calculate every member's share of the whole. You can accomplish this important task in four ways:

1. By hand, with one or more club members using NAIC's *Accounting Manual* and prepared forms.

2. Electronically, with one or more members using NAIC Club Accounting Software.

3. By hiring an outside bookkeeper or accountant to maintain the books for the club.

4. By using a combination of 1 and 3, with an outside service doing the monthly valuation statement and members' records and a club member keeping cash records.

Under each of these alternatives, the financial partner is ultimately responsible for club record keeping—even if that means only overseeing everyone else's reports. The financial partner might also work with a co-treasurer or assistant.

We recommend, in the interest of protecting yourself as well as the club, that every member of the group be somewhat familiar with the process of record keeping. Every member should also be prepared to audit the work of the financial partner if asked to do so. The NAIC Council nearest you offers periodic programs on record keeping and tax reporting. At the very least, the club's financial partner and members of the audit committee should attend these sessions.

This discussion of record keeping is aimed at all members of the club and deals only with the valuation of members' interests. For a more complete explanation of club accounting, study NAIC's *Accounting Manual*. NAIC's Club Accounting Software is designed to be used with the *Accounting Manual*.

GETTING A TAX IDENTIFICATION NUMBER

The first step is getting your Tax Identification Number. Write or phone the nearest U.S. Treasury office and ask for Form SS-4. This is a simple information card that asks for officer names, addresses, and Social Security numbers, as well as the name of your club. You will then be assigned a Tax Identification Number, which is used on all tax filings. You also need to provide the number to your broker and the transfer agents for the securities your club buys. All security transactions and all dividend income received are reported to the IRS under this number. When individual members report their share of income on their individual tax returns, the Tax Identification Number is included so that the reported amounts can be cross-referenced to the club's return.

We recommend the *unit value system* for keeping track of members' proportionate equity in the club. At first review, the system may seem unnecessarily complicated to new clubs. But when you compare it with other methods, you will ultimately agree that this is the most accurate and reliable method to use.

You might wonder, "Why do we have to go through complex calculations when all the members contribute the same amount each month?" In virtually every club there comes a time when one or more members will want to make a more substantial contribution than the minimum amount required. The unit value system permits this and allows the larger contributor to remain in the club with all members' interests fairly valued.

The system allows for flexibility. When a member wants to withdraw funds, the unit value system enables you to calculate and reset proportionate shares without trouble. Likewise, a member might not be able to make a contribution every month; you need a system that allows adjustment of proportionate ownership in a way that is accurate and fair to all.

The unit value system also permits the club to accept a new member at any time without requiring him or her to make a lump-sum payment to match the funds already contributed by long-time members. You have to realize that, for several reasons, you won't be able to maintain identical share values between all members. With this system in use, your club can attract and retain all the members you want without imposing a financial barrier.

CLUB ACCOUNTING IS DIFFERENT

The valuation of an investment club member's interest is different from valuation in other businesses, because the worth of club assets is constantly fluctuating due to stock market changes. In addition, most clubs are partnerships, so each person owns part of the total assets rather than shares of stock, as in a corporation. All of the assets must be valued whenever members deposit additional funds, which is monthly in most clubs. Each member's account consists of two parts: the accumulation of cash deposits and a valuation record of his or her deposits, which includes the sum of profits and losses.

Preparation of a *Valuation Statement* is the first step in valuing new capital deposited in the club. This statement lists the assets of the club at their market value as of the valuation date. As a convenience to the financial partner—or out of necessity, if an outside accountant or bookkeeper is being used—the Valuation Statement customarily is prepared several days before the membership meeting. Most clubs base valuation on the closing price of listed securities, or the bid price of over-the-counter securities. Sample statements are shown later in this chapter.

TWO METHODS

You can develop a record of each member's interest in one of two ways. Under the first method, each member's account is credited or debited with the proportionate amount of value change in the club's assets since the last statement. An example of this method appears in Figure 21-1.

The total value of the club and members' accounts as of January 21 is $43,652.45. The club's Valuation Statement total for the February meeting is $42,925.54. During the month since the January valuation, the club's asset value dropped $726.91. This decline is distributed to the members based on each one's proportionate financial interest in the club.

In the illustration, column 1 lists the balances forward, from column 6 on the previous month's Valuation Statement. Column 2 translates the figures

Figure 21-1

Member	(1) Value of Acct., Jan. 21	(2) % of Total Value	(3) Distribution of (Decrease) or Increase in Value	(4) Member's New Balance	(5) Deposited This Month	(6) Member's Balance, End of Feb. 28 Meeting
Adam	$ 5,456.56	12.5	$ (90.86)	$ 5,365.70	$ 10.00	$ 5,375.70
Mary	6,782.40	15.5	(112.69)	6,669.71	20.00	6,689.71
Charlotte	5,456.56	12.5	(90.86)	5,365.70	10.00	5,375.70
David	5,456.56	12.5	(90.86)	5,365.70	10.00	5,375.70
Edward	6,221.10	14.3	(103.94)	6,117.16		6,117.16
Frances	3,015.14	6.9	(50.16)	2,964.98	50.00	3,014.98
Georgiana	4,627.42	10.6	(77.05)	4,550.37	30.00	4,580.37
Harry	6,636.71	15.2	(110.49)	6,526.22	20.00	6,546.22
	$43,652.45	100.0	$(726.91)	$ 42,925.54	$150.00	$ 43,075.54

in column 1 into percentages of the total. Column 3 distributes the loss of $726.91 by applying the percentages obtained in column 2. Column 4 is the sum of columns 1 and 3. Column 5 lists the members' deposits made at the February 28 meeting. Column 6 is the sum of columns 4 and 5 and represents the new balance forward, to be transferred to column 1 in March.

With this method, each member can see what he or she would receive if the club were liquidated as of the valuation date.

Most clubs prefer the second method, because fewer calculations are required. This is the method described in the Club Accounting Kit and used in the computer program. With this method, you establish a "unit of value" for determining ownership in the club. This amount is typically $10. Each new deposit made by a member is valued to reflect the changes from the prior deposit.

Each member's account consists of a record of cash deposited and "valuation units" credited to his or her account. Any member's liquidating value can be readily computed at any time by multiplying the member's total valuation units by the established dollar value of a unit.

Let's look at an illustration. Assume that a club has twelve members. At the initial meeting, each member invests $10. The valuation unit is set at $10, so each member is credited with 1 valuation unit. When a member invests $20, he or she receives 2 additional valuation units; an investment of $25 will bring 2.5 additional valuation units.

This method eliminates the need to compute percentages, since cash, whether earned from investments or newly deposited, is assigned a value based on the unit size—$10 in our example. To determine the total proportionate value of any account at any time, simply divide the number of units in the account by the total units held by the club.

Another way to look at the valuation unit method is to apply it to market buying power. When a stock is selling for $10 a share, you can buy one share with one unit of the same value. When the stock rises to $11, however, the regular contribution is not enough to purchase a whole share; your $10 will buy only .909 shares ($10 divided by $11). You can't actually buy fractional shares in the market; you and your fellow club members will pool your funds to make full-share purchases. We raise this point only to illustrate how the unit value system simplifies the tracking of proportionate ownership in the club for each member—even when different amounts are contributed over time.

The Valuation Statement assigns a varying portion of a valuation unit in return for the fixed sum invested; the portion changes as contributions vary *and* as market values grow or shrink.

SAMPLE STATEMENTS

The first Valuation Statement for a twelve-member club might look like the one shown in Figure 21-2. The statement reflects the club's condition at the

Figure 21-2

Investment Club 600 Valuation Statement Prepared July 12, 199x, for Club Meeting July 19, 199x

Company	No. of Shares	Cost per Share	Total Cost	Price per Share This Date	Total Value
Moore Steel Co.	20	$5.58	$111.55	$5.125	$102.50
Cash on hand					8.45
Total value of club this date					$110.95
Total number of valuation units to date					12.00

(This is the number of units at the beginning of the July meeting)

Value of each unit this date ($110.95 ÷ 12 units) $9.25

Number of units each $10.00 deposited at July 19 meeting
  will purchase ($10.00 ÷ $9.25) 1.081

Figure 21-3

Investment Club 600 Valuation Statement Prepared August 9, 199x, for Club Meeting August 16, 199x

Company	No. of Shares	Cost per Share	Total Cost	Price per Share This Date	Total Value
Moore Steel Co.............20		$5.58	$111.55	$5.50	$110.00
XG Products, Inc..........22		4.91	108.15	4.25	93.50
Cash on hand...					20.30
Total value of club this date					$223.80
Total number of valuation units to date...					24.972*
Value of one unit ($223.80 ÷ 24.972)..					$8.96
Number of units $10.00 purchases ($10.00 ÷ $8.96)					1.116
Members' total investment					$240.00

* The "total number of valuation units to date" of 24.972 is derived as follows:

Valuation units as of beginning of July meeting...	12.000
12 members deposit $10.00 each at July meeting, each purchasing 1.081 units (12 × 1.081)...	12.972
Total units at beginning of August meeting...	24.972

beginning of the second meeting. Each $10 paid in by members at the second meeting will purchase 1.081 valuation units in the club. Assuming that every member pays in $10, 1.081 units will be added to each member's account, making a total of 2.081 units for each member (without calculating any value changes from invested fund profits) and 24.972 units for the entire club. To determine the value of one unit, divide the total value of the club by the total number of valuation units in the club.

Assuming all members of the club make another investment at the second meeting, the Valuation Statement at the beginning of the third meeting would appear as in Figure 21-3.

Maintain a record of both the total number of valuation units in the partnership and the total number of units owned by each member. You will need to keep total club figures on one sheet and set up a separate sheet for each member's account value.

CONVERTING TO THE UNIT VALUE SYSTEM

Many clubs that have operated under a different procedure may decide to convert to the unit value system. Here is NAIC's recommended procedure for converting:

1. Prepare a Valuation Statement as shown in this chapter.

2. Divide the total value of the Valuation Statement by $10, and take the quotient as the number of valuation units in the club.

3. Allocate these valuation units to your members.

   a. When everyone has an equal interest, divide the total number of valuation units by the total number of members to determine the valuation units for each member.

   b. When interests are unequal, calculate the percentage of the value of each member's account to the total value of the club. Determine the number of each member's valuation units by applying his or her percentage of ownership to the total number of valuation units.

4. After determining the total number of valuation units for the club and the number for each member, with the unit value set at $10, calculate this month's receipts. For each $10 received, add one valuation unit to each member's account and to the grand total.

5. For future meetings, divide the total of your liquidating statement by the new total of valuation units, determining the value of one unit. Divide $10 by the new unit value; the resulting figure will be the number of units that $10 will purchase at the next meeting.

MAINTAINING CONSISTENT RECORDS

The financial partner can verify the consistency of club accounts by confirming that the sum of all the individual records matches the total shown in the *Valuation Units Control Ledger* (Figure 21-4). The Valuation Units Control Ledger records on one sheet all members' actual cash deposits in the club and the members' total number of valuation units.

The first three rows represent regular deposits by members.

The information listed in columns 1–4 is recorded before the meeting from the Valuation Statement. Some clubs show the statement date in column 1; others list the meeting date; and some clubs list both dates, since only columns 2, 3, and 4 reflect data as of the Valuation Statement date. The remaining columns represent actual contributions received from members at the meeting.

Row 4 shows how club records might appear after a year of operation, shortly before you record the annual distribution of earnings.

Figure 21-4

FORM 1 DATE	2 VALUATION STATEMENT TOTAL	3 UNIT VALUE	4 NO. UNITS $10.00 OR $ PURCHASES	5 TOTAL PAID IN THIS MONTH	6 MEMBERS' ORIGINAL INVESTMENT	7 MEMBERS' ORIGINAL INVESTMENT PLUS EARNINGS DISTRIBUTED BY PARTNERSHIP	8 UNITS PURCHASED THIS MONTH	9 TOTAL UNITS
VALUATION UNITS CONTROL LEDGER								
(1) 6-21-9X	—	10.00	1.000	120.00	120.00	120.00	12.000	12.000
(2) 7-19-9X	110.95	9.25	1.081	120.00	240.00	240.00	12.972	24.972
(3) 8-16-9X	223.80	8.96	1.116	120.00	360.00	360.00	13.392	38.364
(4) 12-20-9X	749.79	9.86	1.014	120.00	840.00	840.00	12.168	88.236
THIS IS THE DATE THE VALUATION STATEMENT WAS PREPARED OR DATE OF THE CLUB MEETING	THIS IS THE TOTAL CLUB VALUE AS SHOWN ON THE MONTHLY VALUATION STATEMENT	THIS IS THE AMOUNT IN COL. (2) ÷ TOTAL IN (9) FROM PRECEDING MONTH	THIS IS THE RESULT OF DIVIDING $10 BY THE ENTRY IN COL.(3)	THIS IS THE ACTUAL CASH PAID IN BY THE MEMBERS	THIS IS THE ACCUMULATED TOTAL OF ACTUAL CASH PAID IN BY MEMBERS	THIS IS THE SAME AS COL. (6) UNTIL THE FIRST DISTRIBUTION OF CLUB EARNINGS TO MEMBERS	COL.(5) ENTRY (120.00 + $10=12 (2.) 12X 1.014 FROM COL. (4)=12.168	THE SUM OF THE LAST ENTRY OF COL. (8) AND THE PREVIOUS ENTRY IN THIS COLUMN
TO RECORD DISTRIBUTION OF LOSS FOR YEAR OF $11.88 OR $.1346 PER UNIT AS FOLLOWS:								
(5) 12-31-9X	857.01	9.71	1.029	—	840.00	828.12	(1.224)	87.012
VALUATION	$857.01	$10.00			$840.00 − $11.88	FROM DIST. OF EARNINGS		88.236 LESS
TOTAL AT	÷	÷				SHEET		1.224
12-31-9X	88.236	9.71				$11.88 ÷ 9.71 = 1.224		87.012
TO RECORD DISTRIBUTION OF 199X EARNINGS TOTALING $348.92 OR $.4538 PER UNIT								
(6) 12-31-9X+4	10648.37	13.85	0.722	—	7400.00	8075.34	25.193	7940.28
(7) 3-18-9X+5 (TOTALS BEFORE WITHDRAWAL OF FRANK VESTOR)					8760.00	9435.34		878.964
(8) 3-18-9X+5 (WITHDRAWAL OF FRANK VESTOR)						411.40	(32.965)	845.999
(9) 3-18-9X+5 (NEW BALANCES)					7600.00	9023.94		845.999

Row 5 demonstrates the distribution of the loss at the end of the first year. The earnings are assigned to each member's account since the income (loss) is taxable (deductible) and must be reported by the individual members on their personal tax returns. As long as a member leaves the account money on deposit, it is treated as part of his or her tax-paid invested capital—assuming that member has reported the profits on his or her tax return and paid taxes on them.

Row 6 shows distributed earnings of $348.92 added to column 7. This column represents total cash invested in the club by partners plus realized earnings left in the club after payment of taxes.

The earnings of $348.92, divided by the unit value from column 3, $13.85, reflects a total of 25.193 valuation units being purchased by the year's total earnings. The 25.193 units are recorded in column 8 and added to create a new total in column 9.

The distribution of earnings is divided among all the members in proportion to their investment in the club. The next chapter describes a convenient form and procedure for making this distribution.

After row 6 is completed, you calculate a new unit value for funds deposited by members at the meeting based on the December 25 statement. This is done by dividing the total liquidating value by the new unit total of 794.028. Entries corresponding to those in the Valuation Units Control Ledger are made in each Individual Valuation Units Ledger, as shown in Figure 21-5, line 7 for Frank N. Vestor.

Each partnership club is required by tax law to distribute taxable income to members at the end of each calendar year. While most members do not withdraw that income, once taxes are paid on it, it becomes part of their tax-paid investment in the club. The distribution of units is not required by law.

Row 8 of the Control Ledger illustrates the withdrawal of funds by a member. He withdraws 32.965 units worth $12.48 each at the time, for a total of $411.40. Tax regulations require that the tax base be reduced by the value withdrawn, which in this case is $411.40 in cash. The "Members' Original Investment" column (column 6) is a historical record, and we suggest that this record be left intact. You should not use the withdrawal to adjust the original deposit amount.

For partial withdrawals, no tax liability is incurred until the member has drawn out more than his or her tax-paid investment in the club.

Figure 21-5

INDIVIDUAL VALUATION UNITS LEDGER

NAME FRANK N. VESTOR   5478 Sixth Street, Detriot, MI 48225

	DATE PAID	UNIT VALUE	NO. UNITS $10.00 OR $ PURCHASES	PAID IN THIS MONTH	TOTAL PAID IN TO DATE	TOTAL PAID IN TO DATE INCLUDING SAVINGS REINVESTED	VALUATION UNITS PURCHASED THIS DATE	TOTAL VALUATION UNITS
(1)	6-21-9X	10 00	10 00	1 0-	1 0-	1 0-	10 00	10 00
(2)	7-19-9X	9 25	10 81	1 0-	2 0-	2 0-	10 81	20 81
(3)	8-16-9X	8 96	11 16	1 0-	3 0-	3 0-	11 16	31 97
(4)	12-20-9X	9 84	10 16	1 0-	7 0-	7 0-	10 16	73 53
	To record distribution of loss for year of $11.88 or $.1246 per unit as follows							
	7.353 units x $.1346 equals total loss of $.99 per member							
(5)	12-31-9X			(99)	7 0-	69 01	(0.102)	72 51
(6)	1-15-9X+2	9 81	10 19	1 0-	32 0-	343 52	10 19	329 65
	To record distribution of 199X+4 earnings at rate of $.4530 per unit							
(7)	12-31-9X+4			37 04	68 0-	929 69	2.674	842 98
(8)	3-18-9X+5 (Total before withdrawal)				75 0-	999 69		893 71
(9)	3-18-9X+5 (Withdrawal of 32.965 units)					(411 40)		(32.965)
(10)	3-18-9X+5 (Total after withdrawal)				75 0-	588 29		564 06

TAX CONSEQUENCES OF PAYING IN CASH OR STOCK

A member withdrawing either all or part of his or her account value may be paid in cash or stock. The tax consequences of how a departing member is paid off should be taken into consideration. IRS rules differ depending on whether the withdrawal is full or partial. See NAIC's *Accounting Manual* and Chapter 22 of this book for details about these rules and recommended methods for handling the transaction.

The transfer of stock is advantageous to both club and member if the member is making a full withdrawal. The club writes off the stock at the value of the member's account rather than the cost of the security. Since this is not a taxable transaction, this method is becoming increasingly popular. A letter to the broker stating the time of transfer, number of shares, and name of the member is all that's required. If the withdrawing member wants cash, he or she merely instructs the broker to sell. The club liquidating statement upon which the value of the withdrawal is calculated should be of the same date as the letter to the broker authorizing the transfer.

When the withdrawing member sells the stock, the tax basis of the stock is not what the club paid for it, but the part of the member's tax basis in the club ascribed to the withdrawal.

Some clubs seek out people, either present members or new members, who are willing to buy the departing member's interest in the club. These individuals pay enough into the club to cover the amount that the club will pay the withdrawing member. The newcomer should never pay money directly to the member leaving the club.

As another alternative, clubs may accept sufficient funds from present or new members so that the club itself pays the withdrawing member.

Only in the first case, when a club sells securities it owns to pay a withdrawing member, does a tax liability arise for the remaining members. The club fares best, tax-wise, by selling stocks with a loss and transferring stocks held at a profit. Withdrawing members are liable in all instances for any profit in their accounts, although they do not assume tax liability for shares transferred to them until they elect to sell them.

Most clubs have no stipulations on the frequency or amount of partial withdrawals that its members are allowed to make. While the vast majority of club members look on their contributions as a means of long-term savings, an occasional need will arise for cash. Normally, the same requirements of notice and fee apply to both partial and complete withdrawals.

NO LUMP SUM REQUIRED OF A NEW MEMBER

When a new partner joins the club, no large initial deposit is needed to catch up with other members. Under the unit valuation plan, the new member may make the same or a similar monthly contribution as other members. The valuation unit determined each month will relate the value of his or her holdings to those of other members; of course, a new member's value will be considerably lower than the value of long-standing members.

HELP FROM NAIC

NAIC's Club Accounting Software is designed to help anyone with a PC become a full-fledged club treasurer. At least 512 KB of RAM is needed, but 640 KB is recommended. A hard disk is also advised, but a minimum of 720 KB of disk storage will suffice. The software supports CGA, Hercules, EGA, and VGA monitors, as well as both color and monochrome. Any Hewlett-Packard LaserJet, Epson-compatible printer, or wide-carriage printer may be used. For further information, contact NAIC, P.O. Box 220, Royal Oak, MI 48068, ATTN: Computer Software.

Consultants willing to keep club books advertise in *Better Investing.* They are also known to officers of NAIC's regional councils and, in some cases, to NAIC headquarters. These services charge as little as $7 per month, plus any costs such as faxing reports. For further information, contact NAIC headquarters.

CHAPTER 22

REPORTING TAXABLE INCOME

*T*ax reporting is a chore for every individual, corporation, and partnership. It requires keeping complete, meticulous records, comprehending endless forms and regulations, and meeting deadlines. Investment clubs, like other entities, have to be aware of the tax rules that apply to them and to their members.

Comprehensive instructions on tax computation and reporting requirements can be found in NAIC's *Accounting Manual.* Our purpose here is to introduce you to the overall tax and reporting requirements you assume when you start an investment club.

At the end of each taxable year, a partnership calculates the profit earned during the year. It does not pay federal income taxes, but reports the overall results to the IRS, as well as each member's portion of the total. This applies to income from dividends, interest, and capital gains. Club members are personally liable for payment of their share of the club's income.

One rule that many people have trouble understanding is the difference between *profit* and *withdrawal.* As a partnership, your club is only the conduit for the collective transactions of all members. If it earns profits through dividends, interest, and capital gains, those are divided up and reported according to each person's share of the total. You are liable for the taxes on your share.

For example: Let's say that no one in your club withdraws any money during the year. You all agree to leave your earnings on account to reinvest. You are still taxed on your share of the profits; just because you didn't withdraw those profits doesn't mean you can get around paying taxes on them. The same rule applies if you withdraw more than you earn in any one year. Suppose that last year your share of club earnings was $400, but you have accumulated a fairly large amount of money over the years, so you withdraw $5,000. You are only taxed this year on your $400 earnings. The $5,000 withdrawal is a different matter. The sum of deposits you have made in the club plus earnings you have paid taxes on is your tax basis in the club. Any withdrawal less than your tax basis is tax free. Any amount over your tax basis is taxed as a long-term capital gain as long as the club is more than one year old. Most states that collect an income tax duplicate the federal rules to some degree, although some states have different rules for reporting income. Be sure to check with your state taxing agency for any special rules. Also, the rules for taxation and treatment of withdrawals applies to individual accounts only. If your investment club account is part of an IRA or other tax-deferred retirement account, special penalties and taxes may apply to withdrawals.

FILING REQUIREMENTS

Partnerships must file tax forms 1065 and K-1 for each member.

When the club's income is calculated, it is divided among the members based on their proportionate shares. Because members hold interests of varying amounts and the club income falls into two different tax classes, this process requires a number of computations. Investment club income typically comes from two sources:

1. Dividends from securities owned by the club.
2. Capital gains from sales of securities.

Some clubs may also have interest income, which must be accounted for separately.

The dividend income is taxable as ordinary income. If your club had both short-term gains and short-term losses during the year, they are combined, and only the net short-term gain, if any, will be taxed as ordinary income. As this edition is written, long-term capital gains are taxable as ordinary income, at a maximum tax rate of 28 percent; this—like all tax rules—is subject to change in the future, so check with your tax advisor before filing your returns. Long-term gains and losses are netted and reported as a single item.

In the *Earnings Distribution Statement* that follows (Figure 22-1), one member—Fred Hill—withdrew part of his funds during the year. Fred's withdrawal has been subtracted from the taxable income for the year to determine the remaining taxable amount for each member.

The importance of such an adjustment becomes increasingly evident as the amount withdrawn grows larger. Consider a case where several members withdraw all of their capital. Without this adjustment, the remaining partners have to pay taxes on earnings that were distributed to other partners. They would consequently pay far more taxes than they should.

To prepare the Distribution Statement, list all of the partners' names in column 1. In the next column, copy the number of valuation units listed in each partner's account from the Individual Valuation Units Ledger. The total of column 2 should be the same as the total number of valuation units shown in your Valuation Units Control Ledger.

The illustrated *Income and Expense Statement* (Figure 22-2) provides the figures to be placed on the Earnings Distribution Statement row 9. Total dividend income is listed at $279.15, short-term capital gains at $45.25, long-term capital gains at $202.93, total expenses at $161.17, and net profit at $366.16.

FRED HILL'S CALCULATION

Fred Hill made his partial withdrawal on November 26. The distribution of income and expenses to his withdrawal is shown in row 10. The club calculated and recorded these figures on Fred's Individual Valuation Units Ledger at the time he made his withdrawal. To calculate these items for Fred, take the sum of each item at the time of his withdrawal and divide it by the total number of valuation units in the club. The result is the amount per unit. Then multiply these answers by the number of units Fred withdrew, to determine the total of each. The remaining balances to be distributed are shown in row 12 of the Distribution Statement. If more than one withdrawal had been made during the year, each one would be listed and deducted from the taxable income for the year in row 10. Only the earnings that remain to be distributed to current members would be shown in row 11.

You are now ready to calculate the total profit per valuation unit (column 7, row 12), derived by dividing the adjusted net profit for the year—$348.92 (column 7 total)—by the total number of valuation units—768.835 (column 2). The total profit per unit is $0.4538. Since this figure includes

Figure 22-1
Earnings Distribution Statement

(1)	(2) No. of Valuation Units	(3) Dividends	(4) Short-Term Capital Gains	(5) Long-Term Capital Gains	(6) Total Club Expenses	(7) Year's Net Profit	(8) Val Units Purchased If Profit Is Held
(9) Taxable income for year		$279.15	$45.25	$202.93	$161.17	$366.16	
(10) Partial withdrawal by Fred Hill on Nov. 26		8.83	2.19	9.94	3.72	17.24	
(11) Taxable income remaining to be distributed		$270.32	$43.06	$192.99	($157.45)	$348.92	
Bob Smith	63.510	22.33	3.56	15.94	(13.01)	28.82	2.081
Arthur Black	63.510	22.33	3.56	15.94	(13.01)	28.82	2.081
Mary Brown	63.510	22.33	3.56	15.94	(13.01)	28.82	2.081
Paul Hill	63.510	22.33	3.56	15.94	(13.01)	28.82	2.081
Lilly Hill	52.111	18.32	2.90	13.11	(10.65)	23.68	1.709
Rosilyn Rhodes	63.510	22.33	3.56	15.94	(13.01)	28.82	2.081
Joe Rodgers	63.510	22.33	3.56	15.94	(13.01)	28.82	2.081
Faye Dearson	63.510	22.33	3.56	15.94	(13.01)	28.82	2.081
Donald Luis	63.510	22.33	3.56	15.94	(13.01)	28.82	2.081
Nellie Neil	63.510	22.33	3.56	15.94	(13.01)	28.82	2.081
Ed Echels	63.510	22.33	3.56	15.94	(13.01)	28.82	2.081
Frank Vestor	81.624	28.70	4.56	20.48	(16.70)	37.04	2.672
TOTAL	768.835	$270.32	$43.06	$192.99	($157.45)	$348.92	25.193
(12) Per unit		.3516	.0560	.2510	(.2048)	.4538	

Value of unit before distribution $13.85

Value of unit after distribution $13.41

Figure 22-2
Investment Club 671
Income and Expense Statement
January 1, 199x thru December 31, 199x

INCOME:

Dividends	$279.15	
Sale of securities:		
Net short-term	45.25	
Net long-term	202.93	
Total income		$527.33

EXPENSE:

Expenses of delegates to NAIC Convention	$65.72	
Dues to National Association of Investment Clubs	19.50	
Postage, paper, and supplies	25.31	
Subscriptions to business publications	35.00	
Miscellaneous	15.64	
Total expense		161.17
Net profit		$366.16

income from dividends, short-term capital gains, and long-term capital gains as well as expenses to be deducted from taxable income, it's necessary to break it down to these items. The IRS does not permit partnerships to report just "net" income or loss.

In columns 3, 4, 5, and 6 you follow the same procedure. The column total is divided by the total number of valuation units to get the total per unit. Round the answer to the fourth decimal point to reduce the amount of penny adjusting required later on. To find each individual's share of dividend income (column 3), multiply the number of units owned by the amount per unit, $0.3516. When all of the figures have been inserted in each column, add the columns to double-check that the individual figures add up to the column total. Since you are working with fractional amounts, you might need to adjust individual results by a penny or two to arrive at the exact column total.

DISTRIBUTING EARNINGS
TO INDIVIDUAL ACCOUNTS

Members generally leave their earnings in the club rather than taking annual withdrawals, and the earnings are then distributed to individual accounts as additional valuation units. In our example, we assume that the club's total value is $10,648.37 and that there are 768.835 valuation units in the club. Therefore, the value of a unit is $13.85.

To convert the earnings in column 7 into the valuation units shown in column 8, we divide each figure in column 7 by the $13.85 unit value. We now have a new total of 794.028 valuation units (768.835 plus 25.193) with a per-unit value of $13.41 ($10,648.37 divided by 794.028).

It's necessary to distribute the cash value of earnings per year to each member's account in order to reflect the additional tax-paid investment of club members. Since members report this income on their personal tax returns, it becomes part of their tax-paid investment (tax basis) in the club just like their monthly deposits.

When the club's books are closed at year-end, the total profit of $366.16 will be put into the *surplus account* (unrealized gains disbursed). From this account, the $348.92 belonging to the remaining members is then transferred to the *paid-in-by-members* account and into the individual account of each member.

MEMBER TAX RETURNS

Each member of the club is given a copy of the Earnings Distribution Statement, which contains all of the information he or she needs to file a personal tax return. However, each member also must be given a K-1 form to file with his or her personal return.

Keep all of these tax regulations in mind:

1. Unrealized gains and losses (paper gains and losses for securities still held by the club) are not taxable. Taxes become due—or losses can be deducted—only in the year securities are sold.
2. Capital gains are currently treated like ordinary income. The maximum tax rate on long-term capital gains is currently set at 28 percent.
3. Capital losses are offset by short-term and long-term gains. The net amount, when a profit, is taxed at the ordinary income rate.
4. There's a limit to the total amount of net capital losses you can deduct each year. Excesses are carried over and applied to future capital gains, up to the annual deduction limits.
5. Capital gains are offset against capital losses to reduce tax liabilities.

6. If you own more than one lot of a security (shares bought at different times), you should sell high-cost lots in order to reduce gain or increase loss. Sell low-cost lots to increase gain or reduce loss. If it is impossible to establish which securities are being sold through certificates themselves, identify them by designation when the sale is made. Specify in writing to your broker from which purchase you wish stock sold, identifying the shares by purchase date, cost, or both, and see that you receive a detailed written confirmation of the order from your broker.

7. Part or all of the cash dividends paid by certain companies may be classified as return of capital and are not taxable. Be sure to determine whether the dividends your club receives are taxable.

8. In general, stock dividends (dividends paid in the form of additional shares rather than in cash) are not taxable. Tax is postponed until the stock dividend is sold at a gain, when it is subject to the capital gains tax.

9. Cash received in lieu of a fractional share of stock dividend is treated as a capital gain.

10. In calculating gains on stocks sold, the IRS allows you to add commissions you have paid to the purchase price, and to deduct them from the sale price.

11. Costs incurred in connection with investing, such as subscriptions to financial publications, are deductible as itemized miscellaneous deductions for each individual. However, the total on form 1040 in the category of "miscellaneous" has to be more than 2 percent of the individual's adjusted gross income, or there is no deduction.

WHERE TO RECORD ITEMS ON FORM 1040

This section describes each member's reporting requirements for investment club transactions.

Dividend income is entered on Schedule B of form 1040. Write down your share of club dividend income, with the description "Share of qualifying corporation dividends received from investment club partnership, $_____." Any amount paid to the club as dividend income and then reclassified by the issuing corporation as "return of capital" (usually from utilities and insurance companies) is reported in a separate column on the Earnings Distribution Statement and reported by members on their personal returns.

Returns of capital are deducted from total dividend income at the bottom of Schedule B. (They are also deducted from the cost of the security in the club's records.)

When issuers have withheld tax from the club's dividend payment, total dividends are recorded on the Earnings Distribution Statement. The total withheld is recorded in the section of your return where other withheld amounts are listed (the reverse side of form 1040).

Capital gain income and loss are reported on Schedule D of form 1040. Short-term capital gain is entered under Part I of Schedule D on the line for partnership items. Long-term capital gain is entered in Part II. The individual's share of club expenses shown in column 6 of the Earnings Distribution Statement is listed as a separate item in the Miscellaneous Deduction section of Schedule A, as "Share of investment club expenses, $_____."

If your club received interest income during the year, it is shown as a separate item in the Income and Expense Statement and in a special column of the Earnings Distribution Statement. You report interest on Schedule B, Part I of form 1040.

INDIVIDUAL RETIREMENT ACCOUNTS

Investment club members are allowed to use the club account for their IRAs. NAIC has detailed information on the procedure. Refer to Chapter 17.

FILING FORM 1065

Partnerships file a partnership return (form 1065) each year. Form 1065 should be filed promptly and completely. Include a copy of the K-1 form for each member. You can get the form from your nearest IRS office.

The IRS may fine each partner for late or incorrect returns. If the club receives notice of a fine, promptly prepare and send a letter to the IRS office explaining why the form was not filed in a timely manner, and ask that the fine be forgiven. If the request is not granted and you receive a second fine notice, rewrite your letter in response to the second letter and specifically request that your letter be forwarded to the next level of authority. Persist until you find the right person at the IRS with authority to forgive the fine.

All contacts with the IRS should be made in writing; keep copies of correspondence in your files.

STATE AND LOCAL RETURNS

You might be required by state and local law to file state income tax, city income tax, and intangible property tax returns. In some locations, partnerships have the option of paying taxes as an organization and exempting individual members. It usually costs less to pay such taxes at the club level rather than individually. Be sure to check with your tax advisor to be sure you understand all state and local reporting and tax requirements.

CHAPTER 23

APPRAISING YOUR FINANCIAL RESULTS

"If you don't know where you're going, any road will get you there." This bit of cynical wisdom holds a lot of truth, and in your investment club, setting specific money and time goals is the only way to know if you're succeeding. We recommend setting the goal of doubling your money in five years. Why? Because, with proper research and diligence, you can reach this goal. Investment clubs that have subscribed to our philosophy of stock selection have proven over and over that this goal is realistic.

The five-year interval spans the average time between market peaks. It may take as little as three years, or as long as eight years, but five years is the standard we use for measuring peak to peak. Because our selection guidelines show you how to judge the value of stocks, you will be able to maximize profits by applying value tests—not only to stocks you're thinking of buying, but also to stocks you already own.

We suggest you apply these three tests, to judge how well your club is doing:

1. Determine your actual rate of return by using the procedure outlined in this chapter.

2. Evaluate your results against a broadly based market index, such as the S&P 500, which represents the bulk of the total value of NYSE-listed common stocks.

3. Evaluate your results against those of other clubs of the same age by entering NAIC's annual performance survey. Entry forms are in each

May issue of *Better Investing*. Each club is rated on its lifetime earnings rate as well as last year's rate and the club's comparison with the S&P 500 index.

"Success" doesn't demand that you meet or exceed your established standard; setting that goal is only a means of giving yourself a measurement and a focus. As long as your club produces a higher rate of return than you could have achieved through other forms of investing, you're doing a creditable job. And if you're actually earning at the NAIC recommended rate—doubling your money between market peaks—then your club has joined the thousands that have found out for themselves that these ideas work.

PROCEDURE FOR CALCULATING RETURNS

The method we recommend for calculating your rate of return (Figure 23-1) is based on the assumption that member contributions have been made every month in unvarying amounts, exclusive of reinvested dividends. This calculation was developed by Dr. Thomas O. Walton, chairman of the Mathematics Department at Kalamazoo College, under the auspices of Smith-Hague & Co. The method recognizes that the true return on an investment is a combination of dividends and market appreciation.

Figure 23-1

Compound Annual Rate of Increase

Number of Years	3%	4%	5%	6%	7%	8%	9%	10%	12%
1	1.016	1.022	1.027	1.032	1.038	1.043	1.048	1.053	1.064
2	2.063	2.084	2.105	2.126	2.148	2.169	2.191	2.212	2.255
3	3.141	3.189	3.237	3.286	3.336	3.385	3.436	3.487	3.590
4	4.251	4.338	4.426	4.516	4.607	4.699	4.793	4.889	5.084
5	5.395	5.533	5.674	5.819	5.967	6.118	6.273	6.431	6.758
6	6.573	6.776	6.985	7.200	7.422	7.650	7.886	8.128	8.633
7	7.786	8.069	8.361	8.664	8.979	9.305	9.643	9.994	10.732
8	9.036	9.413	9.806	10.216	10.645	11.092	11.559	12.047	13.084
9	10.323	10.811	11.323	11.861	12.427	13.022	13.648	14.305	15.718
10	11.649	12.265	12.916	13.605	14.335	15.107	15.924	16.788	18.666

Use this chart to determine your annual rate of return, and evaluate your results against returns for NYSE stocks and the success rates of similar investment clubs.

Here is a list of the steps to follow:

1. Determine the market value of the individual capital account as of the close of the last fiscal year.

2. Determine the total annual individual investment by multiplying the monthly contribution by 12, not including reinvested dividends.

3. Divide the amount in step 1 by the amount in step 2, to the third decimal place.

4. Determine the number of fiscal years over which the annual contribution has been made.

5. Locate the row in Figure 23-1 corresponding to the number of years in step 4.

6. In the row for the number of years, find the number closest to the quotient referred to in step 3.

7. Read up to the head of the column for the percentage figure representing the compound annual rate of increase in the value of the individual capital account.

8. Examples:

   a. Monthly contribution = $10.

   Value of individual capital account at end of last fiscal year =

Figure 23-1 (Continued)

Compound Annual Rate of Increase

14%	16%	18%	20%	22%	24%	26%	28%	30%	32%
1.074	1.085	1.095	1.105	1.116	1.126	1.136	1.146	1.156	1.166
2.299	2.343	2.387	2.431	2.477	2.522	2.567	2.613	2.659	2.705
3.695	3.803	3.912	4.023	4.137	4.253	4.370	4.490	4.612	4.736
5.278	5.497	5.711	5.933	6.163	6.399	6.642	6.894	7.152	7.418
7.098	7.460	7.834	8.225	8.634	9.060	9.505	9.970	10.454	10.958
9.170	9.738	10.339	10.975	11.649	12.361	13.113	13.907	14.746	15.631
11.602	12.333	13.295	14.275	15.327	16.453	17.658	18.947	20.326	21.799
14.231	15.446	16.783	18.235	19.815	21.527	23.385	25.398	27.579	29.941
17.280	19.003	20.899	22.987	25.290	27.820	30.601	33.656	37.009	40.688
20.777	23.128	25.756	28.690	31.969	35.622	39.693	44.225	49.268	54.874

$ 912.12.

Number of fiscal years contribution was made = 6.

Multiply $10 by 12 = $120.

Divide $912.12 by 120 = 7.601.

Locate the number closest to 7.601 in the row for 6 years (the closest number is 7.650). Read up to 8 percent, which equals the annual rate of increase.

b. Monthly contribution = $20.

Value of individual capital account at end of last fiscal year = $2,017.58.

Number of years contribution was made = 7.

Multiply $20 by 12 = $240.

Divide $2,017.58 by 240 = 8.406.

Locate the number closest to 8.406 in the row for 7 years, which is 8.361. Read up to 5 percent.

You should note that these answers are approximate and not precise. A ballpark figure is sufficient to indicate if your results are in the right direction and if they are sufficient to bring you close to your goal.

If you meet with initial success, don't allow yourself or fellow club members to become overconfident. As English novelist Samuel Butler said, "Money is like the reputation for ability—more easily made than kept." And don't be discouraged if you're not ahead of the game from the start. Clubs typically lose money the first year or two, until the effect of reinvested capital gains and dividends begins to have an effect. Remember, you're in the market for the long term.

Commenting in *The Wall Street Journal,* Charles R. Schwab, founder of the major discount brokerage, reminded readers that researchers have convincingly demonstrated that stocks provide superior returns over extended holding periods. Despite this evidence, most people contributing to employer-sponsored defined-contribution plans direct their retirement funds into fixed-rate investments. Schwab wrote, "I find this disturbing. By taking the low-risk, low-reward path, millions of Americans are limiting their financial future.... Take charge of your financial future. No one else can do it for you."

More about NAIC

CHAPTER 24

OBJECTIVES AND PROGRAMS

NAIC is founded on the belief that investors succeed when they establish clear programs and standards, and when they follow those programs and standards according to sensible rules. NAIC takes the same advice. We have two important purposes. The first is to encourage people to own stocks directly. The second is to provide a learn-by-doing investment program for everyone who wants to be a self-reliant investor, alone or as a member of an investment club.

ENCOURAGING INDIVIDUAL OWNERSHIP

Approximately 51 million Americans invest as individuals in this country today, and they hold nearly $1.8 trillion in stocks. Yet the individual investor's influence in the market appears to be in decline when you look at the overall market. During the past ten years, individual net purchases and sales of common stock have declined drastically as a percentage of total market volume. In the 1950s the individual was responsible for 80 percent of New York Stock Exchange trading. Now, the situation is reversed: 80 percent of today's trades are institutional; less than 20 percent are individual trades. Similarly, the percentage of individual investors' financial assets in equities plummeted from 43 percent to 18 percent during the past two decades. A rebound from that low began in 1988, but the level is currently only 23 percent.

We believe that institutional investors cannot provide the level of market diversity and liquidity achievable by the actions of many individuals. For this reason, NAIC is working with American corporations to develop an "Own Your Share of America" campaign. The initiative is designed to encourage direct individual share ownership by pointing out the advantages to individuals and public companies, and by simplifying the methods of transfer and ownership of shares.

NAIC also intends to lobby for legislation favorable to individual investors. NAIC backs a capital gains tax program that would do the following:

1. Exempt the first $25,000 of capital gains annually from taxation for individual investors.

2. Grant a lifetime exemption of $500,000 on an individual's overall equity investment.

3. Allow an individual investor to roll over capital gains without taxation until retirement age, and then pay gains as they are realized, in a way similar to deferral rules for investment real estate.

4. Index the tax base of capital gains to offset the effects of inflation.

HELPING WITH INVESTMENT TOOLS

People launch investment programs with a variety of goals in mind. As an investor, you may want to accumulate capital to start a business of your own. Or you might want to fund higher education for your children. Virtually all investors have in mind a financially secure retirement, free of the money worries that plague those who failed to plan for the future. Of course, no investment club program should be undertaken until an adequate savings account for emergencies and suitable insurance coverage has been established.

The accompanying table (Figure 24-1) shows the savings of capital at the rate of $200 per month during the ages 40 through 59 and withdrawal at $5,000 per year plus 3 percent inflation during the ages 60 through 79, with income compounded annually at 7 percent. After nineteen years of withdrawals, a sizable portion of the total assets is still available. In order to plan realistically for your retirement, we recommend that you calculate your own retirement needs based on higher or lower deposits and withdrawals, and based on interest rates you believe to be realistic.

The illustration makes our point that even those investors who wait until middle age to begin an equities investment program can create an important supplement to other sources of retirement income, such as employer pension plans and Social Security.

Figure 24-1
Retirement Statistics

Saving $2,400 Annually			Withdrawing $5,000 Annually plus 3 percent Inflation		
Age	Save	Principal	Age	Withdraw	Principal
40 ....$2,400		$ 2,400	60 ....$5,000		$106,996
41 2,400		5,136	61 5,150		109,335
42 2,400		8,064	62 5,305		111,684
43 2,400		11,196	63 5,464		114,039
44 2,400		14,548	64 5,628		116,394
45 2,400		18,134	65 5,796		118,745
46 2,400		21,971	66 5,970		121,087
47 2,400		26,077	67 6,149		123,414
48 2,400		30,471	68 6,334		125,719
49 2,400		35,172	69 6,524		127,995
50 2,400		40,202	70 6,720		130,235
51 2,400		45,584	71 6,921		132,430
52 2,400		51,343	72 7,129		134,572
53 2,400		57,505	73 7,343		136,649
54 2,400		64,098	74 7,563		138,652
55 2,400		71,153	75 7,790		140,567
56 2,400		78,702	76 8,024		142,384
57 2,400		86,779	77 8,264		144,086
58 2,400		95,421	78 8,512		145,660
59 2,400		104,669	79 8,768		147,089

The NAIC investment philosophy certainly helps you to achieve financial security in the future. We also offer a complete array of services for you individually and as an investment club member. These include:

NAIC Councils. Operating in more than eighty areas around the nation, Councils provide local NAIC members a nearby educational resource. Programs range from instruction in the use of NAIC stock study tools to large Investors Fairs, complete with presentations by corporate officials and investment professionals.

Low-Cost Investment Plan. This is a simple, nearly cost-free opportunity to invest in one or all of the stocks of participating companies.

NAIC Growth Fund, Inc. This is a closed-end mutual fund set up for investment using NAIC principles.

Investors Congress. This is an annual convention featuring lectures, workshops, and seminars by investment professionals, as well as the chance to swap ideas with other investors and take post-meeting tours.

World Federation of Investors Meeting. Held biennially, this get-together in a major overseas business center affords a world view of investing. A post-meeting tour is available for NAIC members wishing to extend their trip.

Investors Expo. We sponsor an annual exposition designed for the public, with corporate displays and information for beginning and advanced investors.

Investment Education Institute. A separate organization established by the Trust. It has worked primarily with the Business School at Wayne State University on investment education subjects. It awards a Distinguished Service Award in Investment Education to selected individuals each year who have made major contributions to investment education.

NAIC Computer Group. About 40 percent of NAIC's membership owns or has access to a computer. Organized to increase investment education through computers, the Computer Group offers NAIC members for an additional fee a newsletter, computerized stock studies, regional seminars, an on-line investor forum and discounts on NAIC investment software. The annual CompuFest highlights the group's many activities.

NAIC Investor Advisory Service. A subscription service providing the individual or club detailed information including a completed Stock Selection Guide study of three corporations each month as investment recommendations.

Better Investing Magazine. One of the nation's most widely read financial publications, *Better Investing* is included in NAIC dues and contains ideas on stocks to study, investment techniques, and investment club news.

Other NAIC Aids

   Investors Manual

   First-Time Investors Manual

   NAIC Stock Study Course

   NAIC Accounting Manual & Accounting Kit

   NAIC Stock Check List

   NAIC Stock Selection Guide and Report

   NAIC Stock Selection Guide

NAIC Giant Stock Selection Guide

NAIC Stock Comparison Guide

NAIC Ratio Calculator

NAIC Portfolio Management Guide

Challenge Tree Comparative Form

PERT (Portfolio Evaluation Review Technique)

A more comprehensive and detailed description of NAIC publications and order forms are available from NAIC.

CHAPTER 25

HISTORY AND ORGANIZATION

*T*he National Association of Investors Corporation is primarily a volunteer organization, with only a small paid staff. The work of NAIC would be impossible without the ability and dedication of those volunteers who serve in so many capacities and in so many locations without compensation.

NAIC was formed in 1951 by representatives of four Michigan investment clubs. One of these, the Mutual Investment Club of Detroit, remains active today. More than 400 of NAIC's member clubs are at least twenty-five years old.

The Association is an independent Michigan not-for-profit organization, free of control by any individual, company, or financial institution.

The trust agreement that marked the organization's beginnings provided for a board of trustees to govern NAIC. The trustees set up a not-for-profit corporation (the N.I.A. Corporation) to be governed by directors elected by the membership. This structure remains in place.

NAIC has three classes of membership: individuals, investment clubs, and corporations. Members pay dues to and are members of the National Association of Investors Corporation, which extends membership to any appropriate Council. NAIC belongs to the World Federation of Investment Clubs, Inc., and thus NAIC members belong to the worldwide group.

The Trust established a separate corporation to operate NAIC's Advisory Service. A nominee partnership was established to expedite the transfer of securities in NAIC's Low-Cost Investment Plan.

In 1990, acting on the suggestion of many members, the Trust established the NAIC Growth Fund, Inc. This is a closed-end investment fund dedicated to NAIC investment principles.

There are two advisory groups assisting different divisions of NAIC. The Board of Advisors counsels the Trust and the National Association of Investors Corporation on matters of policy and investment education. The Corporate Advisory Committee works with the National Association of Investors Corporation and the N.I.A. Corporation in conducting the Investors Expo and in developing new programs and projects.

The accompanying chart (Figure 25-1) depicts the flow of control, membership, and services in the organization.

Figure 25-1

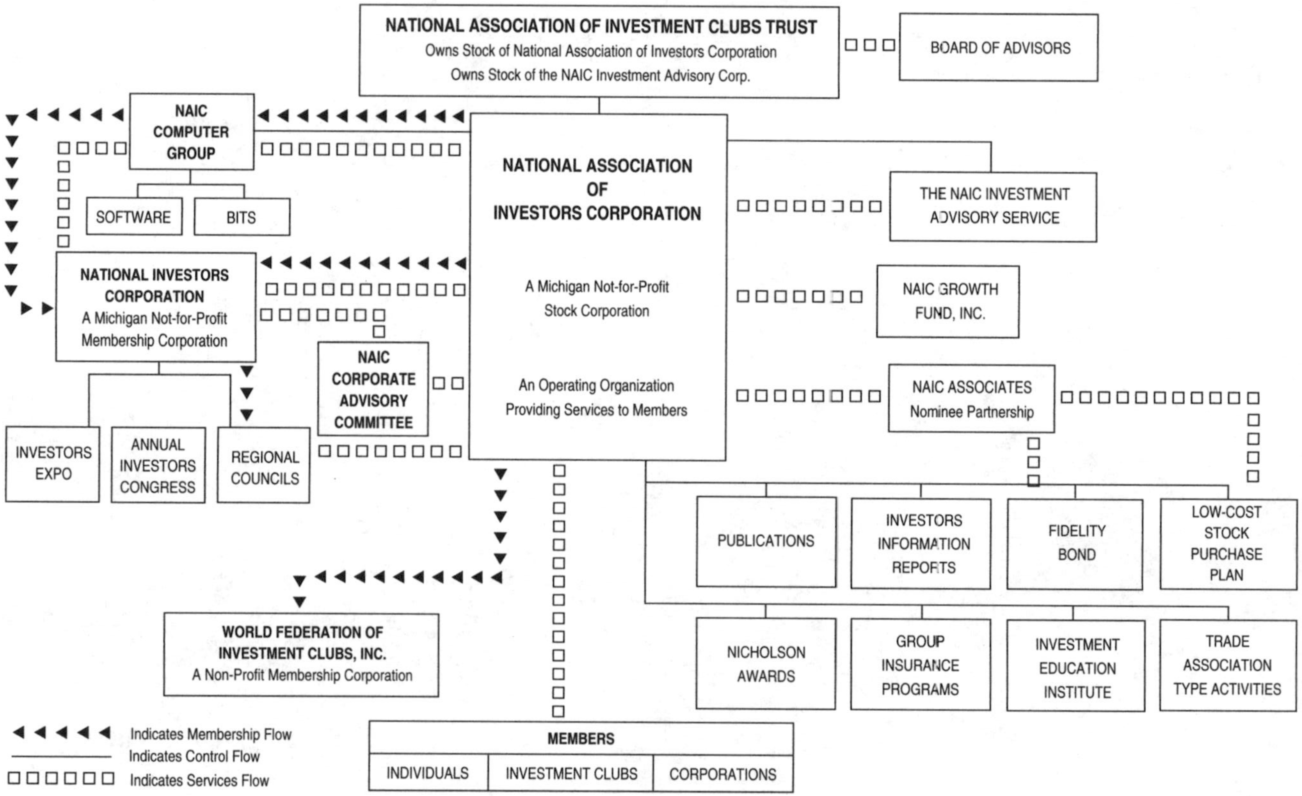

NATIONAL ASSOCIATION OF INVESTMENT CLUBS TRUST
Owns Stock of National Association of Investors Corporation
Owns Stock of the NAIC Investment Advisory Corp.

BOARD OF ADVISORS

THE NAIC INVESTMENT ADVISORY SERVICE

NAIC GROWTH FUND, INC.

NAIC ASSOCIATES Nominee Partnership

NATIONAL ASSOCIATION OF INVESTORS CORPORATION

A Michigan Not-for-Profit Stock Corporation

An Operating Organization Providing Services to Members

PUBLICATIONS

INVESTORS INFORMATION REPORTS

FIDELITY BOND

LOW-COST STOCK PURCHASE PLAN

NICHOLSON AWARDS

GROUP INSURANCE PROGRAMS

INVESTMENT EDUCATION INSTITUTE

TRADE ASSOCIATION TYPE ACTIVITIES

MEMBERS

INDIVIDUALS | INVESTMENT CLUBS | CORPORATIONS

NAIC COMPUTER GROUP

SOFTWARE

BITS

NATIONAL INVESTORS CORPORATION
A Michigan Not-for-Profit Membership Corporation

NAIC CORPORATE ADVISORY COMMITTEE

INVESTORS EXPO

ANNUAL INVESTORS CONGRESS

REGIONAL COUNCILS

WORLD FEDERATION OF INVESTMENT CLUBS, INC.
A Non-Profit Membership Corporation

▼ Indicates Membership Flow
Indicates Control Flow
□ □ □ □ Indicates Services Flow

243

GLOSSARY

*A*bout the abbreviations: *cf.* stands for Latin *confer,* meaning "compare." *q.v.* stands for Latin *quod vide,* meaning "which see," a cross-reference.

Accelerated depreciation.   Provision for recovery of the cost of an asset whose value will decline over a period of time. This is accomplished through deductions against income, with larger deductions taken in earlier years.

Accounts payable.   A current liability; debts owed by a company to its suppliers that must be paid within the course of a year.

Accounts receivable.   A current asset; debts owed to a company by its customers that the company expects to collect within the course of a year.

Accrued taxes.   A current liability; taxes owed by a company to various governmental bodies.

Accrued wages.   A current liability; money owed by a company to its employees.

Accumulated profits.   Same as retained income *(q.v.).*

Acid test ratio.   The sum of a company's cash, accounts receivable, and marketable securities divided by its total current liabilities. A test of financial liquidity.

Amortization.   Reduction of debt through periodic payments consisting of interest and part of principal.

Area method.   A way of drawing the trend line on the Stock Selection Guide chart so that there is an equal amount of area above and below the trend line. (*Cf.* Mid-point method and Best judgment method.)

Asked.   The price demanded by a willing seller. (*Cf.* Bid.)

Asset.   Something of value owned by a company. May be tangible, such as a piece of machinery, or intangible, such as goodwill. (*Cf.* Current asset and Fixed asset.)

Authorized stock.   The total number of shares that a corporation, as indicated in its charter, is authorized to sell. May or may not be the same as outstanding stock (*q.v.*).

Averages.   Selected lists of stock or bonds whose price action is considered representative of the market as a whole. The best-known averages are the Dow Jones and Standard & Poor's.

Balance sheet.   A financial statement detailing, as of a certain point in time, a company's assets, liabilities, and capital. Assets minus liabilities equals net worth, or the equity of the company's stockholders. The balance sheet indicates a company's financial strength and solvency.

Bear.   An investor who anticipates a market decline.

Bear market.   A declining market.

Best judgment method.   A way of drawing the trend line on the NAIC Stock Selection Guide chart, based on the analyst's use of his or her best judgment. (*Cf.* Area method and Mid-point method.)

Beta.   A coefficient that measures volatility relative to the total market, usually as represented by the S&P 500.

Bid.   The price offered by a willing buyer. (*Cf.* Asked.)

Big Board.   Nickname for the New York Stock Exchange, the nation's largest.

Black Monday.   October 19, 1987, when the Dow Jones Industrial Average dropped over 500 points.

Bond.   An instrument of debt. In issuing bonds, a corporation agrees to pay holders a stated rate of interest until principal is repaid on a specified date.

Bond ratio.   That portion of a company's capital structure consisting of bonds, found by dividing the face value of bonds by the total value of bonds, preferred stock, common stock, capital surplus, and retained earnings.

Bondholder.   A creditor. In buying corporate bonds, an individual acquires no portion of ownership in the company, but assumes less risk than a stockholder (*q.v.*).

Book value of common stock.   The value of common stock of a company, found by adding the par value of the common stock, retained earnings, and surplus reserves. Book value per common share may then be determined by dividing this sum by the number of outstanding common shares. Book value has no relation to market value.

Broker.   A firm or individual who arranges a transfer of securities between a buyer and a seller, charging a fee for the service.

Business cycle.   The phases of transition in a free economy, consisting of prosperity, recession, depression, and recovery.

Business ratio.   Also known as current ratio (*q.v.*).

Buy zone.   The computed range on NAIC forms that signals favorable buy prices for the analyzed security.

Capital gain or capital loss.   Profit or loss from the sale of a capital asset, such as securities.

Capital structure.   The total of bonds, preferred stock, reserves, and retained earnings. (*Cf.* Capitalization.)

Capitalism.   An economic system that permits private, rather than public, ownership of the means of production, and free pricing of products.

Capitalist.   Anyone who provides funds for the conduct of a business.

Capitalization.   The total value, as stated in a company's books, of bonds and preferred and common stock outstanding. (*Cf.* Capital structure.)

Cash dividend.   The earnings of a corporation directed by the board to be paid to the stockholders in cash. (*Cf.* Stock dividend.)

Cash flow.   The net income of a company, with the addition of any noncash deductions from income such as depreciation and depletion. Since cash flow represents the actual amount of money generated by a company, it is considered by some analysts to be a more meaningful figure than net income.

Cash flow statement.   A report showing a company's cash flow over selected periods of time. This statement offers the best evidence of a company's debt-paying ability.

Challenge Tree.   An NAIC form used to compare the merits of holding a stock against those of a prospective purchase.

Cheap stock.   Not necessarily a low-priced stock, but one that is selling at a lower price/earnings ratio than would appear justified by corporate results.

Combined yield.   The total return from a stock, consisting of cash and stock dividends and price appreciation.

Common stock.   A representation of ownership in a corporation. Typically, common stockholders elect the company's board of directors, whose responsibilities include declaring of dividends. In case of dissolution of the company, common stockholders have last claim on assets.

Common stock ratio. That portion of a company's capital structure consisting of common stock. The stated value of common stock, any paid-in capital, and retained earnings divided by the total value of bonds, preferred stock, common stock, paid-in capital, and retained earnings.

Consolidated statement. A statement that includes figures for a company and all of its subsidiaries.

Corporation. An entity created by law with perpetual life and limited liability of shareholders.

Cost of goods sold. The cost of labor, materials, and overhead that properly may be assigned to units produced. (*Cf.* Selling, general, and administrative expenses.)

Cost of products sold. Same as cost of goods sold (*q.v.*).

Cost of sales. Same as cost of goods sold (*q.v.*).

Creditor. An individual or entity that lends money to a company, e.g., a bondholder, buyer of commercial paper, or extender of trade credit.

Curb. Nickname for the American Stock Exchange.

Current asset. An asset that can be converted into cash within a year. Current assets are listed in the balance sheet in order of their ease of convertibility to cash: cash, government securities, accounts receivable, and inventories.

Current liability. A liability of a company that must be paid within one year.

Current ratio. A firm's current assets divided by its current liabilities.

Cyclical growth stock. A stock that is very dependent on the business cycle, and reaches new highs in sales and earnings in each succeeding period of prosperity.

Debenture. A bond not secured by any specific property but backed only by the general credit of the issuing company.

Deferred charge. Also known as deferred expense or prepaid expense, an asset that represents payment for a good or service properly chargeable to a future period. Payment of a premium on an insurance policy with several years to run is a common deferred charge.

Deferred expense. Same as deferred charge (*q.v.*).

Depletion.   A charge against earnings derived from a natural resource. Depletion recognizes exhaustion of the resource through its continued conversion into a salable product. Lumber and oil companies are among those listing depletion on their balance sheets. The provision for depletion may exceed the cost of the natural reserve. (*Cf.* Depreciation.)

Depreciation.   Recovery of the cost of an asset that will be worn out over a period of time. (*Cf.* Accelerated depreciation and Straight-line depreciation.)

Dilution.   The effect on earnings and book value per share when the number of shares issued by a company increases disproportionately to growth in company earnings or assets. New shares can be created by the conversion feature in some bonds, debentures, and preferred stock; additional shares can also result from stock dividends, stock splits, options and warrants, and, of course, a new issue. If the book value of new shares is less than that of the old shares, dilution has occurred.

Dividend.   Payment a company makes, in cash or stock, to its shareholders from retained earnings.

Dividend yield.   Found by dividing the cash dividend per share by market price per share. Lower yields are associated with growth companies, and higher yields with more mature companies.

Dollar cost averaging.   Buying a set dollar amount of a security at stated intervals. Over a period of time, the average cost will be lower than the average price of the shares, since more shares will be purchased when the price is low and fewer when the price is high.

Dow Jones Average. (Dow Jones Industrial Average).   Average of the prices of thirty leading industrial stocks. Dow Jones Transportation and Utility averages are also widely watched.

Downside risk.   On NAIC forms, the difference between present price and estimated low price for the next five years.

Earned surplus.   Profits that have been kept in the business rather than being distributed as dividends. Also called undistributed earnings or profits, accumulated profits, retained earnings, or retained income.

Earnings per share.   Of paramount concern to the common shareholder, earnings per share are found by dividing net income after any preferred dividends by the number of shares of common stock outstanding.

Earnings plowback.   Reinvesting earnings in a business rather than paying them out to stockholders in the form of dividends.

Earnings report.   A financial statement (also called income statement or profit and loss statement) that shows a company's operating results over a period of time and gives evidence of the company's profitability.

Economies of scale.   Savings realized by larger corporations, which are able to spread fixed costs over a larger number of units produced.

Equity.   Ownership interest, represented by the net worth of a corporation, or the difference between assets and liabilities.

Equity capital.   Funds furnished by the owners of a business.

Ex dividend.   From the Latin, meaning "without dividend." When a stock is selling ex dividend, the buyer does not receive the soon-to-be-paid dividend; rather, it remains the property of the seller.

Exchange.   A meeting place for the representatives of buyers and sellers of securities.

FIFO.   Abbreviation for first in, first out; a method of inventory valuation. Inventory issued is priced at the cost of the oldest inventory on hand (*Cf.* LIFO.)

Financial leverage.   Same as leverage *(q.v.)*.

Financial risk.   One of the important types of risk confronting investors, it acknowledges that companies may suffer adversity that would affect their ability to make payments to investors and/or creditors. (*Cf.* Interest rate risk and Purchasing power risk.)

Financial statement.   A report depicting a corporation's financial condition as of a given date or financial results for a given period. The most common financial statements are the balance sheet *(q.v.)*, earnings report *(q.v.)*, and cash flow statement *(q.v.)*.

Fiscal period.   A span of time selected as an accounting period. The fiscal year often coincides with the calendar year, although it need not. Companies may follow the business year, closing their books when business activity is slackest. An example is retailers, who close their books in January (following the Christmas selling season).

Fixed asset.   Property of a company that will not be used up or converted into cash within a year's time.

Fixed asset turnover.   A measurement of efficiency, found by dividing fixed assets before depreciation into net sales. The more rapid the turnover, the better.

Fixed cost. A business expense that continues even if production ceases. (*Cf.* Variable cost.)

Fixed income investments. Those investments, including bonds and (usually) preferred stock, for which the company is committed to paying a specific amount of return to investors.

Fixed liability. A debt of a company that will not be paid for a year or more.

Forms 10-K and 10-Q. Filing requirements of the Securities and Exchange Commission. The 10-K may contain more financial information than the annual report, while the 10-Q offers more data than interim reports.

Form 1065. A tax form that must be filed by all investment clubs operating as partnerships.

Formula investing. Investing by prearranged design. Dollar cost averaging (*q.v.*) is a popular type of formula investing.

Free enterprise. Same as Capitalism *(q.v.)*.

Funded debt. Debt carrying a provision that cash must be set aside each year to provide for payment of the debt at maturity.

Funding. A company's conversion of short-term debt into long-term debt.

Government bond. An evidence of U.S. government debt, considered to offer the lowest possible financial risk *(q.v.)*.

Gross Domestic Product. The new statistic offered by the U.S. government to supplant Gross National Product. The value of goods and services produced in the United States during a specified period of time. An important indicator of the state of the nation's economy.

Gross profit. Net sales minus cost of goods sold. The higher the gross profit margin (*q.v.*), the better.

Gross profit margin. Gross profit (*q.v.*) divided by net sales. Also called gross margin.

Gross sales. Sales before deductions for returns and allowances. (*Cf.* Net sales.)

Growth stock. The stock of a company whose growth is faster than that of the economy as a whole.

Goodwill. An asset that arises from business combinations accounted for under the purchase method; represents the cost to a purchaser in excess of the fair value of net assets (equity) of an acquired business. This amount appears in the parent company's balance sheet as an intangible item that is amortized as an expense over a period not to exceed forty years.

Government securities.   U.S. government obligations (bills, notes, and bonds) in which companies invest excess cash. The investments are classified as cash equivalents or marketable securities, depending upon their maturities. Federal agency obligations issued by the Federal Home Loan Mortgage Corporation (Freddie Mac) and the Federal National Mortgage Association (Fannie Mae) are also included in this category.

Hidden asset.   An asset such as a trade secret that does not appear on a company's books.

Hold zone.   On NAIC forms, the calculated price range where securities are neither a buy nor a sell.

Hot tip.   A story suggesting a favorable development for a company. You're likely to get burned if you follow such advice. NAIC's rational approach to investing requires that figures support the story.

Income.   Same as earnings or profit. Net income is the sum remaining after taxes, which may be reinvested in the business or paid out to stockholders in the form of dividends.

Income stock.   A stock offering a liberal yield.

Inflation.   A period during which the purchasing power of the dollar is declining.

Insolvency.   The state that exists for a corporation when liabilities exceed assets, and it is not able to pay its debts.

Inspection method.   Same as Best judgment method (*q.v.*).

Interest.   Payment to a creditor by a borrower for the use of money.

Interest rate risk.   One of the important types of risk confronting investors. Acknowledges that changes in the interest rate may affect the market value of a security. (*Cf.* Financial risk and Purchasing power risk.)

Inventory.   The raw materials, goods in progress, and finished goods of a company.

Inventory turnover.   A measurement of efficiency, found by dividing the cost of goods sold for a period by average inventory at cost for the same period. The faster the turnover, the better.

Invested capital. Same as capital structure (*q.v.*).

IRA. Abbreviation for Individual Retirement Account, a means of deferring taxes on investment income, dividends, and price appreciation. IRAs may be held in investment club accounts.

Leverage. The use of non-equity capital in the hope of increasing the return on equity (*q.v.*).

Liabilities. The claims of creditors. (*Cf.* Current liability and Fixed liability.)

Lien. A claim of a creditor against property of a company. Bonds may be secured by liens against real estate or equipment.

LIFO. Abbreviation for last in, first out; a method of inventory valuation. Inventory issued is priced at the cost of the newest inventory on hand. (*Cf.* FIFO.)

Limited liability. Restriction of liability to the amount invested. Stockholders enjoy limited liability.

Liquid assets. Current assets that can be quickly converted into cash.

Liquidating value. In an investment club, the total number of valuation units multiplied by the dollar value per unit. The current market value of the club.

Liquidity. The ease with which a company's assets can be converted into cash. A business is said to be liquid when it holds a high proportion of liquid assets.

Listed security. A security that has met the requirements for trading on one or more of the nation's stock exchanges. (*Cf.* Off-board security.)

Long-term capital gains. Gains on securities held more than one year. (*Cf.* Short-term capital gains.)

Long-term capital losses. Losses on securities held more than one year. (*Cf.* Short-term capital losses.)

Long-term debt. On the balance sheet, borrowed funds that are due for payment after one year, usually over several years.

Long-term liabilities. Obligations that fall due after one year, including long-term debt, deferred income taxes, and deferred credits.

Lower of cost or market. A conservative rule of accounting that prices an item at the lower of its current market value or the price paid for it.

Market price.   The price at which transactions in a security take place.

Market timing.   The strategy used by the speculator who hopes to buy low and sell high by going in and out of the market.

Market value.   Current value of an asset; its sale price on the open market. Used in financial statements to value marketable securities and inventories.

Maturity.   The date on which an obligation falls due.

Merchandise turnover.   The same as inventory turnover (*q.v.*).

Mid-point method.   An approach to determining the trend line on the NAIC Stock Selection Guide chart where the average figures for the first and last five-year periods are used to locate the trend line. (*Cf.* Area method and Best judgment method.)

Mortgage.   One form of long-term debt on the balance sheet. Represents an obligation of a company secured by specific assets, generally plant, property, and equipment.

Multiple.   Another term for price/earnings ratio (*q.v.*).

Net before taxes.   Same as pre-tax profit (*q.v.*).

Net income.   Profit after taxes.

Net interest margin.   The profit margin for financial institutions, found by dividing net interest revenues by average earning assets.

Net sales.   Gross sales (*q.v.*) minus returns and allowances. Synonymous terms are revenues, gross income, and receipts.

Net working capital.   The difference between current assets (*q.v.*) and current liabilities (*q.v.*).

Net worth.   All assets minus all liabilities of a corporation; equivalent to stock, paid-in capital, and retained earnings.

New York Stock Exchange.   The largest auction market securities exchange in the nation.

Non-operating income and expense.   Income and expense of a corporation not connected with the principal business. Sale of property is an example of non-operating income; payment of interest to bondholders is an example of non-operating expense.

Notes payable.   A current liability on the balance sheet for money owed usually to a bank by a company, as evidenced by promissory notes.

Odd lot.   Less than a round lot, which is the established unit of trading in a security. For most issues, from one to ninety-nine shares constitutes an odd lot.

Off-board security.   Same as unlisted or over-the-counter security, one not listed on a stock exchange.

Operating expenses.   Selling, general, and administrative expenses; those costs of doing business that cannot properly be charged against units produced.

Operating profit.   Gross profit minus operating expenses.

Operating ratio.   A measurement of efficiency, calculated as cost of goods sold plus selling, general, and administrative expenses divided by net sales. The smaller the result, the better.

Ordinary income rate.   The rate at which the federal government taxes a particular level of earned income.

Other income and expense.   Same as non-operating income and expense (*q.v.*).

Outstanding stock.   Stock issued and in the hands of owners.

Overhead.   Costs incurred in manufacturing other than those for materials and direct labor. Electrical power is an example.

Over-the-counter market.   Marketplace for securities that, because the issuing companies cannot qualify or do not care to do so, are not listed on any securities exchange.

Paid-in capital.   Capital arising from payments by stockholders, in contrast to earned surplus, which arises from profits.

Pay-out ratio.   The ratio of cash dividends to earnings. Normally, growth stocks pay out a smaller portion of their earnings in dividends than do income stocks.

Peak period method.   A method for computing the trend line on the Stock Selection Guide chart. Under this plan, the trend line goes through the two most recent peaks in performance. (*Cf.* Best judgment method and Area method.)

Percent earned on equity.   Net earnings divided by total capitalization, less any debt. The higher the return, the better.

Percent earned on invested capital.   Net earnings divided by total capitalization. The higher the return, the better.

PERT.   Portfolio Evaluation Review Technique, an NAIC tool permitting investors to keep current on the latest figures on their holdings and to take action as appropriate.

Pink sheets. Report available at brokerage offices that lists current prices for less popular over-the-counter stocks whose worth is not reported in the newspaper.

Plant turnover. Same as fixed asset turnover *(q.v.)*.

Portfolio. All of the securities held by an individual, investment club, or institution.

Portfolio Management Guide. An NAIC tool permitting users to keep watch over the price movement of their holdings.

Preferred stock. Stock with claim on dividends and assets that takes precedence over common stock.

Preferred stock ratio. That portion of a company's capital structure consisting of preferred stock. The stated value of preferred stock divided by the total of bonds, preferred stock, common stock, retained earnings, and capital surplus.

Prepaid expense. A current asset representing an advance payment, generally for services and supplies, that is classified as current on the balance sheet.

Pre-tax profit. Earnings or income before taxes.

Pre-tax profit margin. Profit before taxes divided by sales. The higher the margin, the better.

Price appreciation. The advance in price of a security. Typically, price appreciation results from two factors: increasing earnings and a higher price/earnings ratio.

Price/earnings ratio. The market price of a security divided by the earnings per share. Used to determine if a stock represents value at a given price.

Pro forma. A manner of presenting financial information, showing the combined full-year results of a parent and company acquired during the year.

Profit. Same as earnings or income.

Profit and loss statement. Same as earnings report *(q.v.)*.

Prospectus. In fulfillment of a federal requirement, the prospectus is issued by corporations to give investors considering purchase of a new issue information on solvency, profitability, and other matters.

Purchasing power risk. One of the important types of risks confronting investors. Recognizes that the value of a stock issue may be affected by a change in the value of the dollar. (*Cf.* Financial risk and Interest rate risk.)

Quality. A rating given to bonds and stocks by a recognized rating service. A requirement for Challenge Tree users is to find a challenging security of equal or higher quality.

Quick asset. A current asset readily converted into cash. Cash, marketable securities, and accounts receivable are all quick assets.

Quick asset ratio. Same as acid test ratio (*q.v.*).

Ratio analysis. Appraisal of the quality of a prospective investment through computation of relationships between various balance sheet and income statement items.

Ratio calculator. NAIC tool for doing ratio analysis.

Ratio chart. A graph, such as the one on the Stock Selection Guide, that depicts relative changes or geometric progressions. Used to plot rates of growth in sales and earnings.

Receipts. Same as sales and revenues.

Receivables. A current asset representing amounts owed to a company that are to be collected within the next year.

Refunding. Replacing one bond issue with another of a lower rate when it is to the financial advantage of the corporation to do so.

Registrar. The agent, usually a bank or trust company, responsible for issuing and distributing shares of stock and bonds.

Relative value. For NAIC investors, the current price/earnings ratio (based on EPS for the latest twelve months) as a percent of the historical average price/earnings ratio.

Reserves. Profits that are set aside for certain purposes.

Retained earnings. Same as retained income (*q.v.*).

Retained income. Money a company keeps from net profits in order to finance its operations.

Return. Same as yield (*q.v.*).

Return on book. Percent earned on book value, or return on equity (*q.v.*).

Revenues. Synonymous with sales and receipts.

Risk capital. Refers to the nature of money that should be invested in the stock market, funds not earmarked for specific near-term purposes.

Round lot. The established unit of trading in a security, usually 100 shares. (*Cf.* Odd lot.)

Rule of five. A rule for investors stating that for every five stocks purchased, one will experience unforeseen difficulties, three will perform more or less as expected, and one will far exceed what was forecast for it.

Sales. Same as net sales, revenues, or receipts.

Securities. Written instruments, including stocks and bonds.

Securities and Exchange Commission. A federal agency that regulates the securities business and protects the interests of the investing public.

Sell zone. On NAIC forms, that range of calculated prices indicating that the holding is a candidate for sale.

Selling, general, and administrative expenses. Non-manufacturing expenses such as salaries of executives, commissions paid to salespeople, and advertising and public relations outlays.

Semi-log chart. A chart such as the one used in the Visual Analysis section of the NAIC Stock Selection Guide, where the vertical scale is based on logarithms. Equal vertical distances represent equal percentage changes, regardless of the absolute values involved.

Shareholder. Synonymous with stockholder or shareowner, the owner of one or more shares of a corporation.

Shareholders' equity. Same as equity (*q.v.*).

Short-term capital gains. Gains for tax purposes on securities held one year or less.

Short-term capital losses. Losses on securities held one year or less.

Solvency. Measure of a company's ability to meet its long-term debt obligations. (*Cf.* Liquidity.)

Spread. The difference between a security's bid and asked prices.

Stock Check List. An NAIC form to be used until the investor has gained mastery of the Stock Selection Guide.

Stock dividend. Distribution of stock to shareholders as a dividend on shares held.

Stock Selection Guide. An NAIC form designed to assist investors in making a judgment about whether or not to buy a security.

Stock split. The issuance of a number of shares for each share of stock outstanding. The common purpose of a split is to broaden ownership and increase marketability.

Stockholder. Synonymous with shareholder, the owner of one or more shares of a corporation.

Straight-line depreciation. A depreciation method in which the same amount is deducted every year.

Street name. Refers to securities held in the name of the broker rather than the customer.

Sum of the years' digits. A form of accelerated depreciation (*q.v.*).

Surplus. The difference between assets on the one hand and liabilities and capital stock on the other.

Tax identification number. Mandatory for an investment club. Form SS-4 is submitted for a partnership, and the resulting number is furnished to brokers and transfer agents.

Thin market. A market in which there are few offers to buy or sell a security, characteristic of stocks with a small number of shares outstanding.

Trader. An individual who does a good deal of buying and selling in the hope of realizing short-term profits.

Trading on equity. Same as leverage (*q.v.*).

Transfer agent. A bank or trust company charged with keeping a record of a company's stockholders and with canceling and issuing certificates as shares are bought and sold.

Treasury bill. A U.S. government obligation that matures within a year of issuance.

Treasury bond. A U.S. government obligation that matures more than five years from the date of issuance.

Treasury note. A U.S. government obligation that matures from one to five years from the date of issuance.

Turnover. The volume of trading in a particular security or in the market as a whole.

Undistributed earnings. Same as retained income (*q.v.*).

Undistributed profits. Same as retained income (*q.v.*).

Unit value system. An investment club accounting method that permits varying contributions and partial withdrawals as well as skips in contributions.

Unlisted security. Same as an off-board security (*q.v.*).

Unrealized gain or loss. On paper and not affected by taxes until taken.

Upside/downside ratio.   On NAIC forms, a measurement of risk. Divide the upside potential (*q.v.*) by the downside risk (*q.v.*).

Upside potential.   On NAIC forms, the difference between the calculated high price and the current price.

Valuation statement.   Investment club accounting report that lists assets at market value as of a certain date.

Variable cost.   The expense of a corporation that varies with the amount of goods produced. (*Cf.* Fixed cost.)

Visual Analysis.   That portion of the Stock Selection Guide containing the ratio chart, where sales and earnings trend lines are established and prices recorded.

Wasting asset.   An asset that is exhausted in production. (*Cf.* Depletion.)

Working capital.   The difference between current assets and current liabilities. Generally, the number should be positive.

Working capital ratio.   Same as current ratio (*q.v.*).

Yield.   The per-share dividend divided by the per-share cost of the stock.

APPENDIX B

HOW TO USE THE RATIO CHART AND CALCULATOR

*T*he chart in Section 1 of the Stock Selection Guide, called a ratio or semi-log chart, enables you to determine quickly the rate of growth of a company under study.

The chart is ruled so that a consistent rate of growth appears as a straight line. The compounded growth rates of 5, 10, 15, 20, 25, and 30 percent are drawn on the chart for reference.

On the ratio chart, equal vertical distances represent constant percentage relationships. For example, the distances are precisely the same between 1 and 2, 2 and 4, and 4 and 8—all increases of 100 percent.

The chart includes two complete series of ratio rulings, or cycles. The first cycle begins at 1 and ends at 10. The second cycle begins at this point and goes to 100.

In assigning values to the numbers on the scale, the value corresponding to 1 must be one tenth of the value corresponding to 10 of the first cycle and one hundredth of the value corresponding to 10 of the second cycle. In other words, as you move up a cycle, you must add one zero to each of the numbers.

You can see that you have a wide range of values at your disposal. Depending on the size of the numbers to be plotted, the unit 1 on the ratio chart might represent 10, 100, or even .0001. Whichever value you assign to 1, all other guide numbers must relate. For example, when the base line represents 100 million, the unit 4 becomes 400 million, the 6 stands for 600 million, and 10 becomes 1 billion.

Figure B-1 shows a variety of correct ways to assign values to the lines on a ratio chart. The last two columns (G and H) depict cases in which a multiple other than 10 is used. You may wish to confine your choices to those employing a multiple of 10 at the base line; it makes it easier to ascertain that your relationships are correct throughout the cycles.

Note that a ratio chart makes no provision for zero or negative numbers. The numbers to compare must always be positive. When a company suffers losses, these cannot be expressed on a ratio chart.

Caution is called for in plotting figures. There are ten lines (or divisions) between 1 and 2, 2 and 3, and 3 and 4. But between 4 and 5, 5 and 6, 6 and 7, 7 and 8, 8 and 9, and 9 and 10, there are only five lines. Since there are just half as many lines after the 4 guide number is reached, each line past that point must be assigned twice the value of the lines below. Therefore, if each line between units 1 and 2 equals 1, each line between units 4 and 5 must equal 2.

QUICK CALCULATIONS

After you have recorded data on the Stock Selection Guide, NAIC's Ratio Calculator makes it easy to read many ratios directly from the chart. There's no need for separate and more time-consuming mathematical computations. By using the Ratio Calculator, you may determine price/earnings ratios, pretax profit margin, percent earned on invested capital, and dividend yield.

In Figure B-2, the earnings per share of a company have been plotted as well as the high and low stock prices for the year. Earnings and prices are recorded on the same scale, so that wherever EPS and price intersect, the price/earnings ratio is 10 to 1.

To determine the high P/E ratio, place the Ratio Calculator parallel to the price bar. The Calculator's index line should be on the EPS mark. Read the figure on the Ratio Calculator where the top of the price bar falls. This is the three quarters past the 16 line, or 16 and three quarters to 1.

Find the low P/E by reading the figure on the Calculator where the bottom of the price bar falls. The answer is about 8.6.

If we plot the pre-tax profit figures on the chart in the same cycle as sales, we can use the Ratio Calculator to read the percent of pre-tax profit earned each year. (Figure B-3)

Lay the Ratio Calculator on the vertical time line so that the index line of the Calculator is at the sales point. Read the pre-tax profit percentage from the point on the Calculator. In Figure B-3, the answer is 14 percent.

Figure B-1
How to Number on a Ratio Chart

	A	B	C	D	E		F	G	H
9		90	900	9,000	90,000		9.00		
8		80	800	8,000	80,000		8.00		
7		70	700	7,000	70,000		7.00		
6		60	600	6,000	60,000		6.00		
5		50	500	5,000	50,000		5.00		
4		40	400	4,000	40,000		4.00		
3		30	300	3,000	30,000		3.00		
2		20	200	2,000	20,000		2.00		
		15	150	1,500	15,000		1.50		
10		10	100	1,000	10,000		1.00	20	50
9		9	90	900	9,000		.90	18	45
8		8	80	800	8,000		.80	16	40
7		7	70	700	7,000		.70	14	35
6		6	60	600	6,000		.60	12	30
5		5	50	500	5,000		.50	10	25
4		4	40	400	4,000		.40	8	20
3		3	30	300	3,000		.30	6	15
2		2	20	200	2,000		.20	4	10
1		1	10	100	1,000		.10	2	5
	A	B	C	D	E		F	G	H

Figure B-2

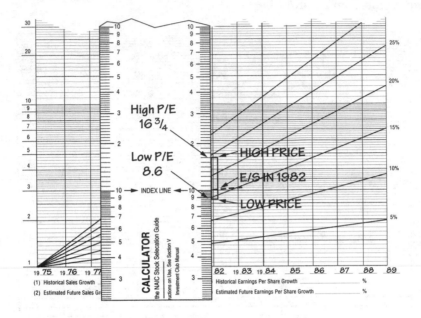

Figure B-3

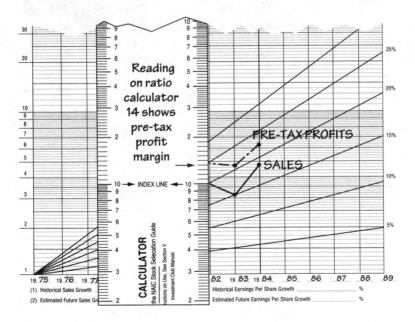

To read the percent earned on invested capital, plot book value per share on the chart in the same cycle as earnings per share. Read the relationship on the Ratio Calculator.

To determine dividend yield, plot dividend per share on the same cycle as price, and read the answer off the Ratio Calculator.

APPENDIX C

HOW TO READ NEWSPAPER STOCK TABLES

Stock prices are quoted daily in most newspapers. Business publications such as the *The Wall Street Journal, Investor's Daily,* and *Barron's* offer more detailed information. However, your local paper probably contains sufficient data for your use.

Prices typically are presented by marketplace. Listed stocks (those traded on an exchange) may be found in the New York Stock Exchange or American Exchange (AMEX) tables. If a regional exchange operates in or near the newspaper's circulation area, a table may also be found for the Pacific, Midwest, Boston, Philadelphia, or Cincinnati exchange. All told, there are about 2,500 listed equities.

Unlisted stocks are those traded over the counter (OTC), the single largest market for stocks. Generally, newspapers report prices only for the most actively traded OTC stocks or those with a local following. There are, after all, more than 50,000 unlisted stocks!

Equities are traded on the basis of eighths of a dollar, a practice dating back to the Spanish real's reign as a world class monetary unit. (The real was the basis for the "pieces of eight" of pirate tales.) Increasingly, stocks are traded in sixteenths or even thirty-seconds.

LISTED STOCKS

Figure C-1 shows how the New York Stock Exchange table probably appears in your newspaper. The high and low prices for the previous fifty-two weeks

Figure C-1

6½	2½	ATT Cap yen wt			...	...	15	5¼	5⅛	5⅛	–	½
69½	42⅞	AbbotLab	ABT	1.00	1.6	25	5738	64¾	63¼	64¼	+	⅝
14⅝	11½	Abitibi g	ABY	.50	...	...	4	12⅞	12¾	12⅞		...
5⅝	3⅜	AcmeElec	ACE		...	27	176	4⅞	4½	4⅞	+	⅛
▲ 9¾	5¼	**AcmeCleve**	**AMT**	.40	4.0	...	951	10	9⅜	10	+	⅝
40	25⅜	Acuson	ACN		...	21	823	30⅞	30½	30⅞	+	¼
20¼	15½	AdamsExp	ADX	1.63e	8.6	...	159	18⅞	18¾	18⅞		...
9⅛	3⅞	AdobeRes	ADB		...	...	2927	5	4⅞	5		...
20⅛	12⅞	AdobeRes pfB			...	...	43	14¼	14	14	–	¼
18	10¾	AdobeRes pfA			...	...	42	12	12	12		...
21⅜	7¼	**AdvMicro**	**AMD**		...	13	29751	20¾	19⅞	20⅝	+	1⅛
48½	23½	AdvMicro pf		3.00	6.3	...	300	47¾	46¾	47½	+	2

appear first, followed by the name of the stock. In the case of Abbott Labs, the high price was $69.50 and the low $42.875.

Be alert for codes following or preceding names. An explanation of the codes usually accompanies the tables. The letter *s* following the name indicates the stock has split during the past fifty-two weeks, or paid a stock dividend of at least 25 percent. The high and low prices have been adjusted to reflect the split. The *g* following Abitibi indicates that the dividend is in Canadian funds. The *pf* following AdobeRes indicates a preferred stock. In *The Wall Street Journal,* the stock symbol follows the name for both NYSE, AMEX, and NASDAQ OTC stocks. All of the other listings shown are common stocks. Following the name is the tape symbol for the stock (e.g., ABT for Abbott Laboratories).

The dividend column depicts the actual cash amount paid annually. If a letter follows the sum shown, the footnotes at the end of the table will explain its meaning. An *a* means the company paid the amount shown plus an extra dividend. The *e* after the dividend for Adams Express indicates there is no regular dividend, but the amount shown was paid last year. If no figure appears in the dividend column, no dividend was paid.

The dividend yield is given as a percentage of the current price. For example, Abbott Labs pays $1.00. When that sum is divided by the current price ($64.25), the yield comes to 1.6 percent. This is the annual cash return on your investment if the dividend remains the same. Dividend yield is based on cash, not on stock dividends. In the example, no yield is shown for ACE, which pays no cash dividend.

The price/earnings ratio comes next. The P/E is the figure you get by dividing the present price by the latest twelve months' earnings per share. No P/E is shown for AMT, a common stock, because the company did not earn a profit in the last twelve months.

The sales figure tells how many shares were traded in the most recent session. The figure is a composite for all exchanges where the security is listed. The 5738 shown for ABT translates to 573,800 shares. Unless a z appears after the sales figure, it is given in hundreds. The z denotes actual sales.

The next three columns show the high, low, and closing prices for the day. For ABT, the high was $64.75, the low $63.25, and the last price $64.25.

The last column represents the change in price from the previous day's close. ABT gained $0.625.

In our example, all of the net changes are fractional, and price fluctuated only moderately during the day's trading. You can be certain no important news concerning any of these companies became known during the session!

OVER-THE-COUNTER STOCKS

OTC stocks are divided into two groups in most publications. The more actively traded are reported in the same manner as the listed stocks. The less actively traded securities will appear as in Figure C-2. A large number of these infrequently traded stocks are listed in what are called pink sheets, since the prices are printed on pink paper. Brokers have these lists.

The dividend follows the stock's name. Sales are presented in hundreds. Only the bid and asked prices are shown. The net change reveals the difference from the previous day's bid price.

Basically, the bid price is what buyers are offering. The asked price represents what sellers are seeking. There is no way to tell the day's trading range. The bid and asked prices, as reported, do not necessarily represent actual transactions, but are intended as a guide to the range within which the securities could have been sold or bought at the time the table was compiled.

As a general rule, an OTC stock buyer pays the asked price; the seller receives the bid price. The difference or spread between the two constitutes profit for the market-making brokerage firm. If the market-maker for Alden buys 100 shares from a selling investor, the firm will pay $3,750. If there is a buyer seeking a round lot, the firm sells the shares for $4,125 and pockets

Figure C-2

Alcoln' s		1665	11 1/2	11 3/4 —	2 3/8
Alden	.12e	2	3 3/4	4 1/8	. . .
AllACm		62	2 1/8	2 1/2 —	1/2
AldCap		16	2 7/8	3 1/8	. . .
AldWste		621	5 7/8	6 1/8	. . .
Alpha1		392	15 1/2	16 —	1/4
Alph1 wtB		100	8	8 1/2 —	1/2
Alphr un		9	8 1/4	9 1/4 —	1/4

$375. There may be more sellers than buyers, however, and the firm must then commit capital to inventory the shares until buyers can be found. If a buyer and seller bid and ask the same price, between the published bid and asked price, the transaction may not take place unless a market-maker accepts the offer.

APPENDIX D

SOURCES
OF FURTHER
INFORMATION

INVESTMENT ADVISORY SERVICES

Donoghue'$ Money Letter. Published by the Donoghue Organization, Inc. This guide to stock funds, bond funds, and money market funds, issued twice monthly, includes mutual fund asset allocation models for conservative, active, or venturesome portfolios.

Emerging and Special Situations. Published monthly by Standard & Poor's with a *New Issues* supplement. Advice for those interested in small capital stocks, including a recommended list.

Growth Stock Outlook. Edited by Charles Allmon. Mailed twice monthly and designed for those "who recognize the risk and rewards of investing in vigorously growing companies."

Handbook for No-Load Fund Investors. Published annually by Sheldon Jacobs of the No-Load Fund Investor advisory service. A directory of more than 1,300 no-load stock and bond funds, along with ten-year performance data on the funds and a section on how to pick and monitor funds.

Handbook of Common Stocks. Published by Moody's, this quarterly provides overviews of more than 900 stocks with high investor interest, including operating data, stock performance, seven- to ten-year comparative earnings per share, dividend and stock price charts, as well as short- and long-term prospects and a discussion of recent corporate developments.

271

Handbook of Dividend Achievers. Published annually by Moody's. Lists companies that have increased their annual dividend payout for ten consecutive years or more.

Handbook of OTC Stocks. This quarterly publication of Moody's provides overviews of actively traded over-the-counter securities. Included are key financial data, history, company descriptions, stock price charts, dividend payments, and a discussion of recent developments.

Hulbert Guide to Financial Newsletters. Edited by Mark Hulbert and issued by the New York Institute of Finance, this reference rates more than 100 investment newsletters by clarity of advice, completeness, relative riskiness, and volatility. The methods and philosophies each newsletter follows are named, and the percent gain or loss on recommended investments is given for both short- and long-term periods.

Industry Review. Published by Moody's and updated semi-annually, this looseleaf service provides comparative key financial and operating data on more than 5,000 corporations covering 145 industry groups.

Moody's Dividend Record Service. Published twice weekly, the service covers more than 12,500 common and preferred dividend-paying stocks, mutual funds, foreign securities, and nonpaying issues.

Morningstar Mutual Funds. Published biweekly in two sections by Morningstar, Inc. The first section classifies 1,242 load and no-load equity and fixed income funds by risk, objective, total return, dividends, and net assets. Portfolio manager changes are included. The second section presents detailed information on 120 or so different funds.

Morningstar Mutual Fund Sourcebook. Annual coverage of 1,800 funds by Morningstar, Inc. One volume is devoted to equity funds and the other to fixed-income funds. Information includes investment criteria, performance data, risk-adjusted ratings, and more.

Mutual Fund Profiles. Published quarterly by Standard & Poor's. Covers 750 funds, comprising general and specialized equity funds, balanced funds, and long-term taxable fixed income mutual funds. Description includes investment policy, performance evaluation, portfolio composition, and five-year historical data.

NAIC Investors Advisory Service. Three stocks are discussed and recommended for purchase each month. A completed NAIC Stock Selection Guide is furnished for each.

Nelson's Earnings Outlook. A compilation of estimated earnings per share based on figures supplied by security analysts who follow particular stocks and industries.

No-Load Fund Investor. Edited by Sheldon Jacobs of the No-Load Fund Investor, Inc. Provides comprehensive coverage of virtually all no-load funds available to the public, plus direct marketed low-loads and closed-ends. Offers performance data for seven periods ranging from the latest month to five years. Includes cash positions and betas.

The Outlook. Published by Standard & Poor's weekly except for legal holidays. Covers the status of the stock market, lists stocks to buy and stocks to avoid, and features a stock from S&P's Master List of Recommended Stocks for Superior Long-Term Total Return.

S&P Earnings Guide. A compilation of estimated earnings per share based on figures supplied by security analysts who follow particular stocks and industries.

S&P Industry Report Service. Provides a comprehensive look at thirty-seven business sectors from aerospace to utilities, offering fundamental and investment forecasts by industry and buy and sell recommendations on individual stocks within the groupings. Lists more than 800 companies by industry.

S&P Stock Guide.   A monthly pocket-size alphabetical guide to more than 5,300 common and preferred stocks, both listed and over-the-counter. Offers forty-eight items of information on each. A special section contains data on 600 leading mutual funds.

S&P Stock Report Services. Popularly known as S&P sheets, the services offer salient statistics on about 4,700 companies listed on the New York, American, and regional stock exchanges, as well as over-the-counter issues.

Stock Market Encyclopedia. Published quarterly by Standard & Poor's. Includes data on 750 companies: industrials, utilities, transportation, and financial firms. A full-page report is included for every stock in the S&P 500.

Value Line Investment Survey. Published by Value Line Publishing, Inc. Follows 1,700 stocks and ninety-seven industries in three sections. Part 1 is Summary and Index. Part 2, Selection & Opinion, analyzes and forecasts the national economy and the stock market. Part 3 is Ratings & Reports.

Wall Street Digest. Monthly digest of investment advice from leading financial advisors.

NEWSPAPERS AND MAGAZINES

Barron's. A business and financial weekly published by Dow Jones & Company. Contains articles on industries and companies, commentary on stock market activity, information on new issues, a summary of research reports, and a comprehensive statistical section including both current and year-ago earnings information.

Better Investing. Monthly magazine of NAIC containing information designed especially for the self-reliant investor. Features include a stock to study, an undervalued stock, selected portfolios, and regular columnists who provide a variety of investment information and ideas.

Business Week. Published weekly except for one issue in January. Covers the general business scene, with departments focusing on the economy, government, finance, science and technology, and personal business, among other topics. Reviews business books.

FW (formerly *Financial World*). Published biweekly except for a combined Dec./Jan. issue. Departments include market watch, company watch, economic currents, market comments, and special situations.

Forbes. Published biweekly, except for an extra issue in October. Sections include companies/industries, international, money and investing, law and issues, marketing, computers, science and technology, and personal affairs. Also featured are regular columnists.

Fortune. Published biweekly, with three issues in May and October. Coverage includes the economy, innovation, technology, and money and markets. Departments include personal investing.

Investor's Daily. Gives complete market quotes and a variety of statistical information along with news stories.

Kiplinger's Personal Finance Magazine. Published monthly. Topics include spending, taxes, estate planning, investing basics, insurance, and personal finances.

Money Magazine. A monthly publication centering on personal finance. Areas of concern include home ownership, jobs, taxes, insurance, and investing.

The New York Times. The business section, daily and Sunday, is the nation's most comprehensive.

USA Today. A national daily with extensive quotations and business news.

The Wall Street Journal. Published by Dow Jones & Company. Issued Monday through Friday in regional editions, reporting news developments in terms of their significance to business people and investors. The third section, Money & Investing, contains regular features such as Heard on the Street, Abreast of the Market, Digest of Earnings Reports, and Corporate Dividend News.

Wall Street Transcript. Published weekly by Wall Street Transcript Corporation. Provides reprints of investment research reports, round-table discussions, and industry features.

INDEXES AND DIRECTORIES

America's Corporate Families and International Affiliates. Published by Dun & Bradstreet in two volumes, linking U.S. and foreign parents with the domestic and international affiliates.

Brands and Their Companies (1992). Edited by Susan L. Stetler and published by Gale Research Inc. In two volumes, providing access to more than 240,000 consumer brands and about 45,000 manufacturers and importers. Brands are presented in alphabetical order.

Bull & Bear's Directory of Investment Advisory Newsletters. Published annually by Bull & Bear Financial Newspaper, Inc. Lists 445 newsletters in alphabetical order within each category, including international investments, mutual funds, new issues, and stocks. Included are newsletter title, address, phone, description, subscription rates, frequency, and trial subscription offers.

Business and Investment Almanac (1991). Edited by Sumner N. Levine and published by Business One Irwin. A review of the year, including stock market averages, price/earnings ratios, foreign stock markets, mutual fund performance, and more. Includes an explanation of investment and financial terms.

Business Periodicals Index. Published monthly except July by H. W. Wilson Company, with a bound cumulation annually. An index to the contents of several hundred periodicals, including *Barron's, Business Week, Forbes, Fortune,* and *FW* (formerly *Financial World*).

Directory of Companies Offering Dividend Reinvestment Plans. (eighth edition, 1991). Edited by Sumie Kinoshita and published by Evergreen Enterprises. Dividend reinvestment plans listed for more than 1,100 corporations and closed-end investment companies.

Dun's Business Rankings. Published by Dun & Bradstreet. Ranks the top 8,000 firms by sales and employees.

Encyclopedia of Business Information Sources, (eighth edition, 1991–92). Edited by James Woy and published by Gale Research, Inc. A guide to more than 21,000 citations covering 1,000 subjects of interest to businesspeople.

Investment Statistics Locator (1988). Written by Karen J. Chapman and published by Oryx Press. Detailed subject index to the most-used sources of financial and investment data.

Million Dollar Directory: America's Leading Public and Private Companies. Published by Dun & Bradstreet, offers information on more than 160,000 top businesses.

Moody's Complete Corporate Index. Comprehensive index to 28,000 corporations included in *Moody's Manuals.* Published twice yearly.

Moody's Manuals. Six volumes of comprehensive statistical and analytical data covering listed and unlisted industrials, public utilities, transportation companies, banks and finance companies, and international businesses.

New York Times Index. Published semi-monthly by the New York Times Company, with quarterly cumulations and an annual cumulation. Business listings indexed by industry, individual company, and person.

Predicasts F and S Index—United States. Published by Predicasts, Inc. monthly, with weekly supplements. Selectively indexes leading business publications for company activities, industry news, and product information.

Principal International Businesses. Published by Dun & Bradstreet, offering up-to-date information on approximately 50,000 leading enterprises in 133 countries around the world.

Reader's Guide to Periodical Literature. Published by H. W. Wilson Company. A cumulative author/subject index to periodicals of general interest. Published semi-monthly in March, April, September, October, and December and monthly in January, February, May, June, July, August, and November. Bound cumulation issued yearly. Includes *Business Week, Kiplinger's Personal Finance, Forbes, Fortune,* and *Money.*

Reference Book on Corporate Managements. Published by Dun & Bradstreet, lists biographies of top corporate executives.

Register of Corporations, Directors, and Executives. Published annually by Standard & Poor's in three volumes. Volume I lists 55,000 corporations with address; telephone number; name, title, and function of approximately 500,000 officers, directors, and other principals; and a description of company products/services. Volume 2 offers listings of more than 70,000 individuals serving as officers, directors, trustees, and partners. Volume 3 consists of indexes.

Stock Market Encyclopedia. Published quarterly by Standard & Poor's. Includes data on 750 companies—industrials, utilities, transportation, and financial firms. A full-page report is included for every stock in the S&P 500.

Wiesenberger Investment Companies Service. Published annually. Includes general information about funds as an investment medium, as well as descriptions of and data on investment companies.

INDEX

The Value Line Investment Survey®
PO Box 3988, New York, NY 10008-3988

A Special offer from Value Line

Receive a TRIAL subscription to
The Value Line Investment Survey

for ~~$75~~ $55

The most widely used investment publication, hailed as an invaluable information resource by

National Association of Investment Clubs Members

is yours at the special price indicated, when you purchase this book describing the NAIC's investment methods.

As a new Value Line subscriber, you receive the following:

- Full "Investor's Reference Library" containing the most recent full-page reports on all 1,700 companies and 98 industries covered by **The Value Line Investment Survey.**

- Your own copy of "How to Invest in Common Stocks," our guide to using **The Value Line Investment Survey.**

- A copy of **Wall Street Words**, including definitions of over 3,500 terms and special explanations, with case histories and helpful hints.*

- Ten full weeks of current editions, each updating some 130 company reports and seven industry reviews, with new Timeliness™ and Safety Ranks and current data on all 1,700 stocks.

To order, indicate on a card or in a letter your preferred option, with your name, mailing address, and telephone number (with the source code indicated below), and send this information to us, with your payment (check or current credit-card information: VISA, MasterCard or American Express), at the address indicated above.

To qualify for this special offer, you MUST include the following source code: NAIC01

❏ 10-week trial of Value Line for $55 — (available only once every three years to any household; not available to current subscribers)

❏ One year (52 issues) of Value Line for $495 — (regular price: $570)

Please allow four weeks for delivery. Foreign rates upon request. NY residents, please add sales tax. Prices subject to change without notice.
*While supplies last; subject to substitution.

Money-Back Guarantee
If you are not satisfied, for any reason, you may return the materials within 30 days from the start of your new subscription for a full refund. Your subscription to Value Line may be tax-deductible. Consult your tax advisor.